QUANTUM AND WOODY
BY PRIEST & BRIGHT

Q2–
THE RETURN

CHRISTOPHER PRIEST | MD BRIGHT | DEXTER VINES | ALLEN PASSALAQUA

CONTENTS

Quantum & Woody created by MD Bright & Priest

Collection Cover Art: MD Bright

Editor: Alejandro Arbona
Editor-in-Chief: Warren Simons

VALIANT.

Peter Cuneo
Chairman

Dinesh Shamdasani
CEO & Chief Creative Officer

Gavin Cuneo
Chief Operating Officer & CFO

Fred Pierce
Publisher

Warren Simons
VP Editor-in-Chief

Walter Black
VP Operations

Hunter Gorinson
Director of Marketing,
Communications & Digital Media

Atom! Freeman
Director of Sales

Matthew Klein
Andy Liegl
John Petrie
Sales Managers

Josh Johns
Associate Director of Digital Media and Development

Travis Escarfullery
Jeff Walker
Production & Design Managers

Tom Brennan
Editor

Kyle Andrukiewicz
Editor and Creative Executive

Peter Stern
Publishing & Operations Manager

Andrew Steinbeiser
Marketing & Communications Manager

Danny Khazem
Editorial Operations Manager

Ivan Cohen
Collection Editor

Steve Blackwell
Collection Designer

Lauren Hitzhusen
Editorial Assistant

Rian Hughes/Device
Trade Dress & Book Design

Russell Brown
President, Consumer Products,
Promotions and Ad Sales

Geeta Singh
Licensing Manager

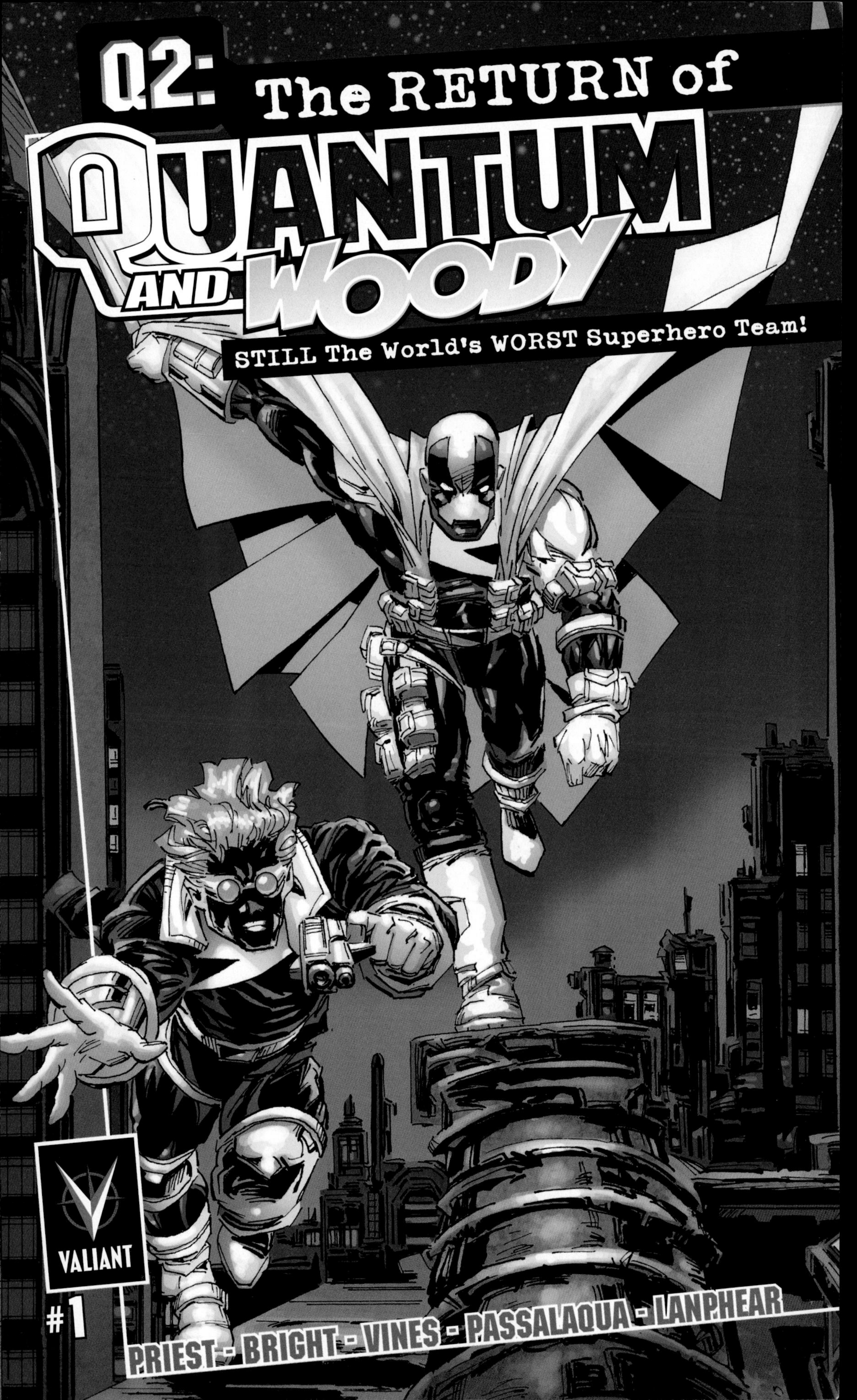

Q2: The RETURN of
QUANTUM AND WOODY
STILL The World's WORST Superhero Team!
VALIANT
#1
PRIEST - BRIGHT - VINES - PASSALAQUA - LANPHEAR

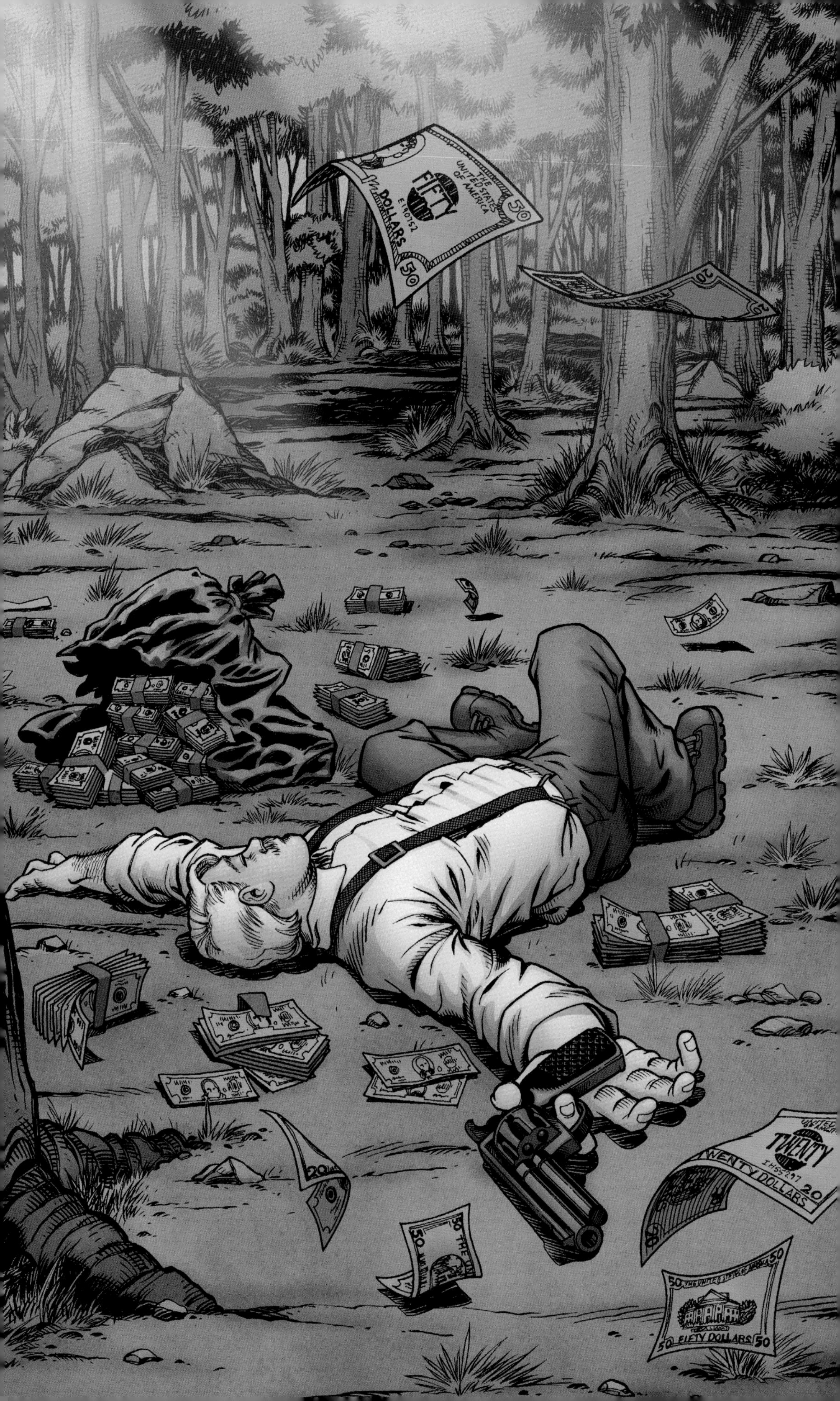

THE UNITED STATES OF AMERICA
FIFTY
DOLLARS
TWENTY
TWENTY DOLLARS
FIFTY DOLLARS

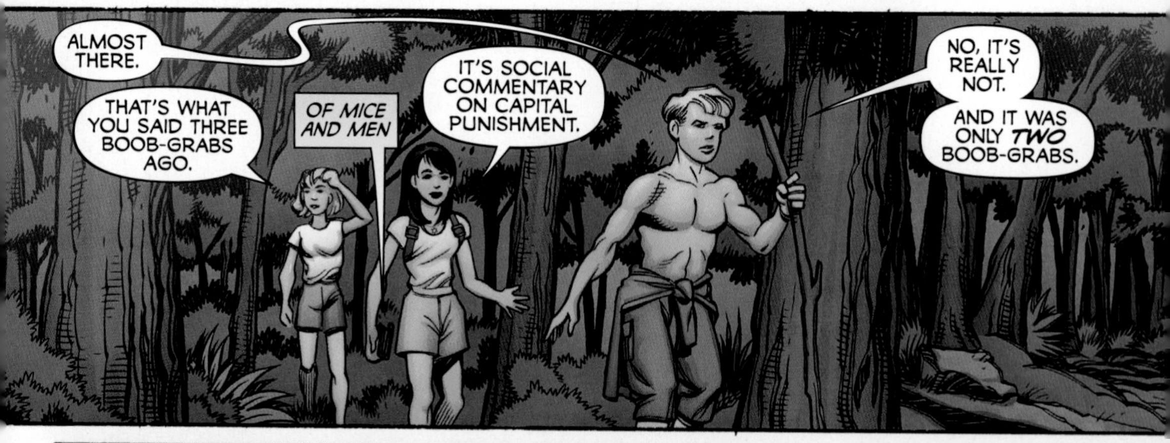
ALMOST THERE.
THAT'S WHAT YOU SAID THREE BOOB-GRABS AGO.
OF MICE AND MEN
IT'S SOCIAL COMMENTARY ON CAPITAL PUNISHMENT.
NO, IT'S REALLY NOT.
AND IT WAS ONLY *TWO* BOOB-GRABS.

"What Have You Done?"

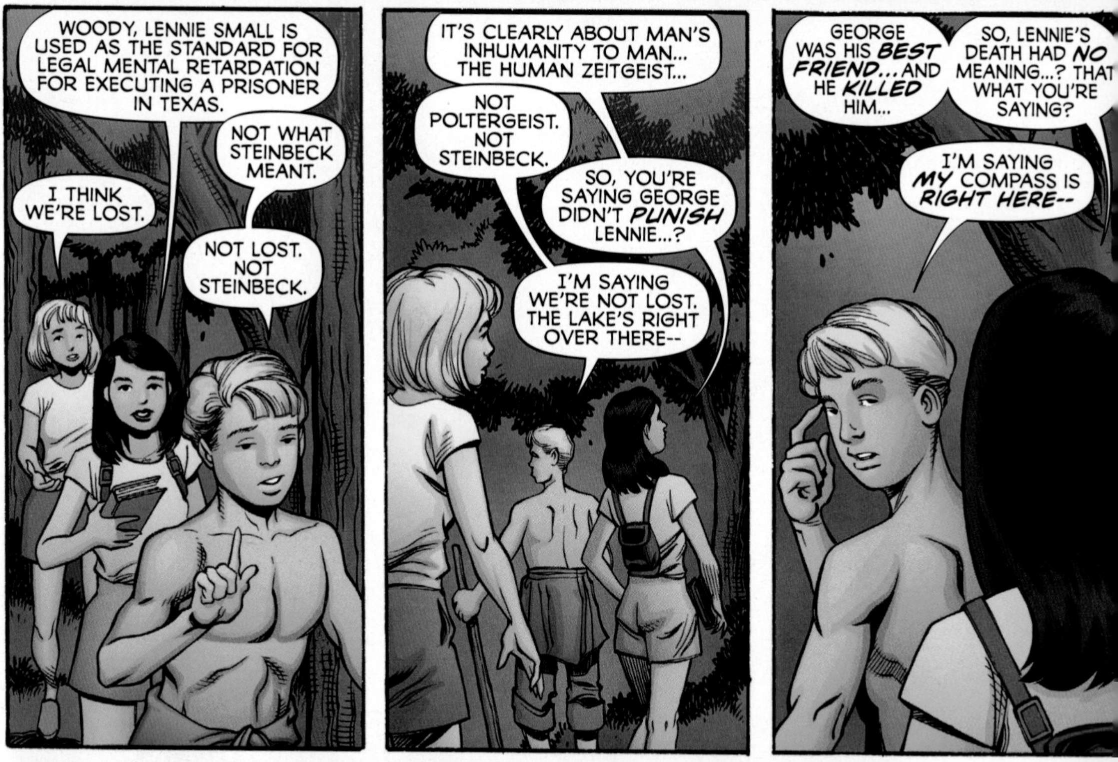
WOODY, LENNIE SMALL IS USED AS THE STANDARD FOR LEGAL MENTAL RETARDATION FOR EXECUTING A PRISONER IN TEXAS.
I THINK WE'RE LOST.
NOT WHAT STEINBECK MEANT.
NOT LOST. NOT STEINBECK.
IT'S CLEARLY ABOUT MAN'S INHUMANITY TO MAN... THE HUMAN ZEITGEIST...
NOT POLTERGEIST. NOT STEINBECK.
SO, YOU'RE SAYING GEORGE DIDN'T *PUNISH* LENNIE...?
I'M SAYING WE'RE NOT LOST. THE LAKE'S RIGHT OVER THERE--
GEORGE WAS HIS *BEST FRIEND*... AND HE *KILLED* HIM...
SO, LENNIE'S DEATH HAD *NO* MEANING...? THAT WHAT YOU'RE SAYING?
I'M SAYING *MY* COMPASS IS *RIGHT HERE*--

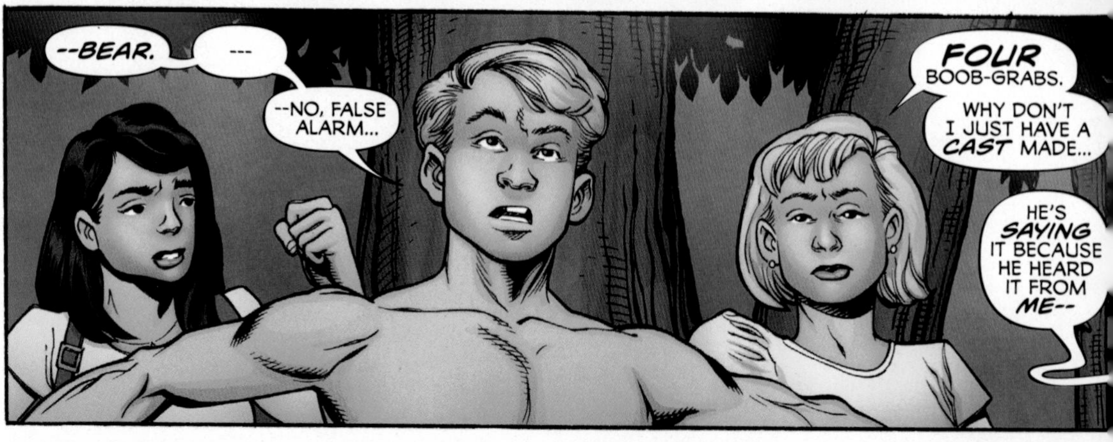
--BEAR.

--NO, FALSE ALARM...
FOUR BOOB-GRABS.
WHY DON'T I JUST HAVE A *CAST* MADE...
HE'S *SAYING* IT BECAUSE HE HEARD IT FROM *ME*--

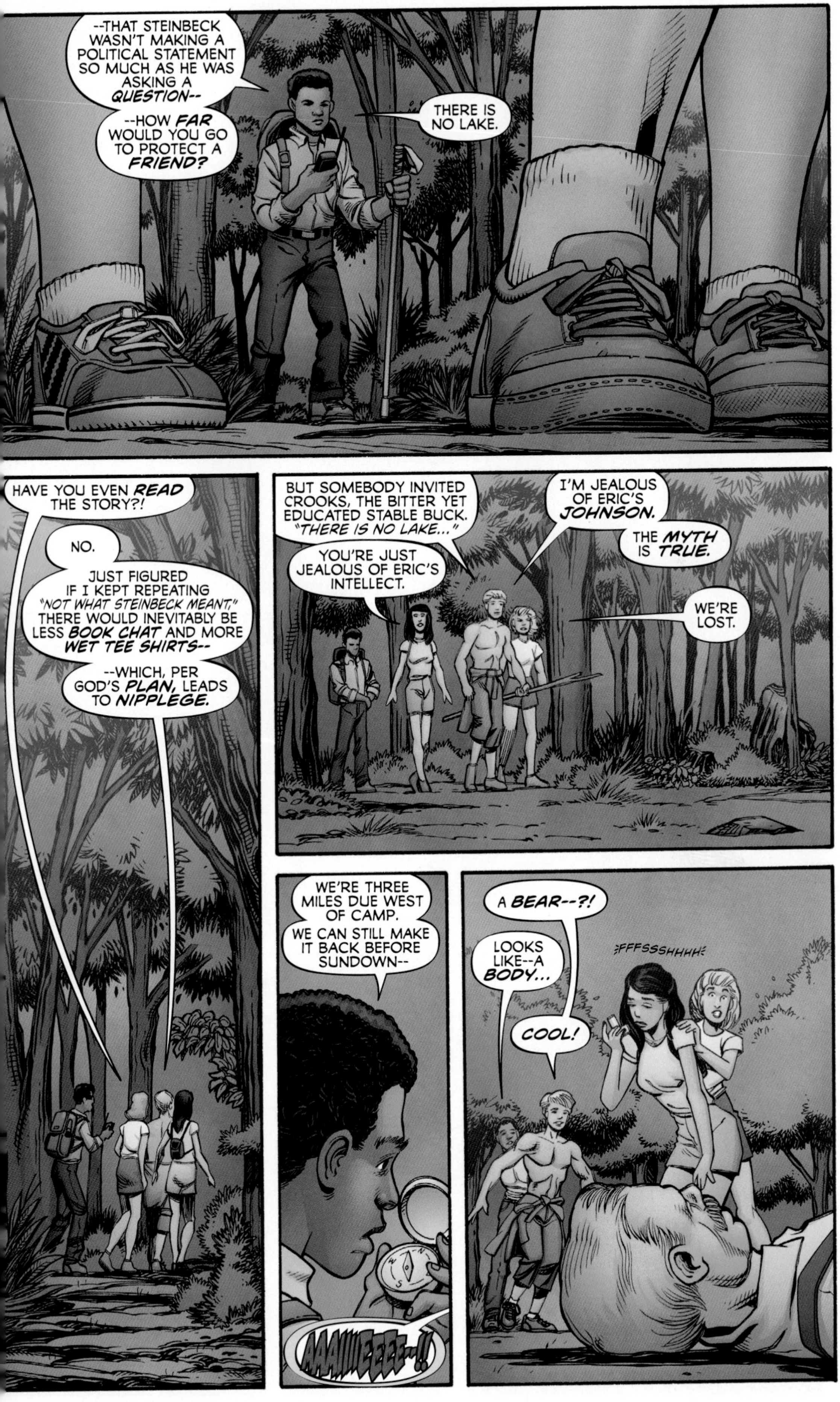

--THAT STEINBECK WASN'T MAKING A POLITICAL STATEMENT SO MUCH AS HE WAS ASKING A *QUESTION--*
--HOW *FAR* WOULD YOU GO TO PROTECT A *FRIEND?*
THERE IS NO LAKE.
HAVE YOU EVEN *READ* THE STORY?!
NO.
JUST FIGURED IF I KEPT REPEATING *"NOT WHAT STEINBECK MEANT,"* THERE WOULD INEVITABLY BE LESS *BOOK CHAT* AND MORE *WET TEE SHIRTS--*
--WHICH, PER GOD'S *PLAN,* LEADS TO *NIPPLEGE.*
BUT SOMEBODY INVITED CROOKS, THE BITTER YET EDUCATED STABLE BUCK. *"THERE IS NO LAKE..."*
YOU'RE JUST JEALOUS OF ERIC'S INTELLECT.
I'M JEALOUS OF ERIC'S *JOHNSON.*
THE *MYTH* IS *TRUE.*
WE'RE LOST.
WE'RE THREE MILES DUE WEST OF CAMP.
WE CAN STILL MAKE IT BACK BEFORE SUNDOWN--
AAAIIIIEEEE--!!
A *BEAR--?!*
LOOKS LIKE--A *BODY...*
COOL!
FFFSSSHHHH

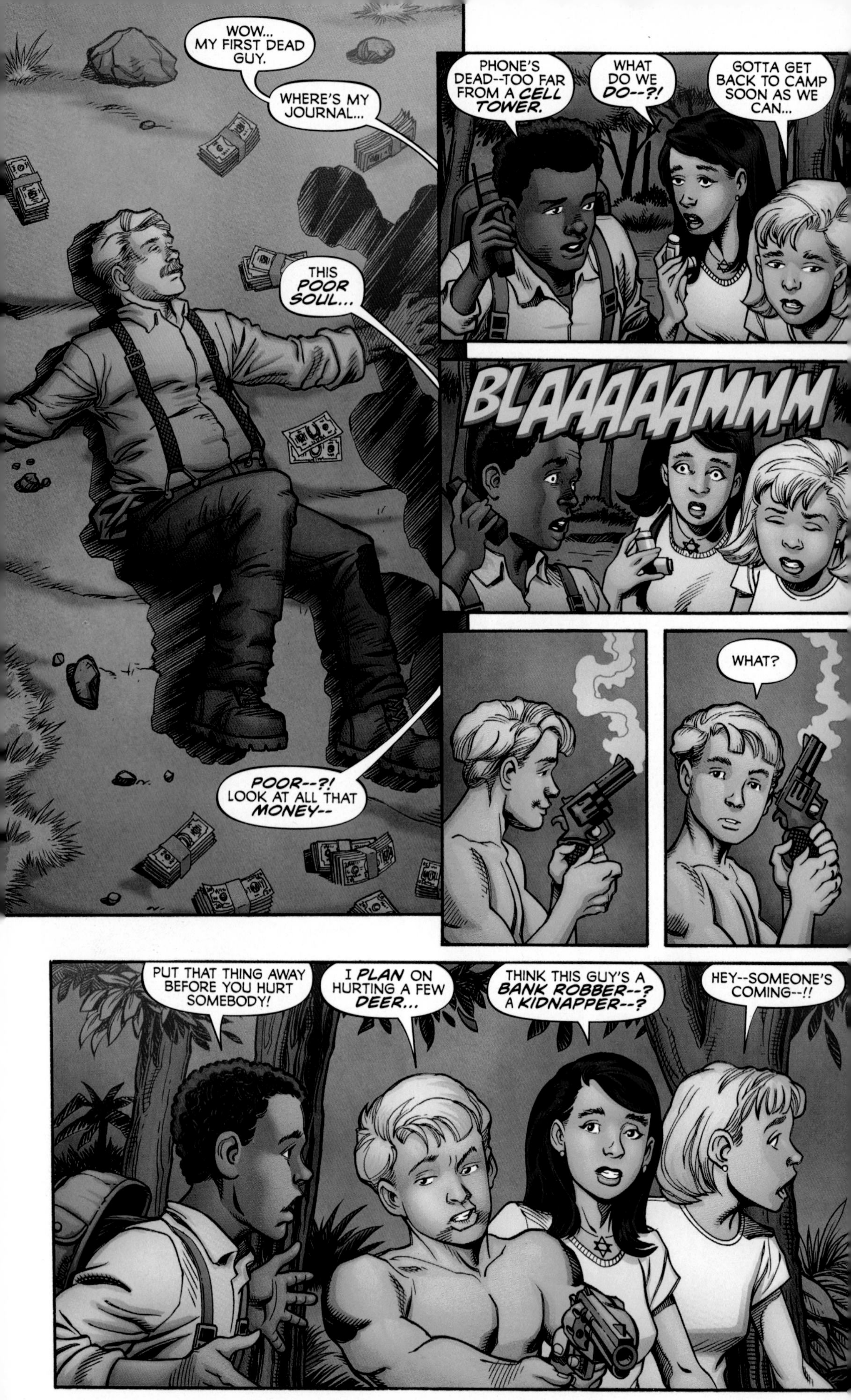

WOW... MY FIRST DEAD GUY.
WHERE'S MY JOURNAL...
THIS POOR SOUL...
POOR--?! LOOK AT ALL THAT MONEY--
PHONE'S DEAD--TOO FAR FROM A CELL TOWER.
WHAT DO WE DO--?!
GOTTA GET BACK TO CAMP SOON AS WE CAN...
BLAAAAAMMM
WHAT?
PUT THAT THING AWAY BEFORE YOU HURT SOMEBODY!
I PLAN ON HURTING A FEW DEER...
THINK THIS GUY'S A BANK ROBBER--? A KIDNAPPER--?
HEY--SOMEONE'S COMING--!!

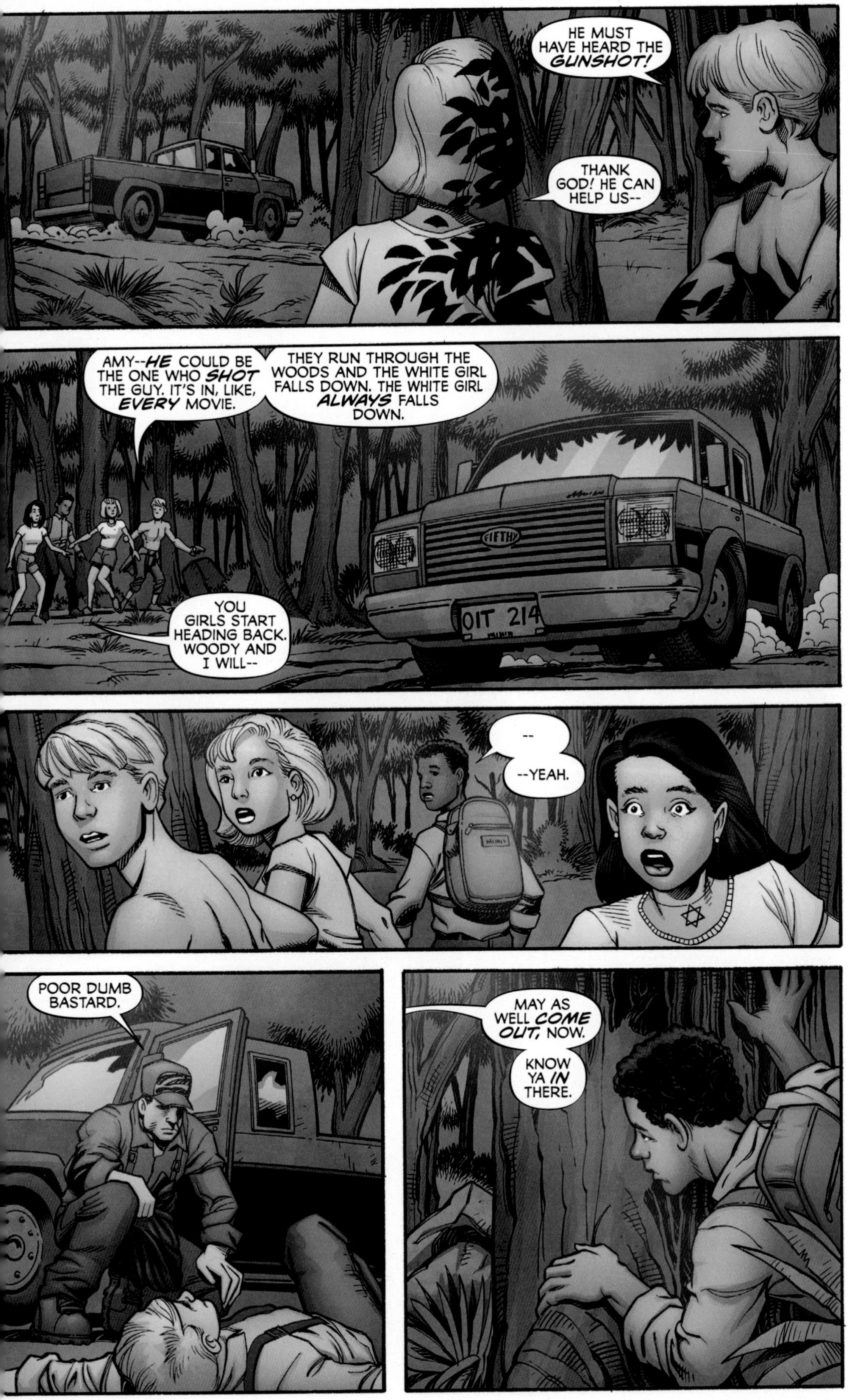
HE MUST HAVE HEARD THE GUNSHOT!
THANK GOD! HE CAN HELP US--
AMY--HE COULD BE THE ONE WHO SHOT THE GUY. IT'S IN, LIKE, EVERY MOVIE.
THEY RUN THROUGH THE WOODS AND THE WHITE GIRL FALLS DOWN. THE WHITE GIRL ALWAYS FALLS DOWN.
FIFTHY
OIT 214
YOU GIRLS START HEADING BACK. WOODY AND I WILL--
--
--YEAH.
POOR DUMB BASTARD.
MAY AS WELL COME OUT, NOW.
KNOW YA IN THERE.

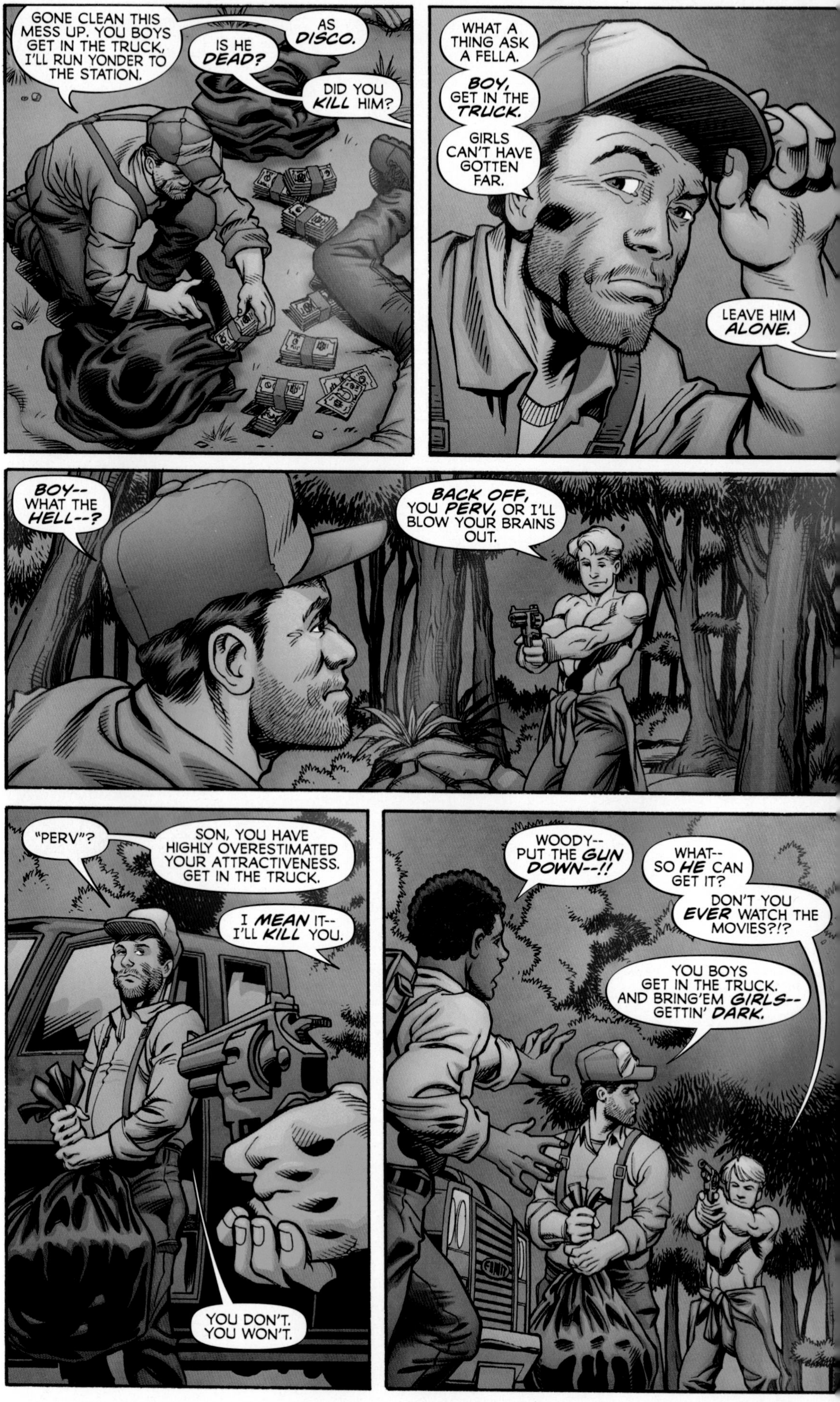
GONE CLEAN THIS MESS UP. YOU BOYS GET IN THE TRUCK, I'LL RUN YONDER TO THE STATION.
AS DISCO.
IS HE DEAD?
DID YOU KILL HIM?
WHAT A THING ASK A FELLA.
BOY, GET IN THE TRUCK.
GIRLS CAN'T HAVE GOTTEN FAR.
LEAVE HIM ALONE.
BOY-- WHAT THE HELL--?
BACK OFF, YOU PERV, OR I'LL BLOW YOUR BRAINS OUT.
"PERV"?
SON, YOU HAVE HIGHLY OVERESTIMATED YOUR ATTRACTIVENESS. GET IN THE TRUCK.
I MEAN IT-- I'LL KILL YOU.
YOU DON'T. YOU WON'T.
WOODY-- PUT THE GUN DOWN--!!
WHAT-- SO HE CAN GET IT?
DON'T YOU EVER WATCH THE MOVIES?!?
YOU BOYS GET IN THE TRUCK. AND BRING'EM GIRLS-- GETTIN' DARK.

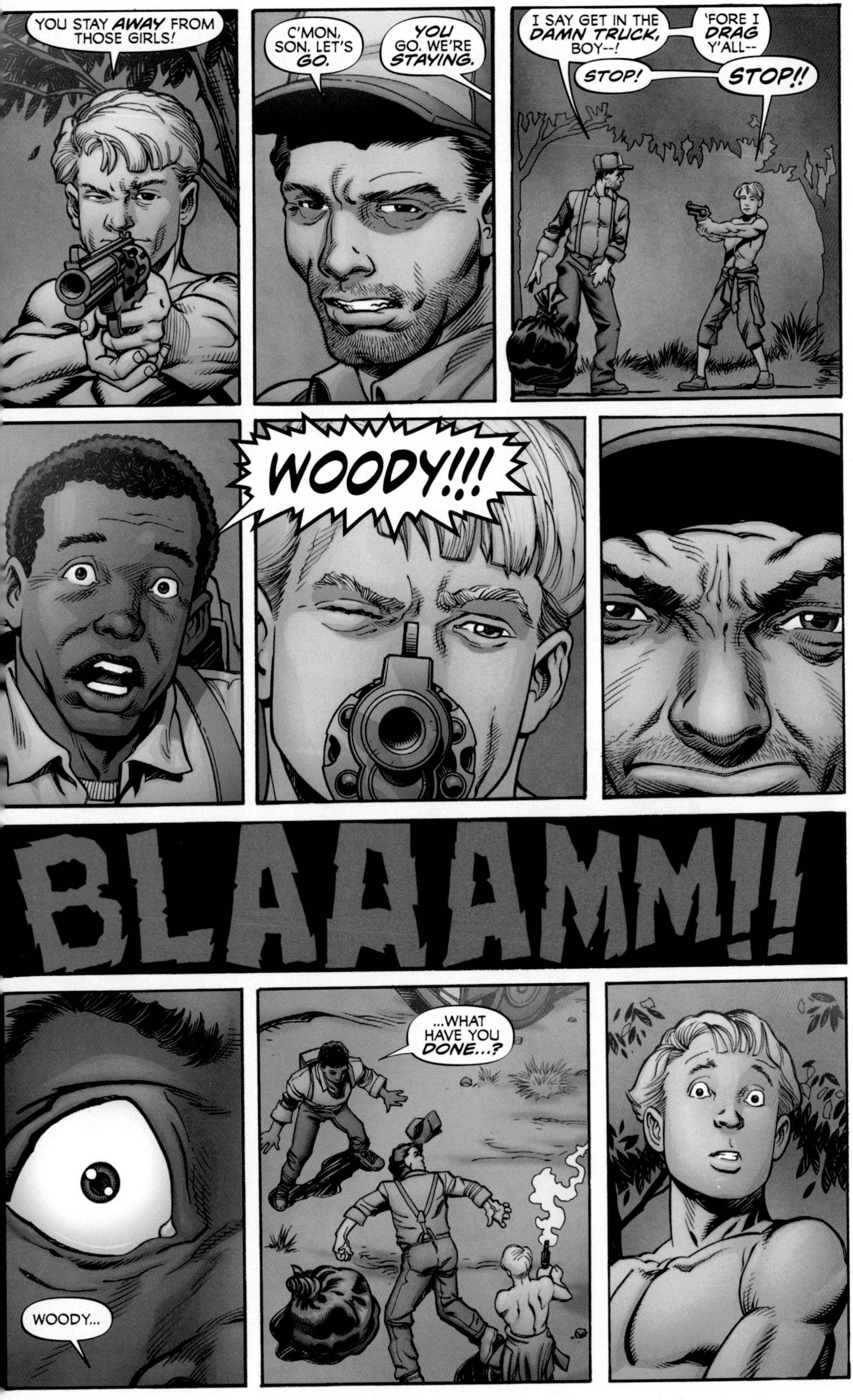
YOU STAY AWAY FROM THOSE GIRLS!
C'MON, SON. LET'S GO.
YOU GO. WE'RE STAYING.
I SAY GET IN THE DAMN TRUCK, BOY--!
'FORE I DRAG Y'ALL--
STOP!
STOP!!
WOODY!!!
BLAAMM!!
WOODY...
...WHAT HAVE YOU DONE...?

"The Wish Of The Land"

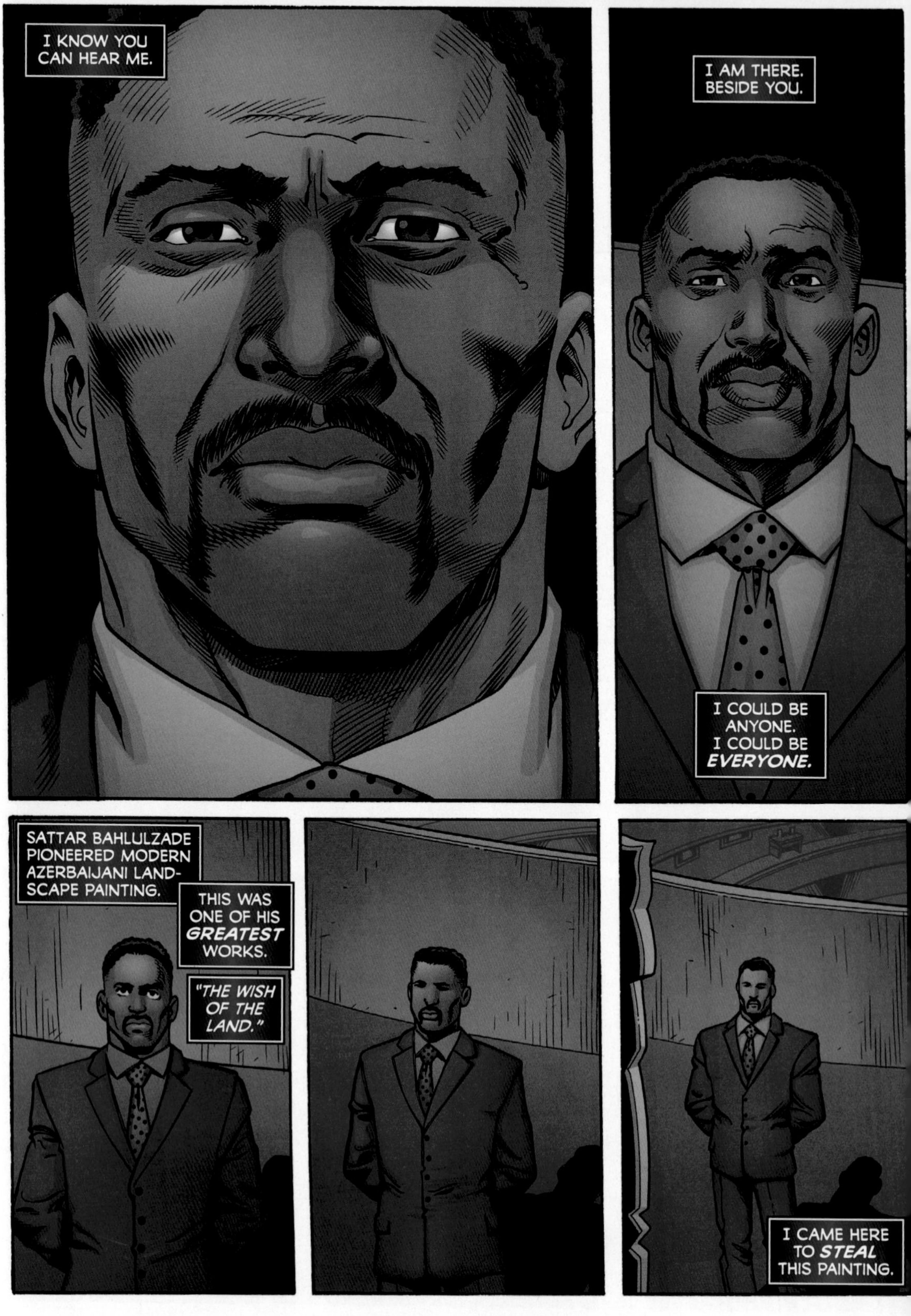

I KNOW YOU CAN HEAR ME.
I AM THERE. BESIDE YOU.
I COULD BE ANYONE. I COULD BE *EVERYONE.*
SATTAR BAHLULZADE PIONEERED MODERN AZERBAIJANI LAND-SCAPE PAINTING.
THIS WAS ONE OF HIS *GREATEST* WORKS.
"THE WISH OF THE LAND."
I CAME HERE TO *STEAL* THIS PAINTING.

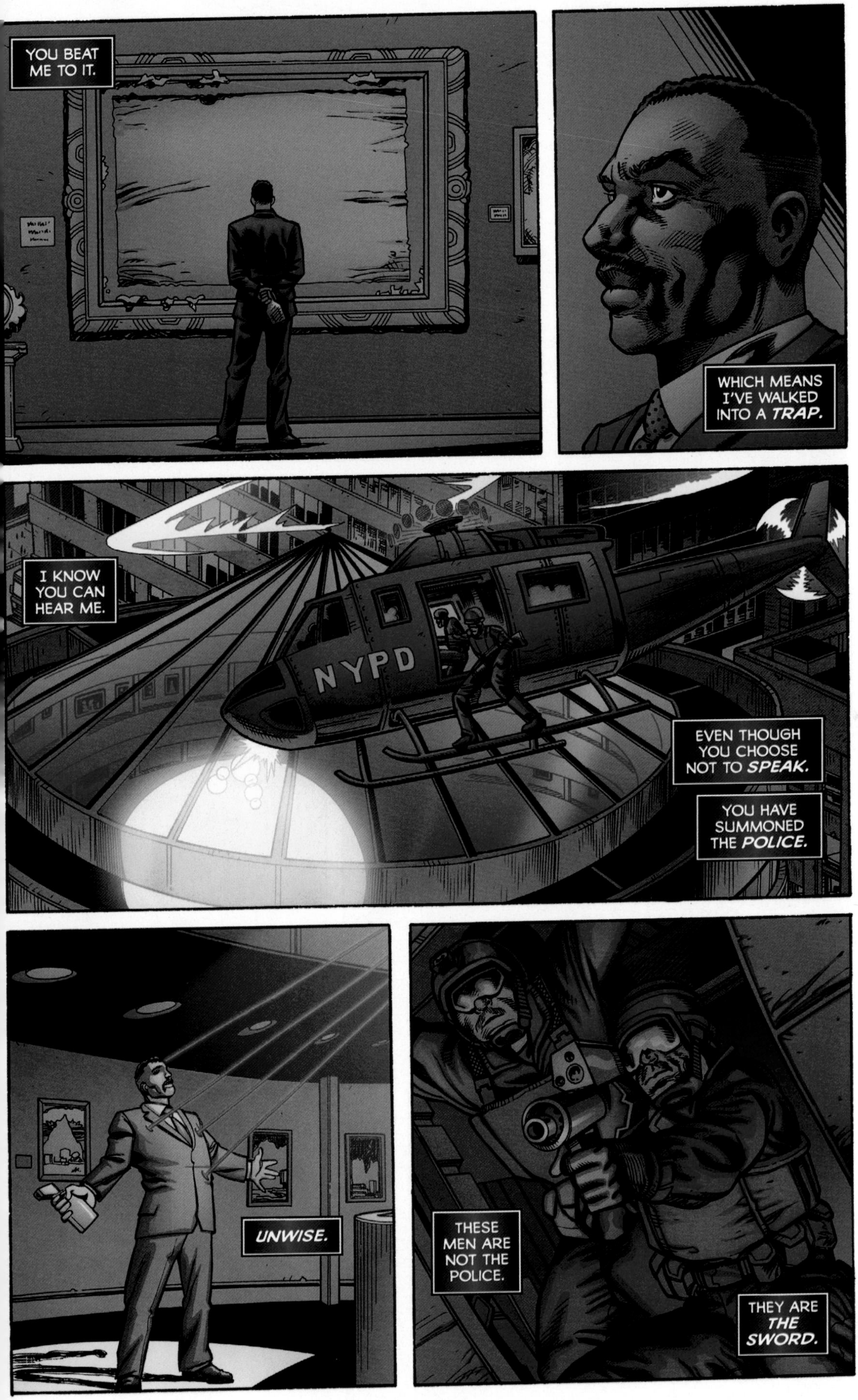
YOU BEAT ME TO IT.
WHICH MEANS I'VE WALKED INTO A *TRAP.*
I KNOW YOU CAN HEAR ME.
NYPD
EVEN THOUGH YOU CHOOSE NOT TO *SPEAK.*
YOU HAVE SUMMONED THE *POLICE.*
UNWISE.
THESE MEN ARE NOT THE POLICE.
THEY ARE *THE SWORD.*

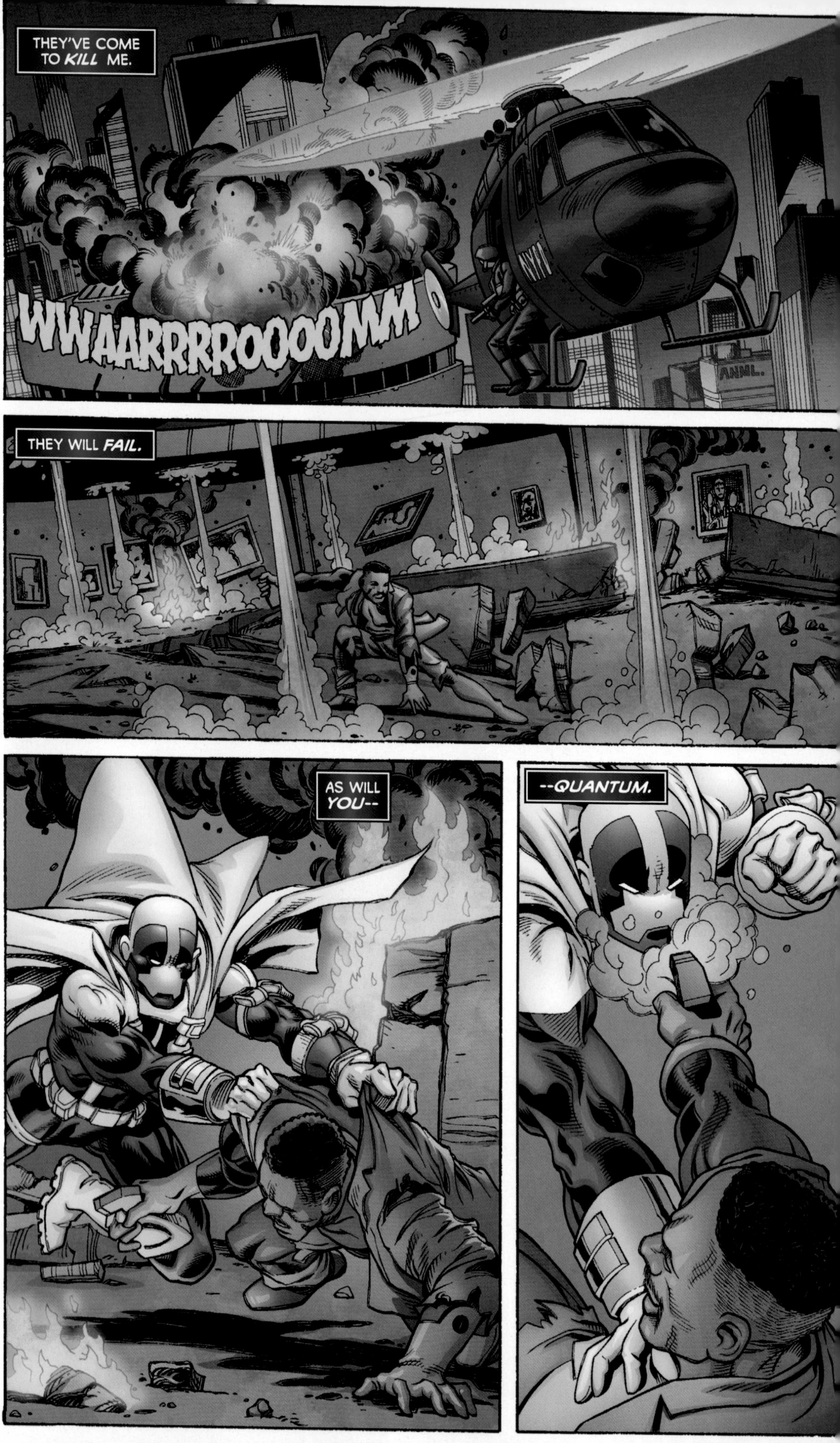
THEY'VE COME TO KILL ME.
WWAARRRROOOOMM
THEY WILL FAIL.
AS WILL YOU--
--QUANTUM.

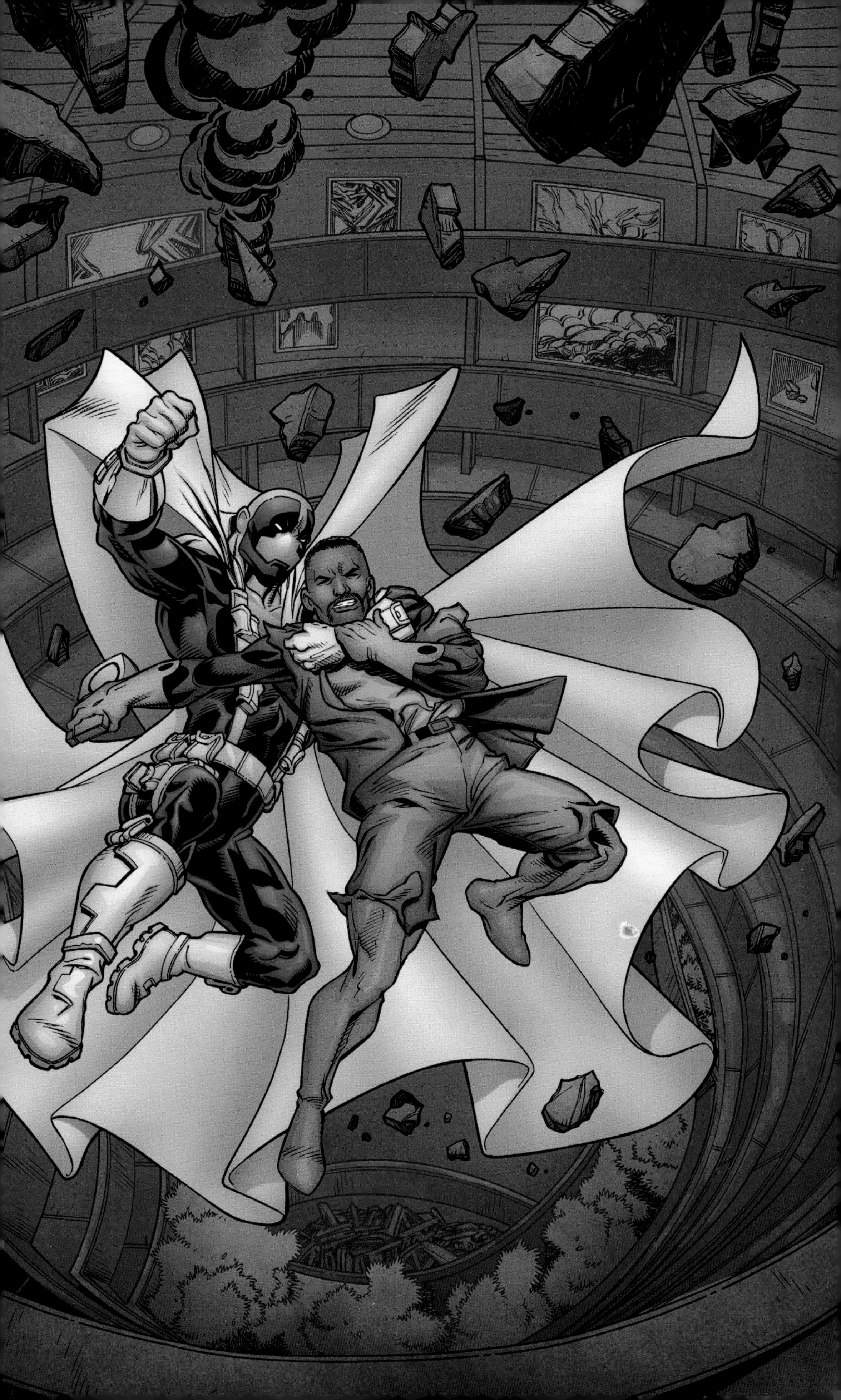

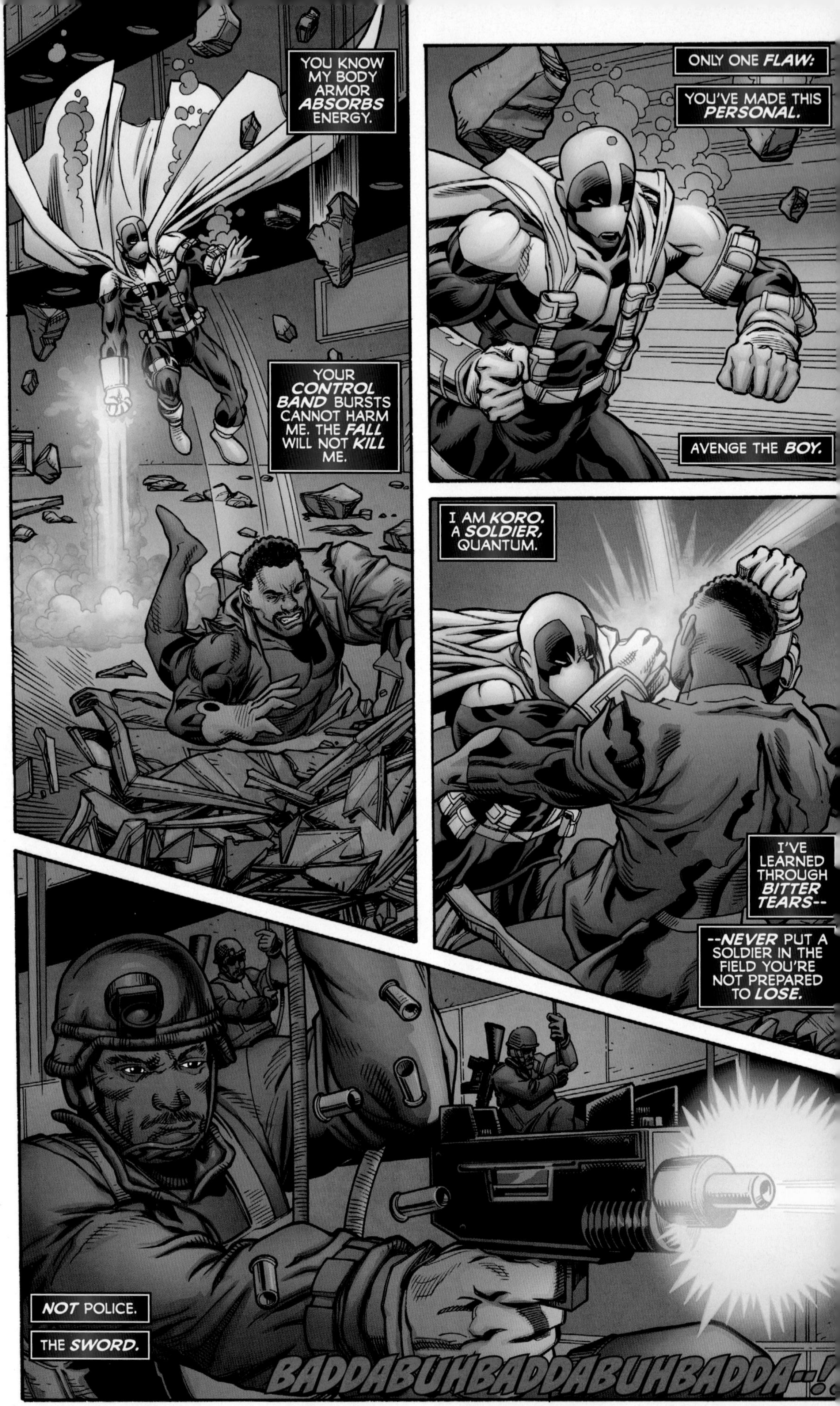
YOU KNOW MY BODY ARMOR *ABSORBS* ENERGY.
YOUR *CONTROL BAND* BURSTS CANNOT HARM ME. THE *FALL* WILL NOT *KILL* ME.
ONLY ONE *FLAW:*
YOU'VE MADE THIS *PERSONAL.*
AVENGE THE *BOY.*
I AM *KORO.* A *SOLDIER,* QUANTUM.
I'VE LEARNED THROUGH *BITTER TEARS*--
--*NEVER* PUT A SOLDIER IN THE FIELD YOU'RE NOT PREPARED TO *LOSE.*
NOT POLICE.
THE *SWORD.*
BADDABUHBADDABUHBADDA--!

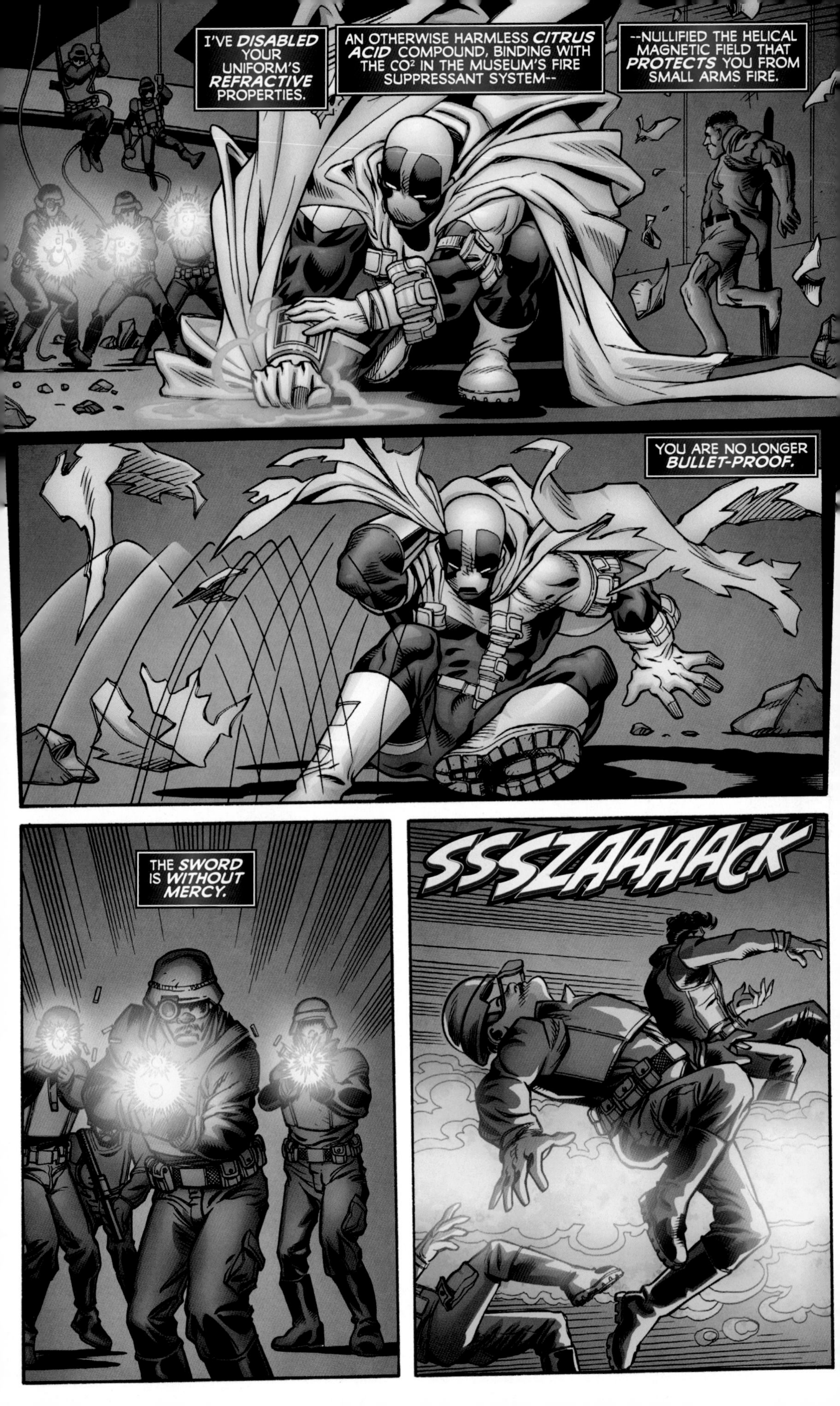
I'VE DISABLED YOUR UNIFORM'S REFRACTIVE PROPERTIES.
AN OTHERWISE HARMLESS CITRUS ACID COMPOUND, BINDING WITH THE CO2 IN THE MUSEUM'S FIRE SUPPRESSANT SYSTEM--
--NULLIFIED THE HELICAL MAGNETIC FIELD THAT PROTECTS YOU FROM SMALL ARMS FIRE.
YOU ARE NO LONGER BULLET-PROOF.
THE SWORD IS WITHOUT MERCY.
SSSZAAAACK

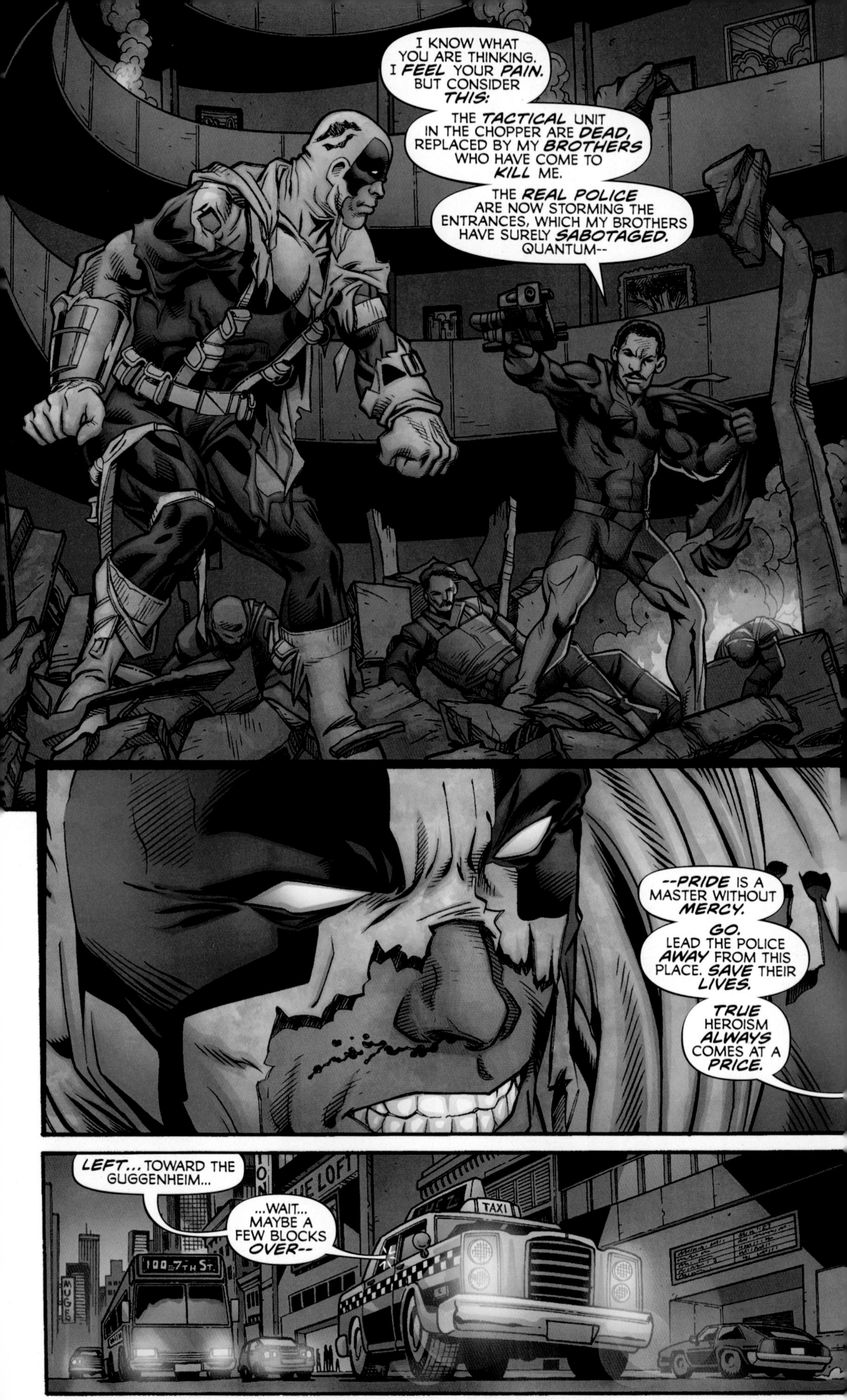

I KNOW WHAT YOU ARE THINKING. I FEEL YOUR PAIN. BUT CONSIDER THIS:
THE TACTICAL UNIT IN THE CHOPPER ARE DEAD, REPLACED BY MY BROTHERS WHO HAVE COME TO KILL ME.
THE REAL POLICE ARE NOW STORMING THE ENTRANCES, WHICH MY BROTHERS HAVE SURELY SABOTAGED. QUANTUM--
--PRIDE IS A MASTER WITHOUT MERCY.
GO. LEAD THE POLICE AWAY FROM THIS PLACE. SAVE THEIR LIVES.
TRUE HEROISM ALWAYS COMES AT A PRICE.
LEFT... TOWARD THE GUGGENHEIM...
...WAIT... MAYBE A FEW BLOCKS OVER--
TAXI

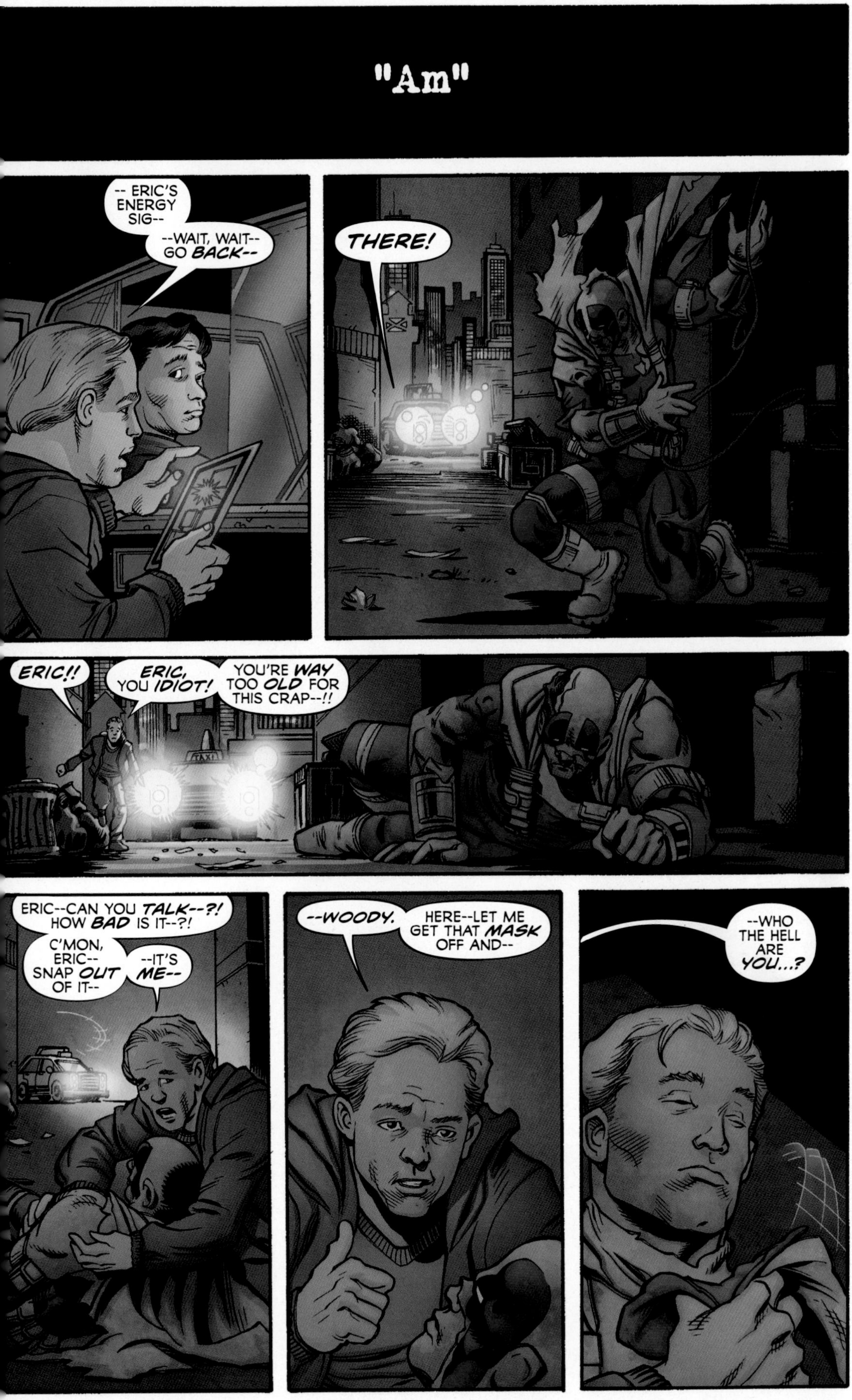
"Am"
-- ERIC'S ENERGY SIG--
--WAIT, WAIT-- GO BACK--
THERE!
ERIC!!
ERIC, YOU IDIOT!
YOU'RE WAY TOO OLD FOR THIS CRAP--!!
TAXI
ERIC--CAN YOU TALK--?! HOW BAD IS IT--?!
C'MON, ERIC-- SNAP OUT OF IT--
--IT'S ME--
--WOODY.
HERE--LET ME GET THAT MASK OFF AND--
--WHO THE HELL ARE YOU...?

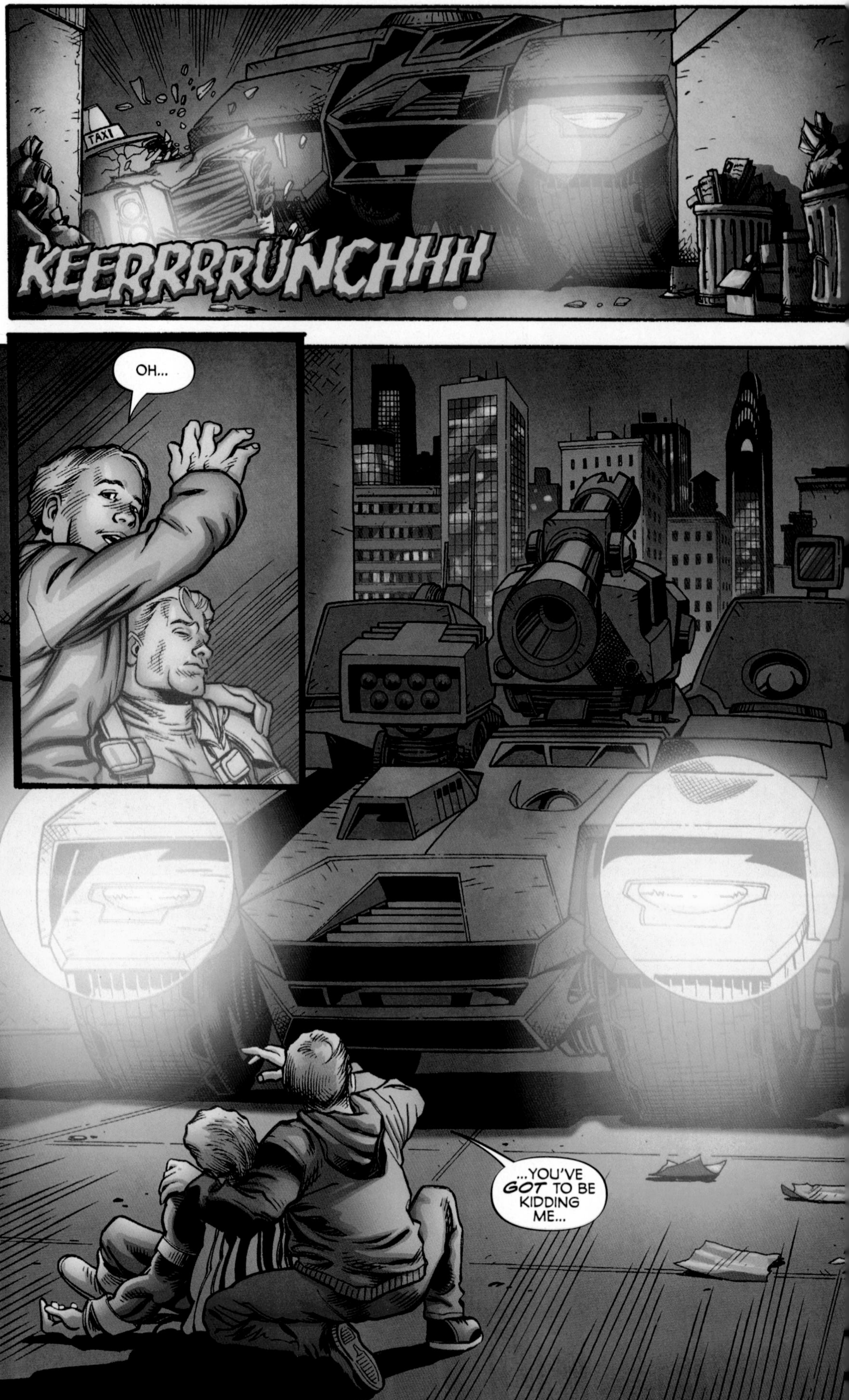
KEERRRRUNCHHH
TAXI
OH...
...YOU'VE *GOT* TO BE KIDDING ME...

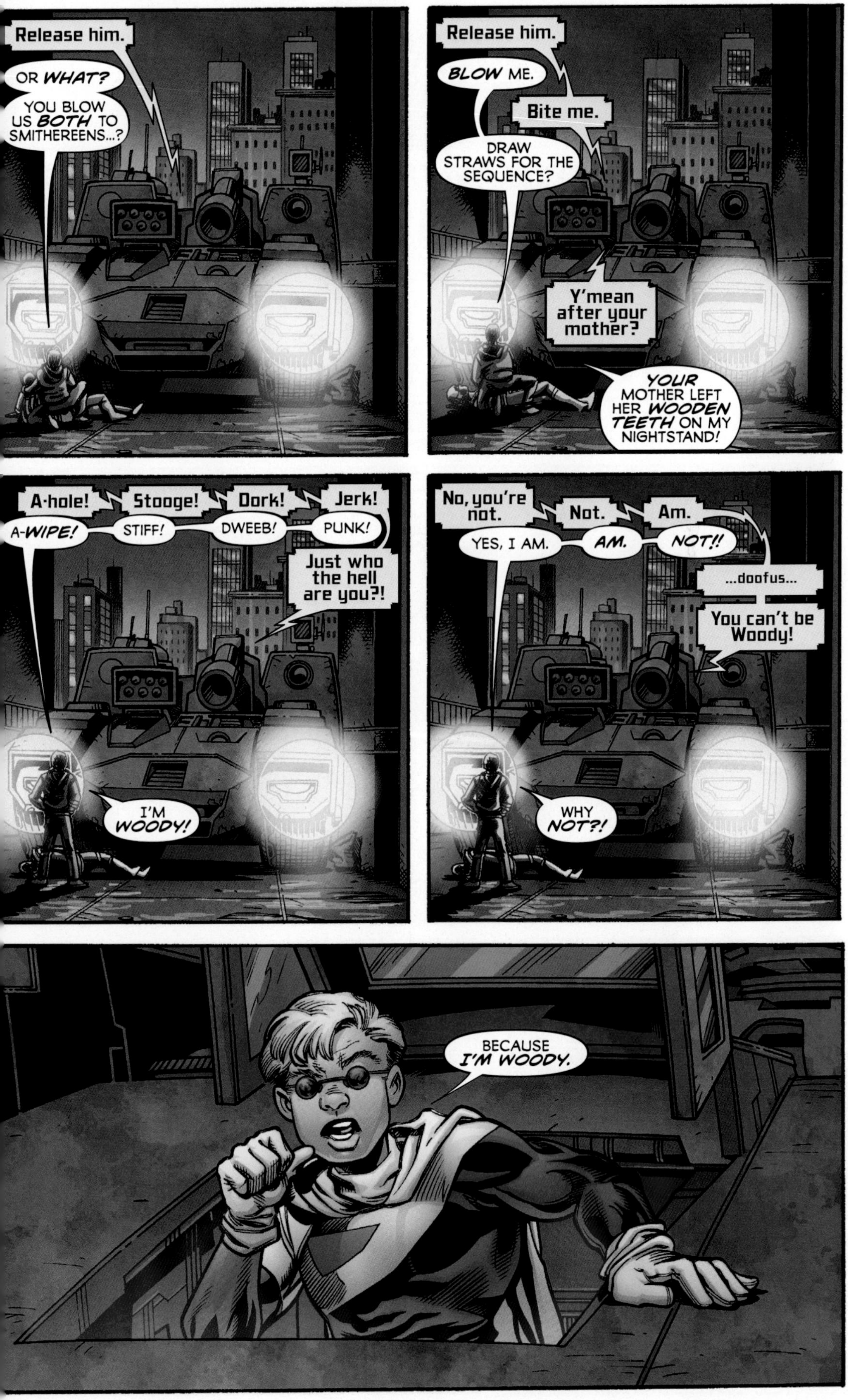
Release him.
OR WHAT?
YOU BLOW US BOTH TO SMITHEREENS...?
Release him.
BLOW ME.
Bite me.
DRAW STRAWS FOR THE SEQUENCE?
Y'mean after your mother?
YOUR MOTHER LEFT HER WOODEN TEETH ON MY NIGHTSTAND!
A-hole!
A-WIPE!
Stooge!
STIFF!
Dork!
DWEEB!
Jerk!
PUNK!
Just who the hell are you?!
I'M WOODY!
No, you're not.
YES, I AM.
Not.
AM.
Am.
NOT!!
...doofus...
You can't be Woody!
WHY NOT?!
BECAUSE I'M WOODY.

"Obligatory Flashback Sequence"

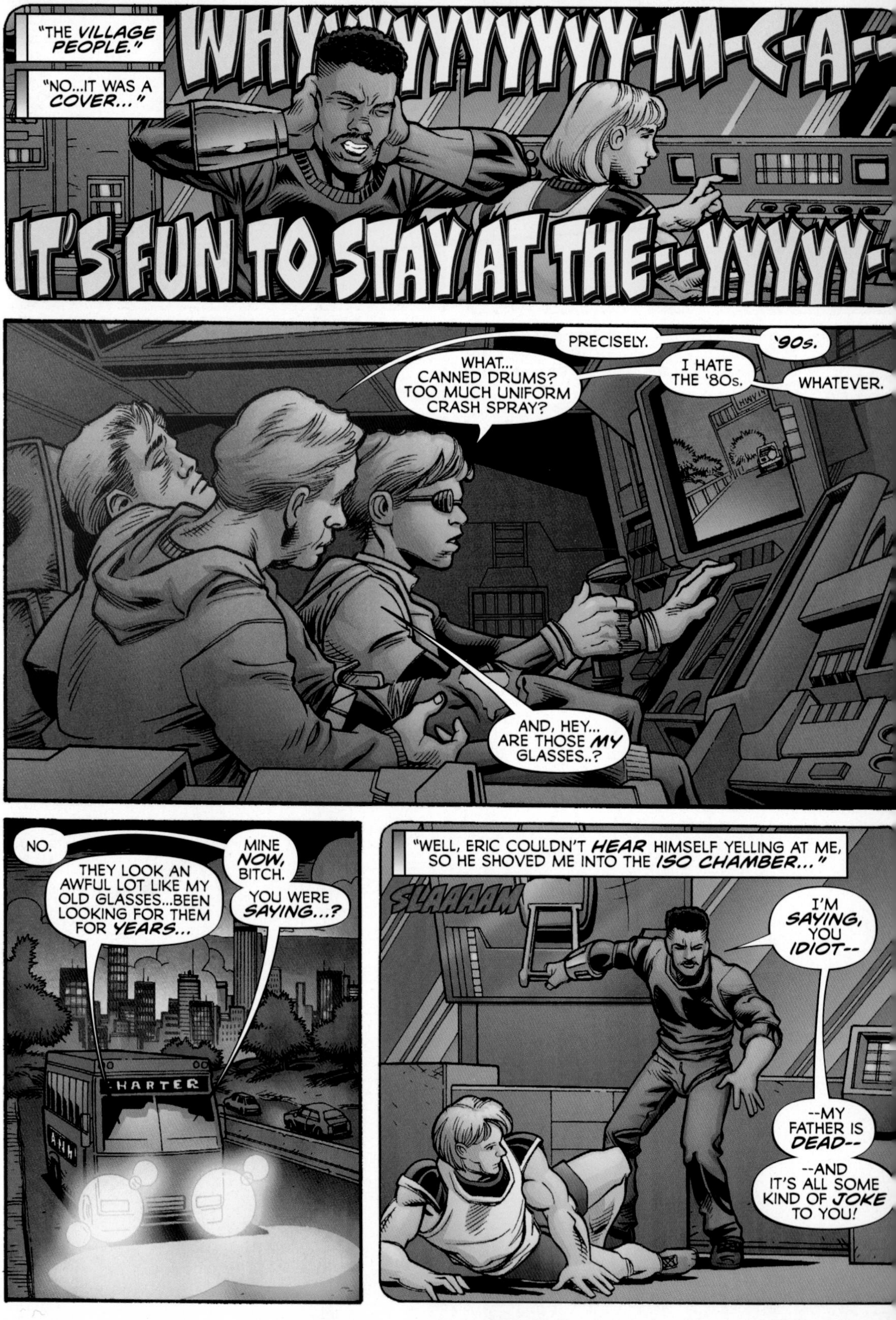
"THE VILLAGE PEOPLE."
"NO...IT WAS A COVER..."
WHYYYYYYYYY-M-C-A--
IT'S FUN TO STAY AT THE--YYYYY-
WHAT... CANNED DRUMS? TOO MUCH UNIFORM CRASH SPRAY?
PRECISELY.
I HATE THE '80s.
'90s.
WHATEVER.
AND, HEY... ARE THOSE MY GLASSES..?
NO.
THEY LOOK AN AWFUL LOT LIKE MY OLD GLASSES...BEEN LOOKING FOR THEM FOR YEARS...
MINE NOW, BITCH.
YOU WERE SAYING...?
HARTER
"WELL, ERIC COULDN'T HEAR HIMSELF YELLING AT ME, SO HE SHOVED ME INTO THE ISO CHAMBER..."
SLAAAAM
I'M SAYING, YOU IDIOT--
--MY FATHER IS DEAD--
--AND IT'S ALL SOME KIND OF JOKE TO YOU!

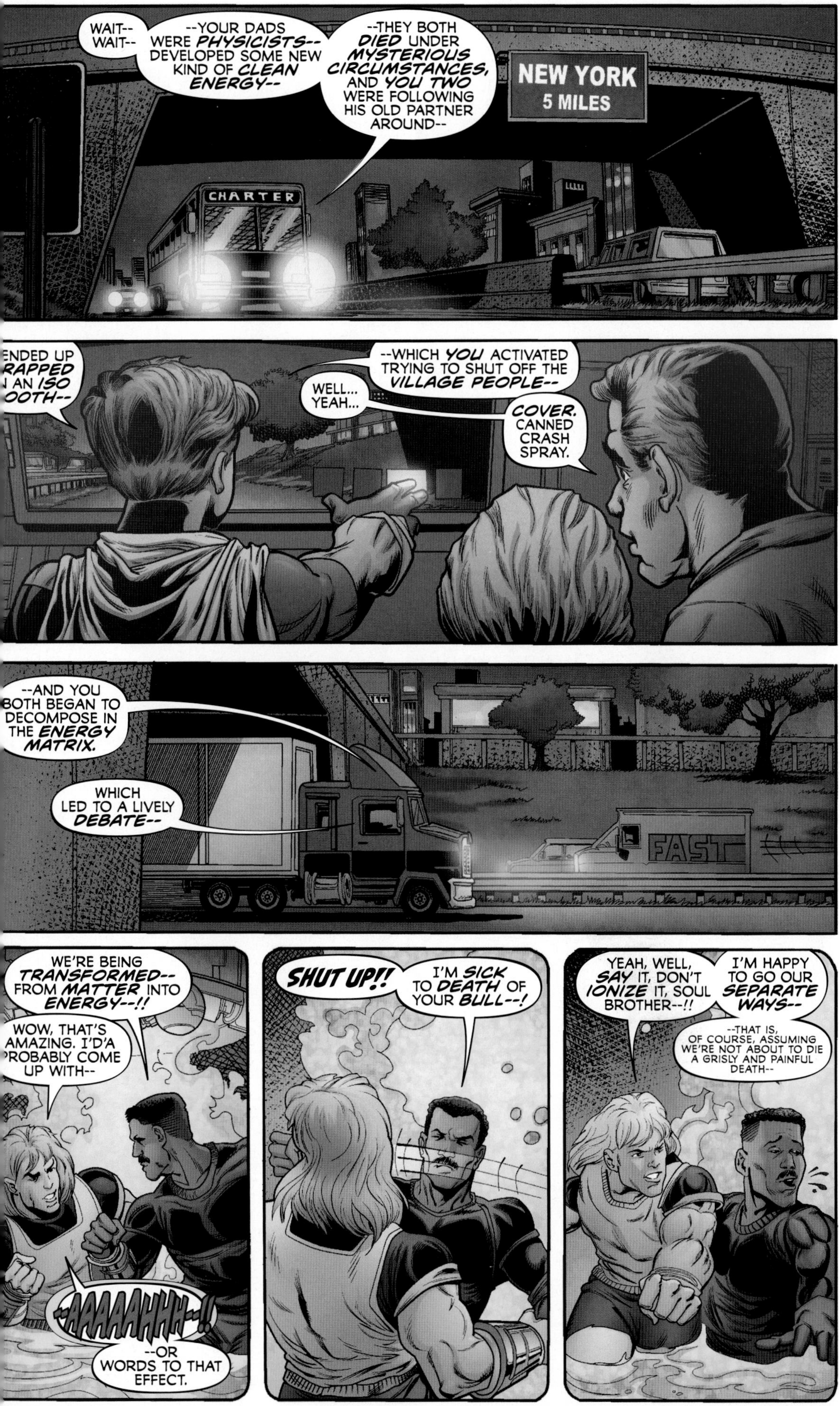

WAIT-- WAIT--
--YOUR DADS WERE PHYSICISTS-- DEVELOPED SOME NEW KIND OF CLEAN ENERGY--
--THEY BOTH DIED UNDER MYSTERIOUS CIRCUMSTANCES, AND YOU TWO WERE FOLLOWING HIS OLD PARTNER AROUND--
NEW YORK 5 MILES
CHARTER
ENDED UP RAPPED N AN ISO OOTH--
--WHICH YOU ACTIVATED TRYING TO SHUT OFF THE VILLAGE PEOPLE--
WELL... YEAH...
COVER. CANNED CRASH SPRAY.
--AND YOU BOTH BEGAN TO DECOMPOSE IN THE ENERGY MATRIX.
WHICH LED TO A LIVELY DEBATE--
FAST
WE'RE BEING TRANSFORMED-- FROM MATTER INTO ENERGY--!!
WOW, THAT'S AMAZING. I'D'A PROBABLY COME UP WITH--
-AAAAAHHH--!!
--OR WORDS TO THAT EFFECT.
SHUT UP!!
I'M SICK TO DEATH OF YOUR BULL--!
YEAH, WELL, SAY IT, DON'T IONIZE IT, SOUL BROTHER--!!
I'M HAPPY TO GO OUR SEPARATE WAYS--
--THAT IS, OF COURSE, ASSUMING WE'RE NOT ABOUT TO DIE A GRISLY AND PAINFUL DEATH--

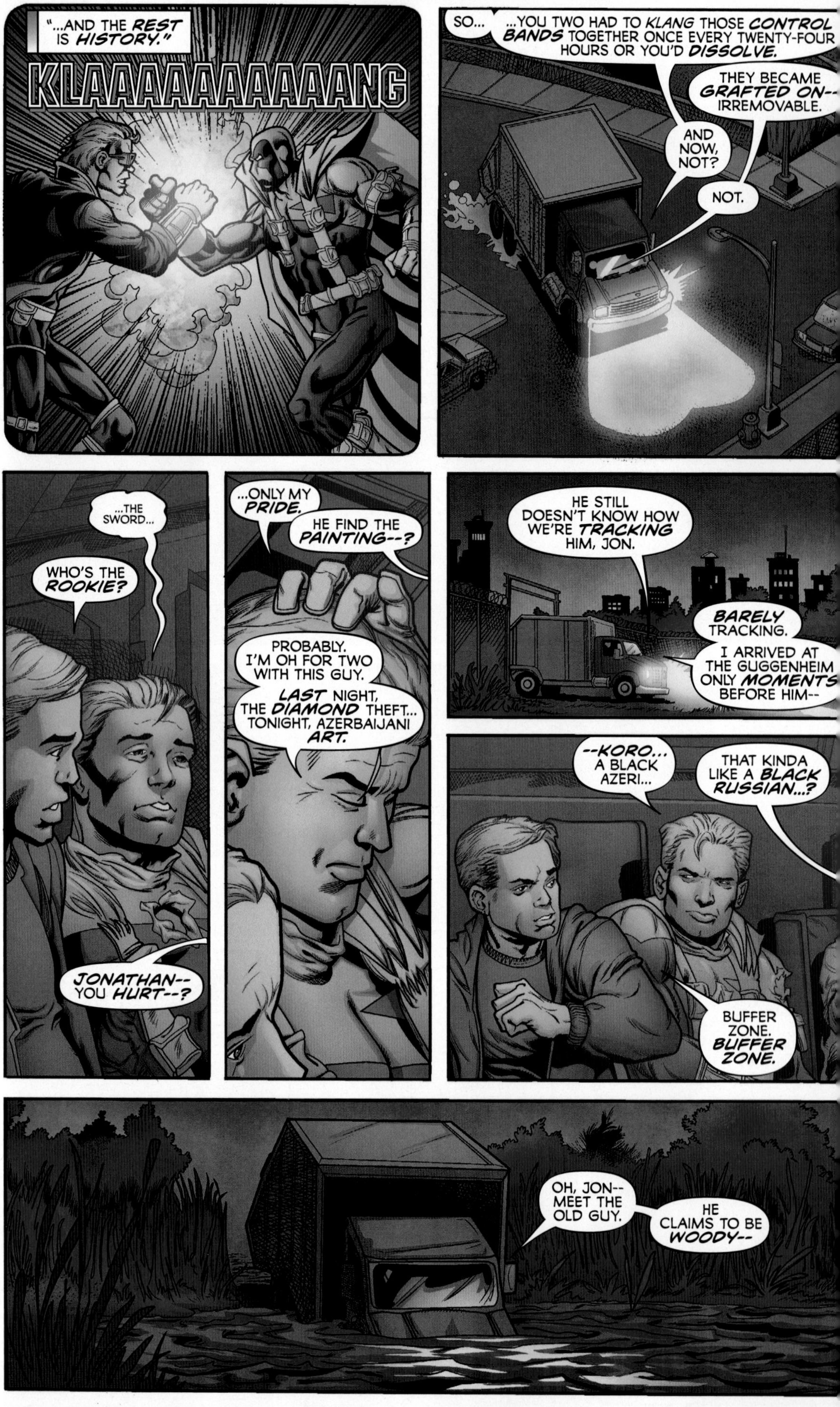
"...AND THE REST IS HISTORY."
KLAAAAAAAAAAANG
SO...
...YOU TWO HAD TO KLANG THOSE CONTROL BANDS TOGETHER ONCE EVERY TWENTY-FOUR HOURS OR YOU'D DISSOLVE.
THEY BECAME GRAFTED ON-- IRREMOVABLE.
AND NOW, NOT?
NOT.
...THE SWORD...
WHO'S THE ROOKIE?
JONATHAN-- YOU HURT--?
...ONLY MY PRIDE.
HE FIND THE PAINTING--?
PROBABLY. I'M OH FOR TWO WITH THIS GUY.
LAST NIGHT, THE DIAMOND THEFT... TONIGHT, AZERBAIJANI ART.
HE STILL DOESN'T KNOW HOW WE'RE TRACKING HIM, JON.
BARELY TRACKING.
I ARRIVED AT THE GUGGENHEIM ONLY MOMENTS BEFORE HIM--
--KORO... A BLACK AZERI...
THAT KINDA LIKE A BLACK RUSSIAN...?
BUFFER ZONE. BUFFER ZONE.
OH, JON-- MEET THE OLD GUY.
HE CLAIMS TO BE WOODY--

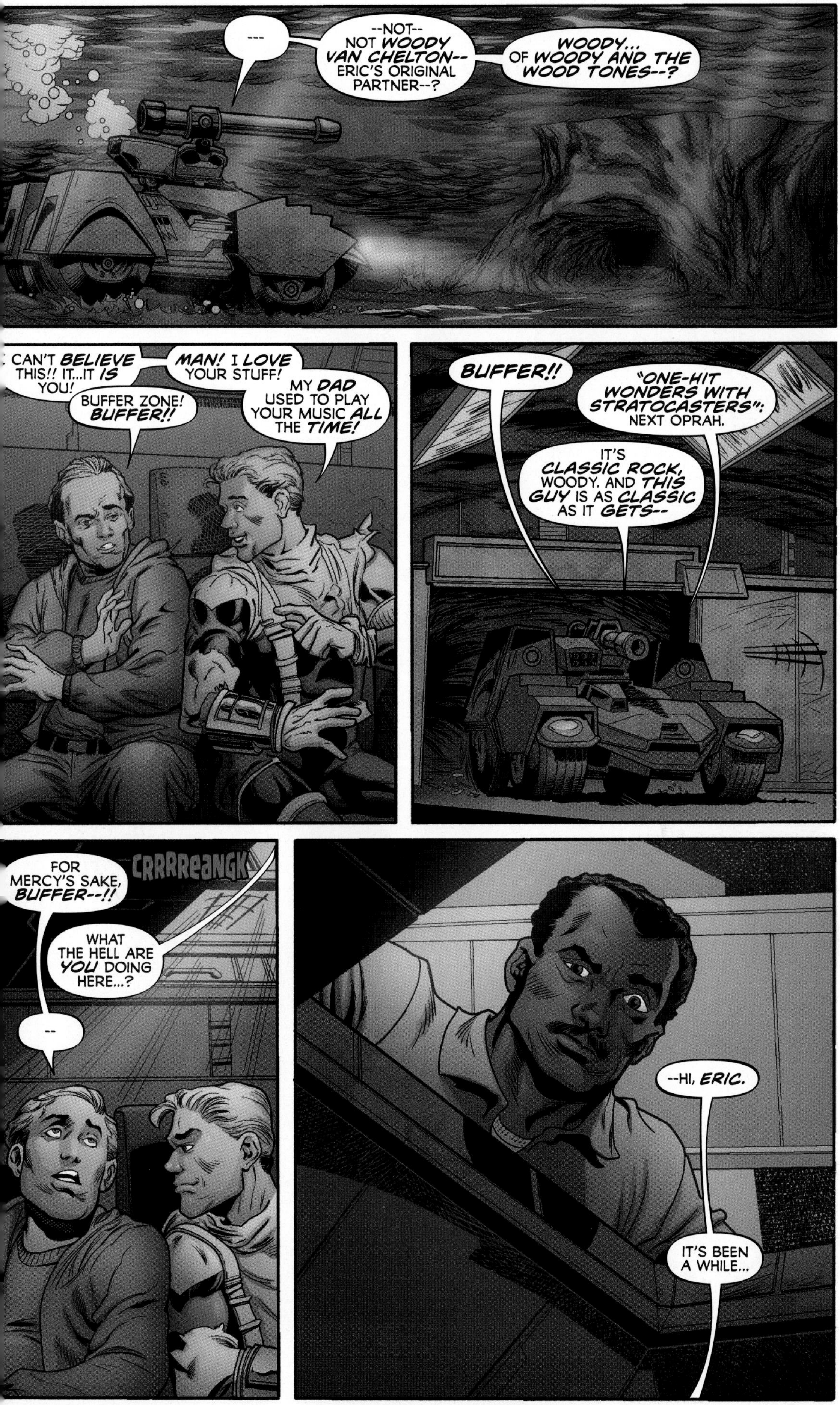

--NOT-- NOT WOODY VAN CHELTON-- ERIC'S ORIGINAL PARTNER--?
WOODY... OF WOODY AND THE WOOD TONES--?
CAN'T BELIEVE THIS!! IT...IT IS YOU!
MAN! I LOVE YOUR STUFF!
BUFFER ZONE! BUFFER!!
MY DAD USED TO PLAY YOUR MUSIC ALL THE TIME!
BUFFER!!
"ONE-HIT WONDERS WITH STRATOCASTERS": NEXT OPRAH.
IT'S CLASSIC ROCK, WOODY. AND THIS GUY IS AS CLASSIC AS IT GETS--
CRRRREANGK
FOR MERCY'S SAKE, BUFFER--!!
WHAT THE HELL ARE YOU DOING HERE...?
--
--HI, ERIC.
IT'S BEEN A WHILE...

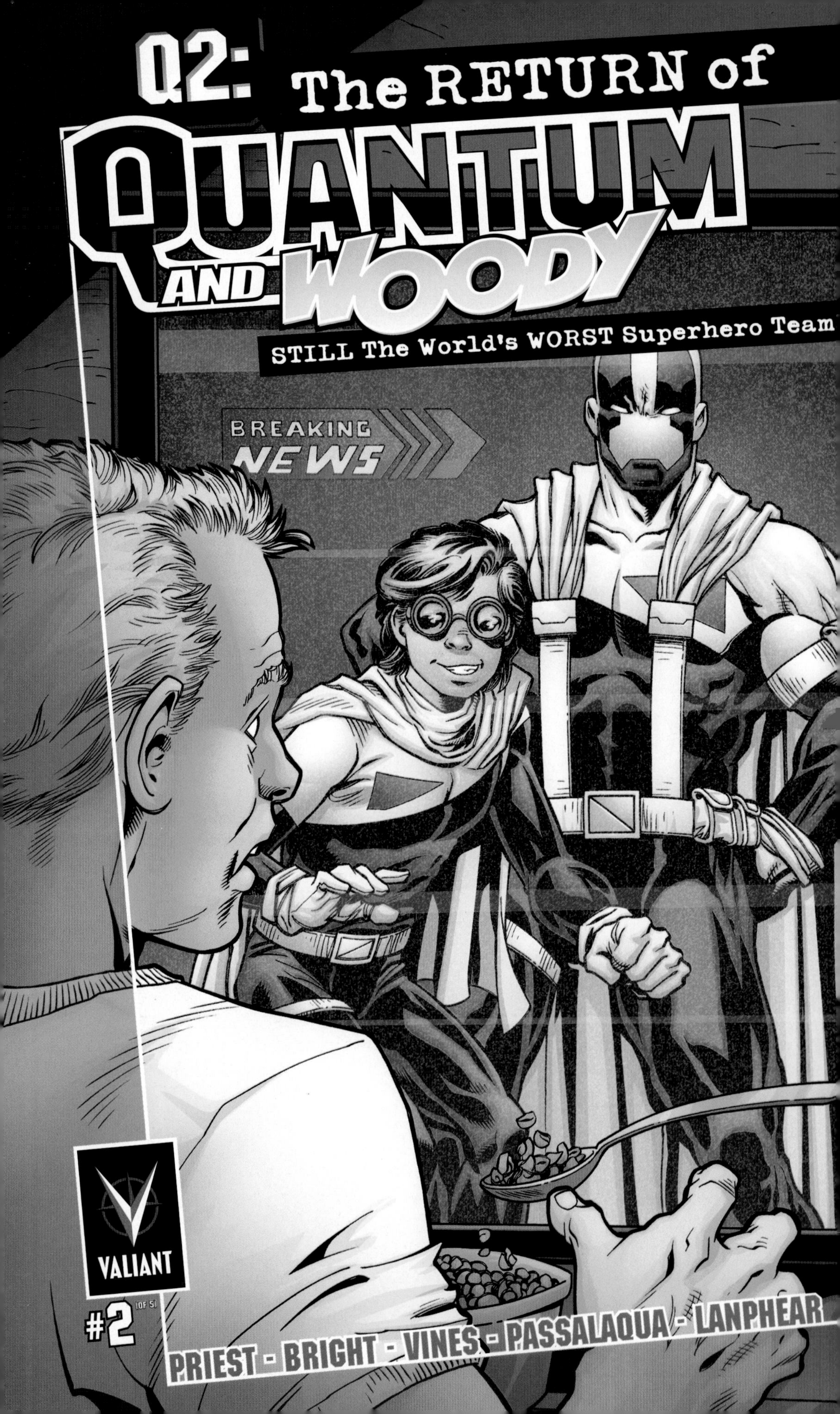

Q2: The RETURN of
QUANTUM AND WOODY
STILL The World's WORST Superhero Team
BREAKING NEWS
VALIANT
#2 (OF 5)
PRIEST - BRIGHT - VINES - PASSALAQUA - LANPHEAR

"Quesadilla"

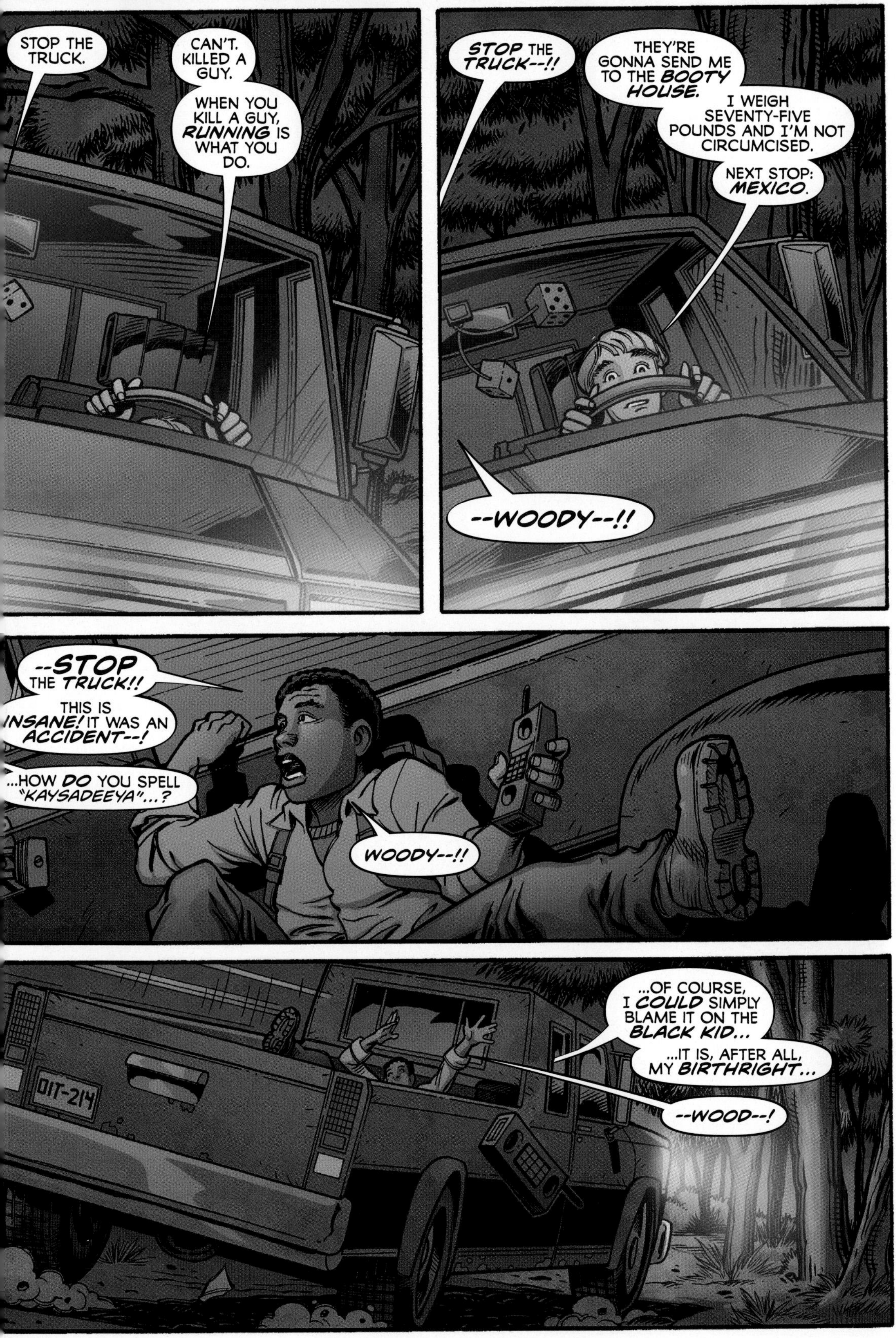

STOP THE TRUCK.
CAN'T. KILLED A GUY.
WHEN YOU KILL A GUY, RUNNING IS WHAT YOU DO.
STOP THE TRUCK--!!
THEY'RE GONNA SEND ME TO THE BOOTY HOUSE.
I WEIGH SEVENTY-FIVE POUNDS AND I'M NOT CIRCUMCISED.
NEXT STOP: MEXICO.
--WOODY--!!
--STOP THE TRUCK!!
THIS IS INSANE! IT WAS AN ACCIDENT--!
...HOW DO YOU SPELL "KAYSADEEYA"...?
WOODY--!!
DIT-214
...OF COURSE, I COULD SIMPLY BLAME IT ON THE BLACK KID...
...IT IS, AFTER ALL, MY BIRTHRIGHT...
--WOOD--!

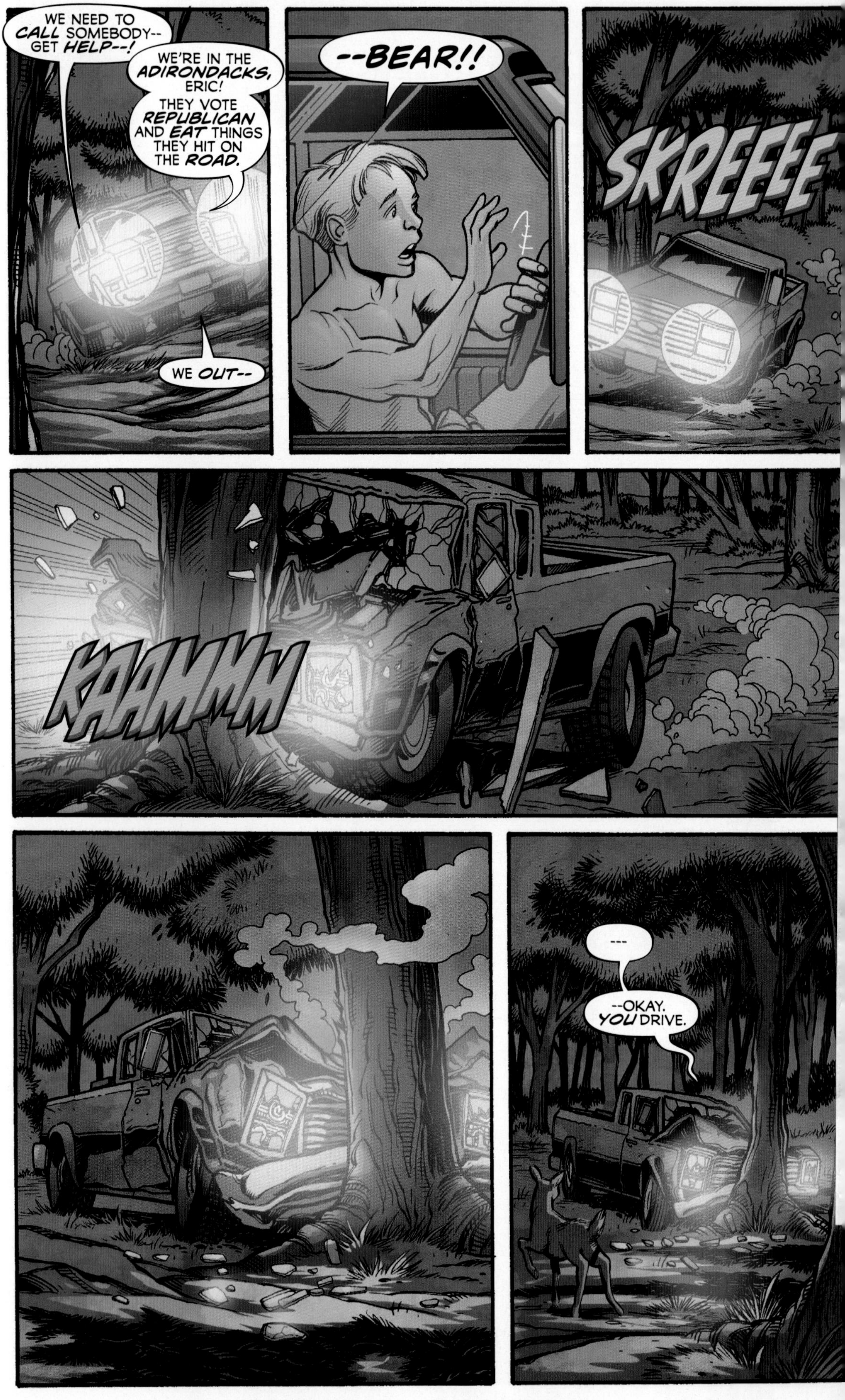
WE NEED TO CALL SOMEBODY-- GET HELP--!
WE'RE IN THE ADIRONDACKS, ERIC!
THEY VOTE REPUBLICAN AND EAT THINGS THEY HIT ON THE ROAD.
WE OUT--
--BEAR!!
SKREEEE
KRAMMM

--OKAY. YOU DRIVE.

"Heroes"

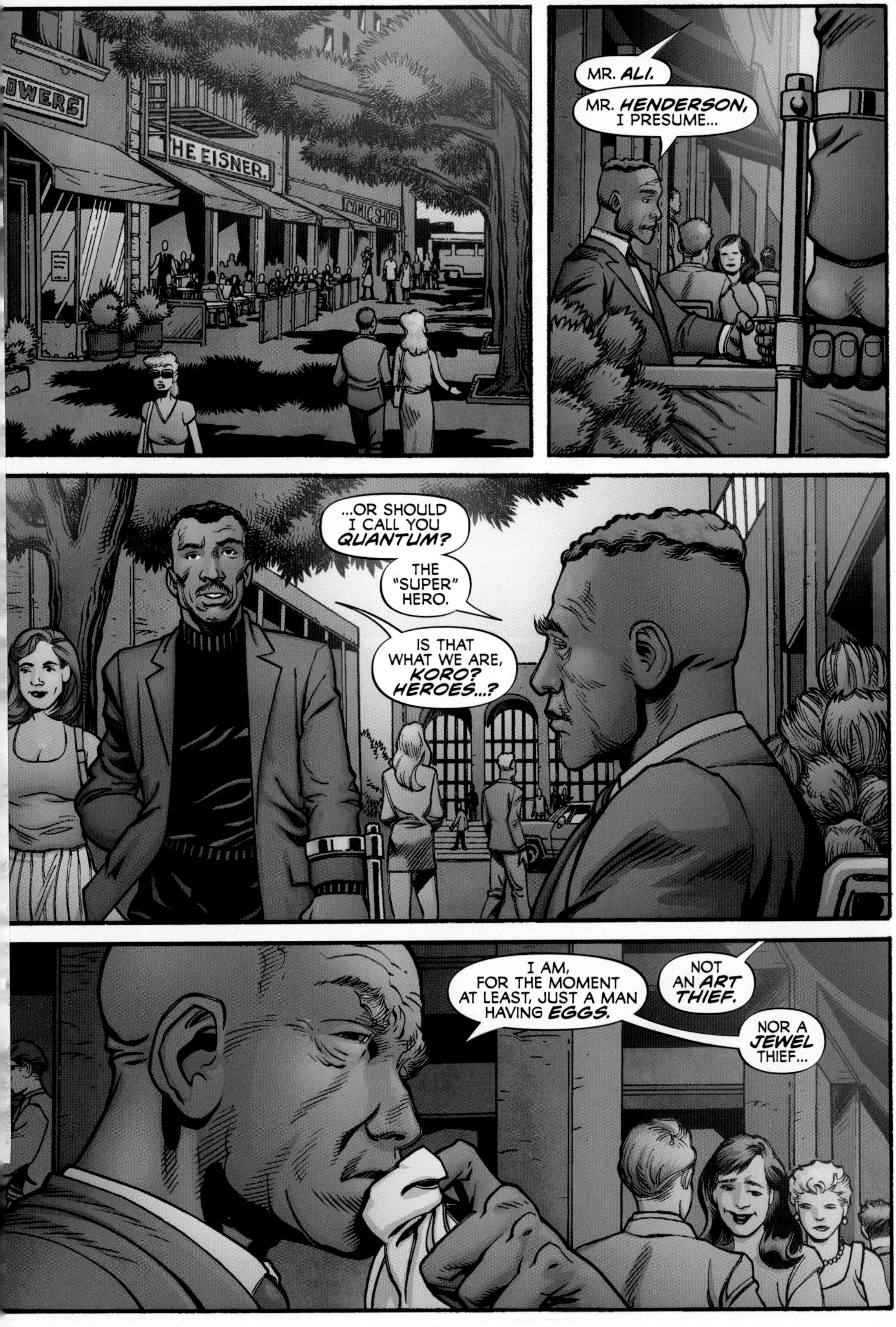
COMIC SHOP
MR. ALI.
MR. HENDERSON, I PRESUME...
...OR SHOULD I CALL YOU QUANTUM?
THE "SUPER" HERO.
IS THAT WHAT WE ARE, KORO? HEROES...?
I AM, FOR THE MOMENT AT LEAST, JUST A MAN HAVING EGGS.
NOT AN ART THIEF.
NOR A JEWEL THIEF...

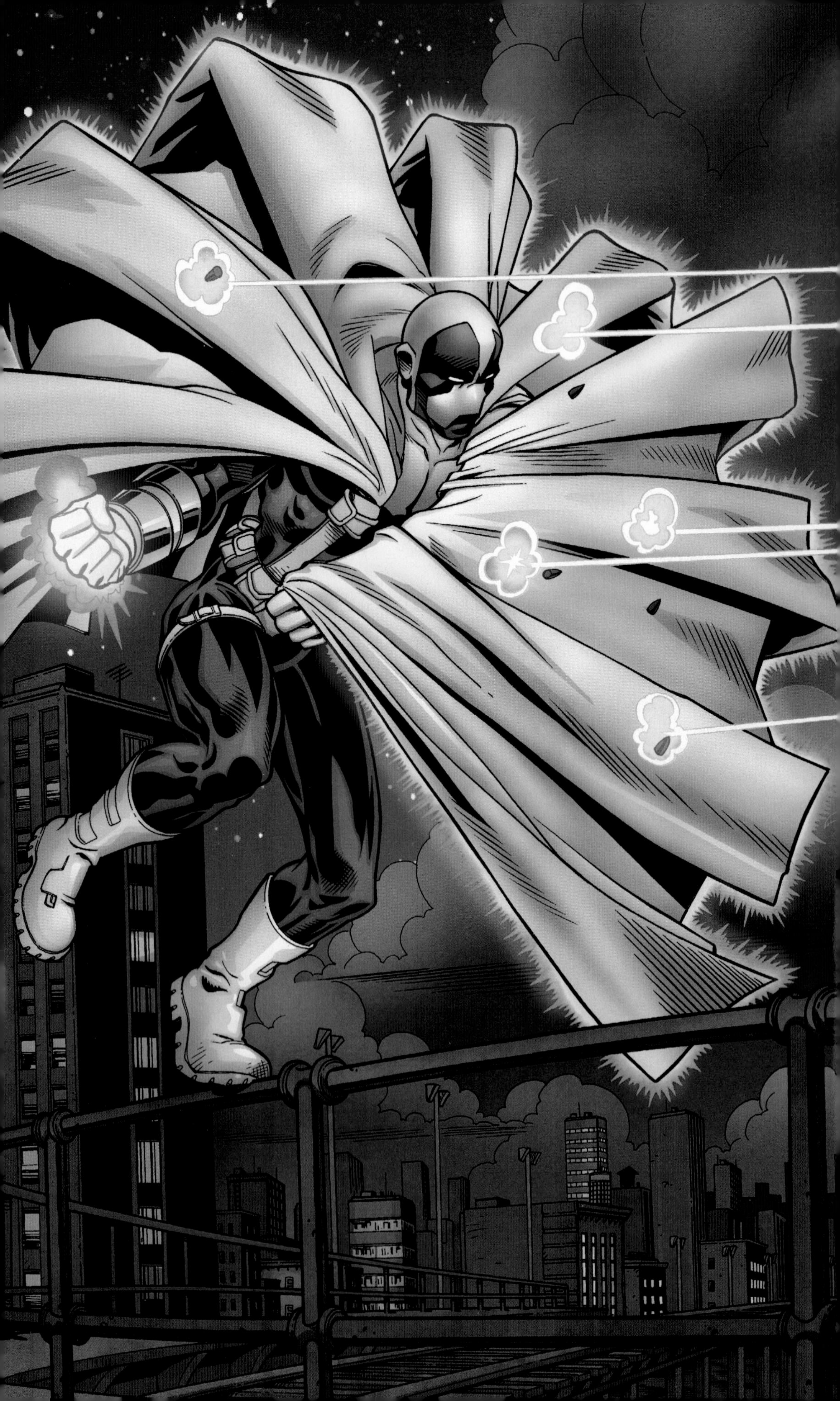

"The Jewel Thief"

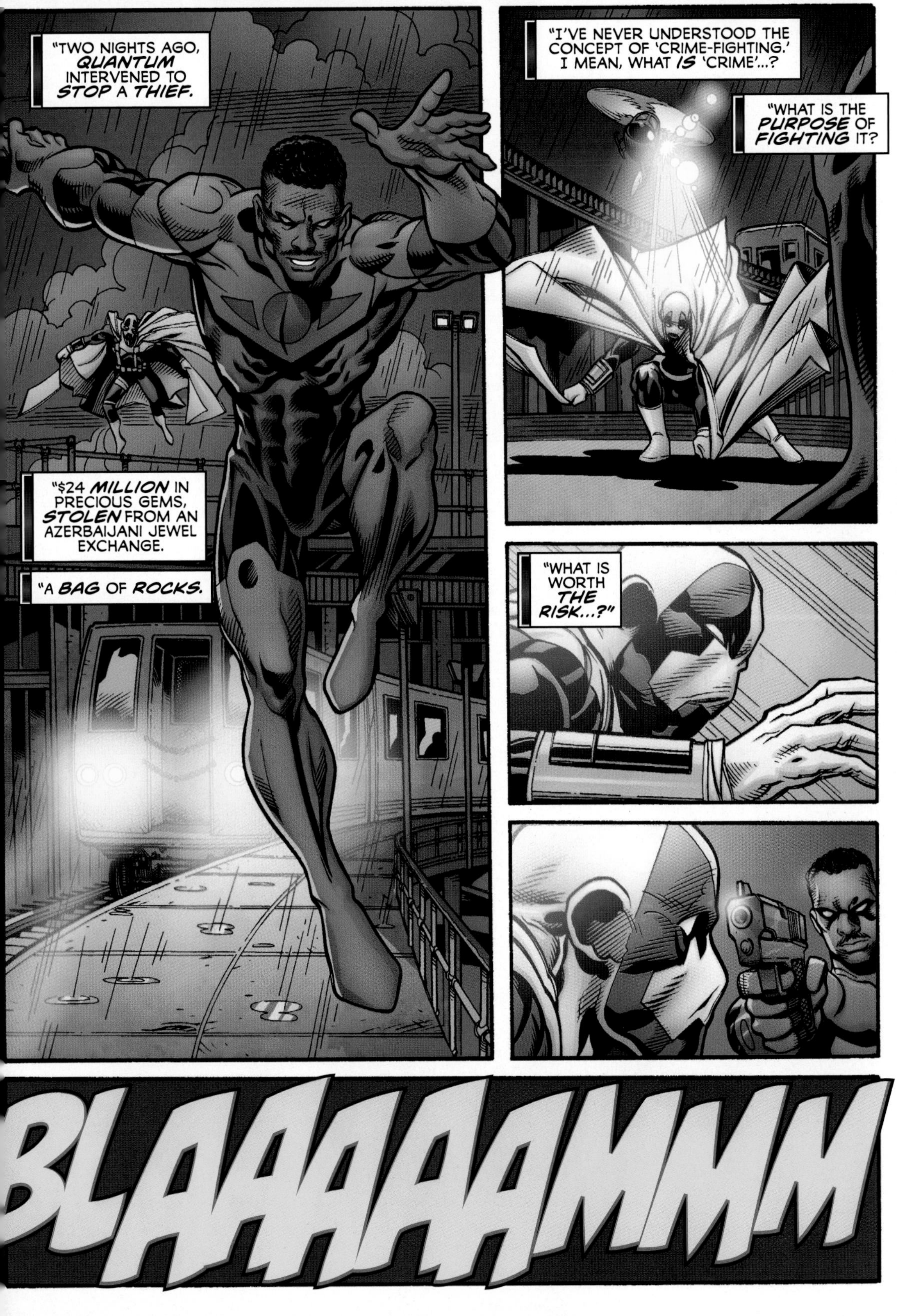

"TWO NIGHTS AGO, QUANTUM INTERVENED TO STOP A THIEF.
"$24 MILLION IN PRECIOUS GEMS, STOLEN FROM AN AZERBAIJANI JEWEL EXCHANGE.
"A BAG OF ROCKS.
"I'VE NEVER UNDERSTOOD THE CONCEPT OF 'CRIME-FIGHTING.' I MEAN, WHAT IS 'CRIME'...?
"WHAT IS THE PURPOSE OF FIGHTING IT?
"WHAT IS WORTH THE RISK...?"
BLAAAAMMM

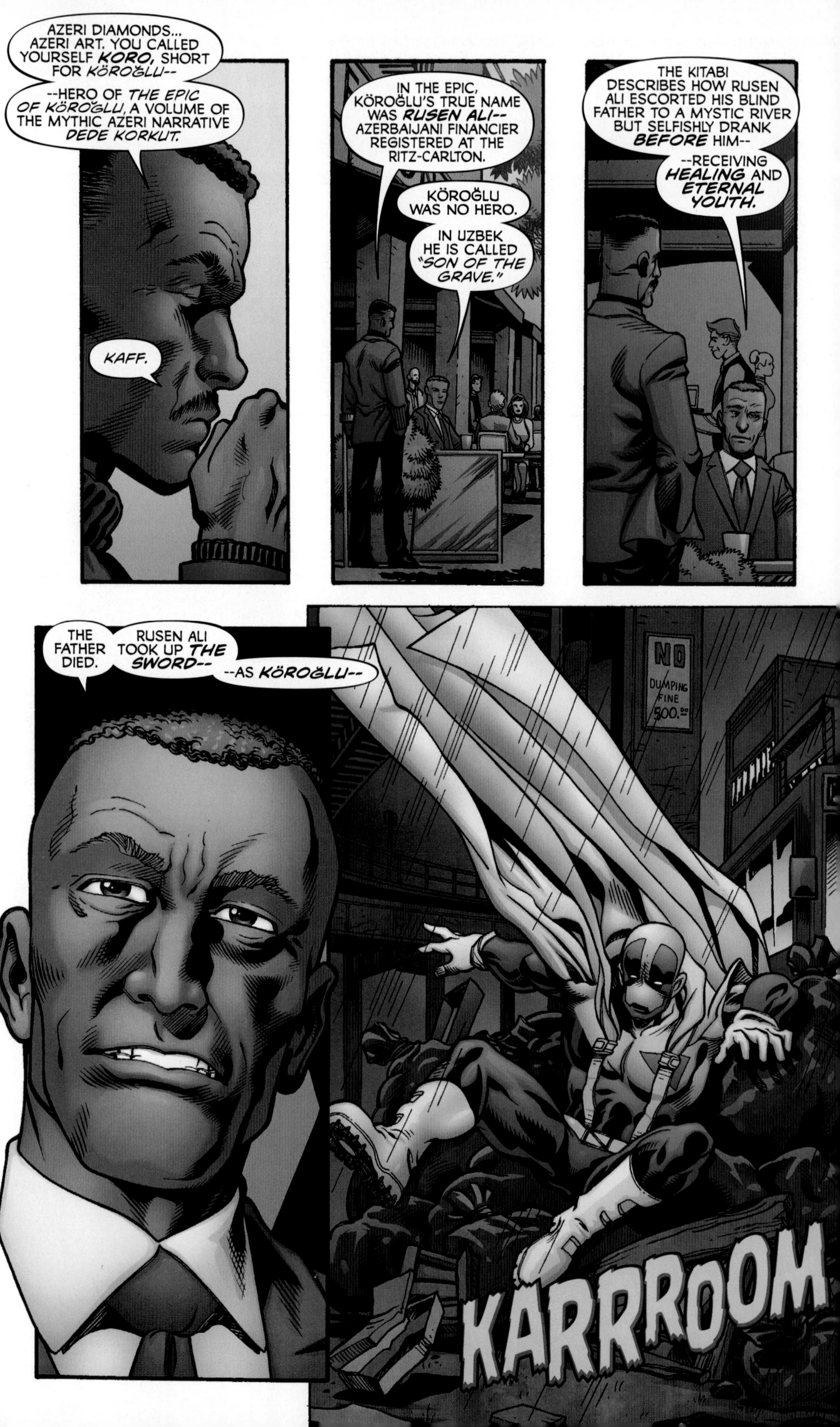

AZERI DIAMONDS... AZERI ART. YOU CALLED YOURSELF KORO, SHORT FOR KÖROĞLU--
--HERO OF THE EPIC OF KÖROĞLU, A VOLUME OF THE MYTHIC AZERI NARRATIVE DEDE KORKUT.
KAFF.
IN THE EPIC, KÖROĞLU'S TRUE NAME WAS RUSEN ALI-- AZERBAIJANI FINANCIER REGISTERED AT THE RITZ-CARLTON.
KÖROĞLU WAS NO HERO.
IN UZBEK HE IS CALLED "SON OF THE GRAVE."
THE KITABI DESCRIBES HOW RUSEN ALI ESCORTED HIS BLIND FATHER TO A MYSTIC RIVER BUT SELFISHLY DRANK BEFORE HIM--
--RECEIVING HEALING AND ETERNAL YOUTH.
THE FATHER DIED.
RUSEN ALI TOOK UP THE SWORD--
--AS KÖROĞLU--
NO DUMPING FINE $500.00
KARRROOM

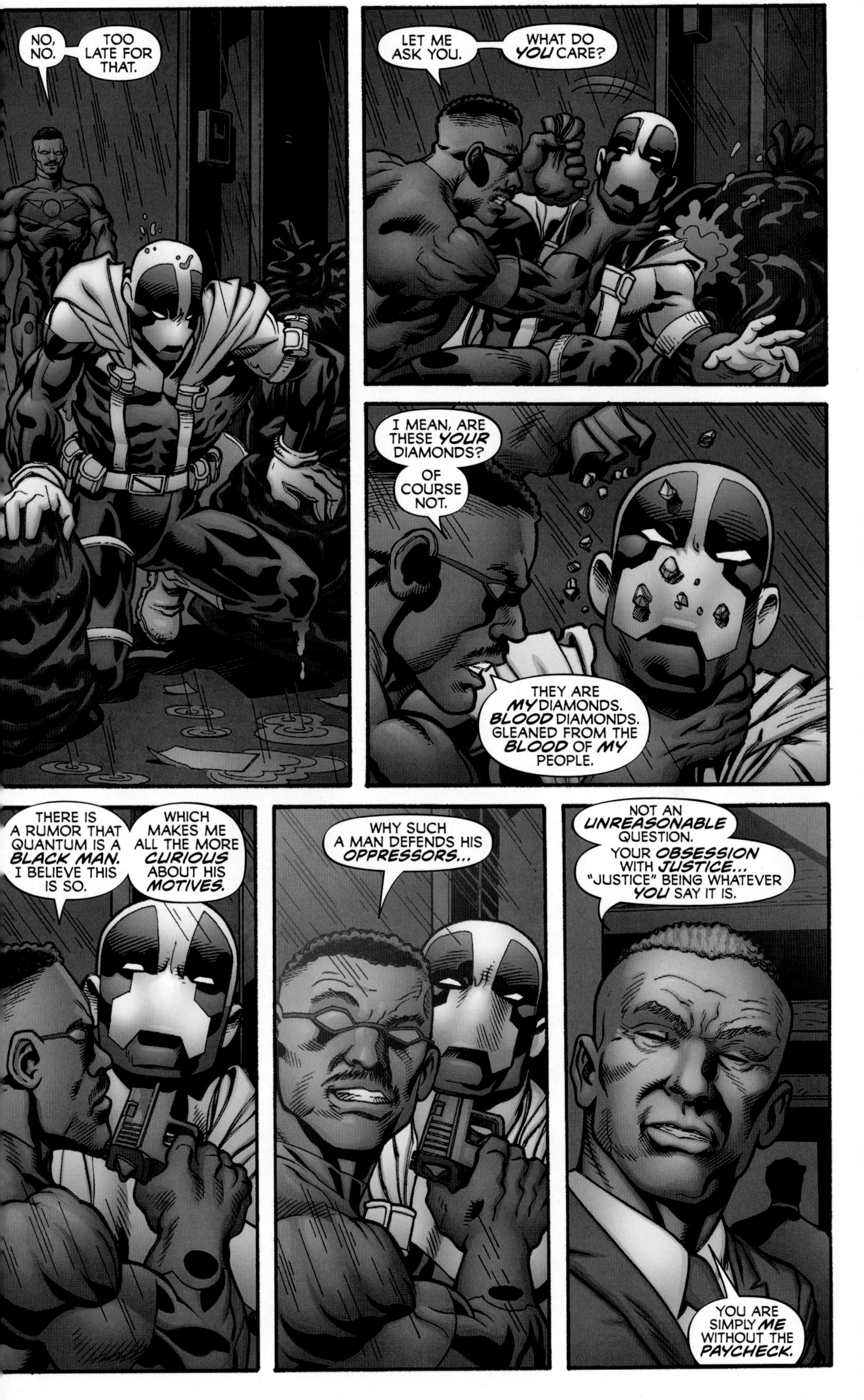
NO, NO.
TOO LATE FOR THAT.
LET ME ASK YOU.
WHAT DO *YOU* CARE?
I MEAN, ARE THESE *YOUR* DIAMONDS?
OF COURSE NOT.
THEY ARE *MY* DIAMONDS. *BLOOD* DIAMONDS. GLEANED FROM THE *BLOOD* OF *MY* PEOPLE.
THERE IS A RUMOR THAT QUANTUM IS A *BLACK MAN.* I BELIEVE THIS IS SO.
WHICH MAKES ME ALL THE MORE *CURIOUS* ABOUT HIS *MOTIVES.*
WHY SUCH A MAN DEFENDS HIS *OPPRESSORS...*
NOT AN *UNREASONABLE* QUESTION.
YOUR *OBSESSION* WITH *JUSTICE...* "JUSTICE" BEING WHATEVER *YOU* SAY IT IS.
YOU ARE SIMPLY *ME* WITHOUT THE *PAYCHECK.*

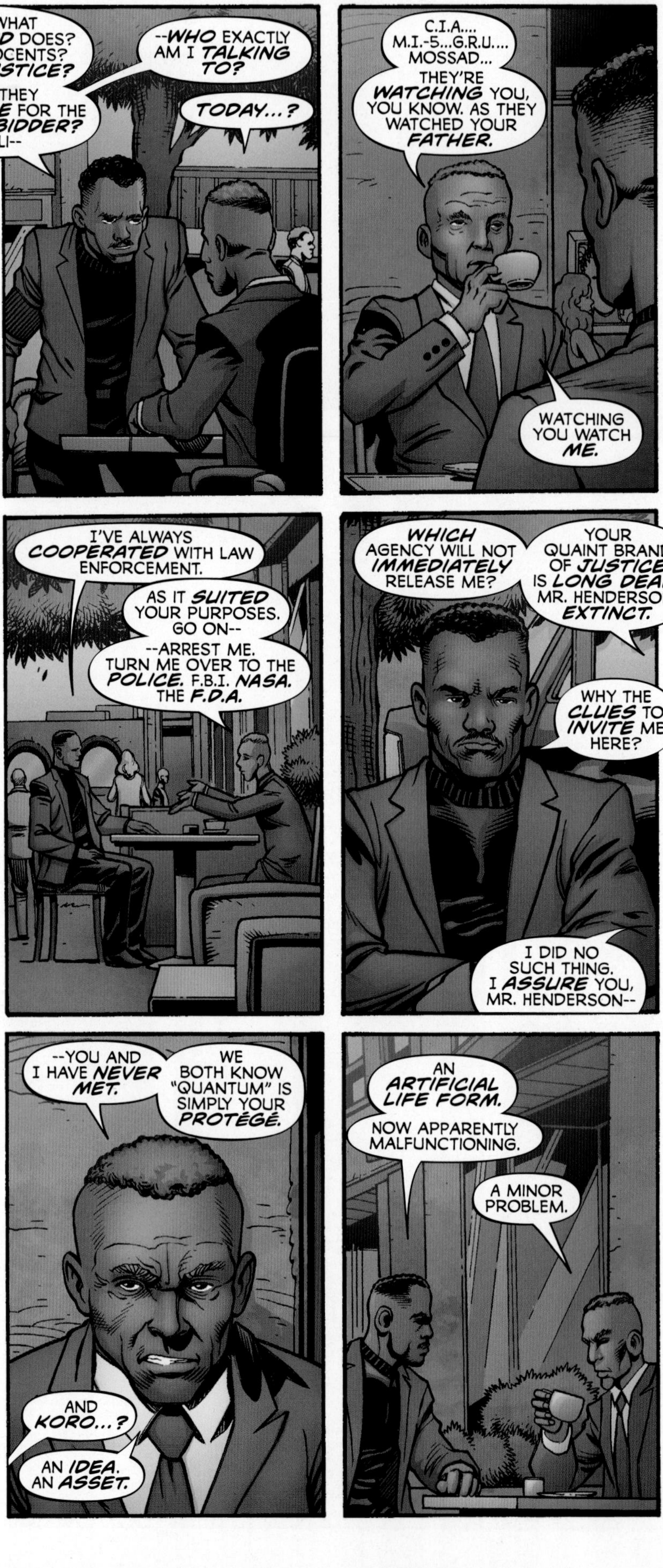

IS THAT WHAT THE SWORD DOES? DEFEND INNOCENTS? DISPENSE JUSTICE?
OR DO THEY JUST WHORE FOR THE HIGHEST BIDDER? MR. ALI--
--WHO EXACTLY AM I TALKING TO?
TODAY...?
C.I.A.... M.I.-5...G.R.U.... MOSSAD...
THEY'RE WATCHING YOU, YOU KNOW. AS THEY WATCHED YOUR FATHER.
WATCHING YOU WATCH ME.
I'VE ALWAYS COOPERATED WITH LAW ENFORCEMENT.
AS IT SUITED YOUR PURPOSES. GO ON--
--ARREST ME. TURN ME OVER TO THE POLICE. F.B.I. NASA. THE F.D.A.
WHICH AGENCY WILL NOT IMMEDIATELY RELEASE ME?
YOUR QUAINT BRAND OF JUSTICE IS LONG DEAD, MR. HENDERSON. EXTINCT.
WHY THE CLUES TO INVITE ME HERE?
I DID NO SUCH THING. I ASSURE YOU, MR. HENDERSON--
--YOU AND I HAVE NEVER MET.
WE BOTH KNOW "QUANTUM" IS SIMPLY YOUR PROTÉGÉ.
AND KORO...?
AN IDEA. AN ASSET.
AN ARTIFICIAL LIFE FORM.
NOW APPARENTLY MALFUNCTIONING.
A MINOR PROBLEM.

"One Hit"

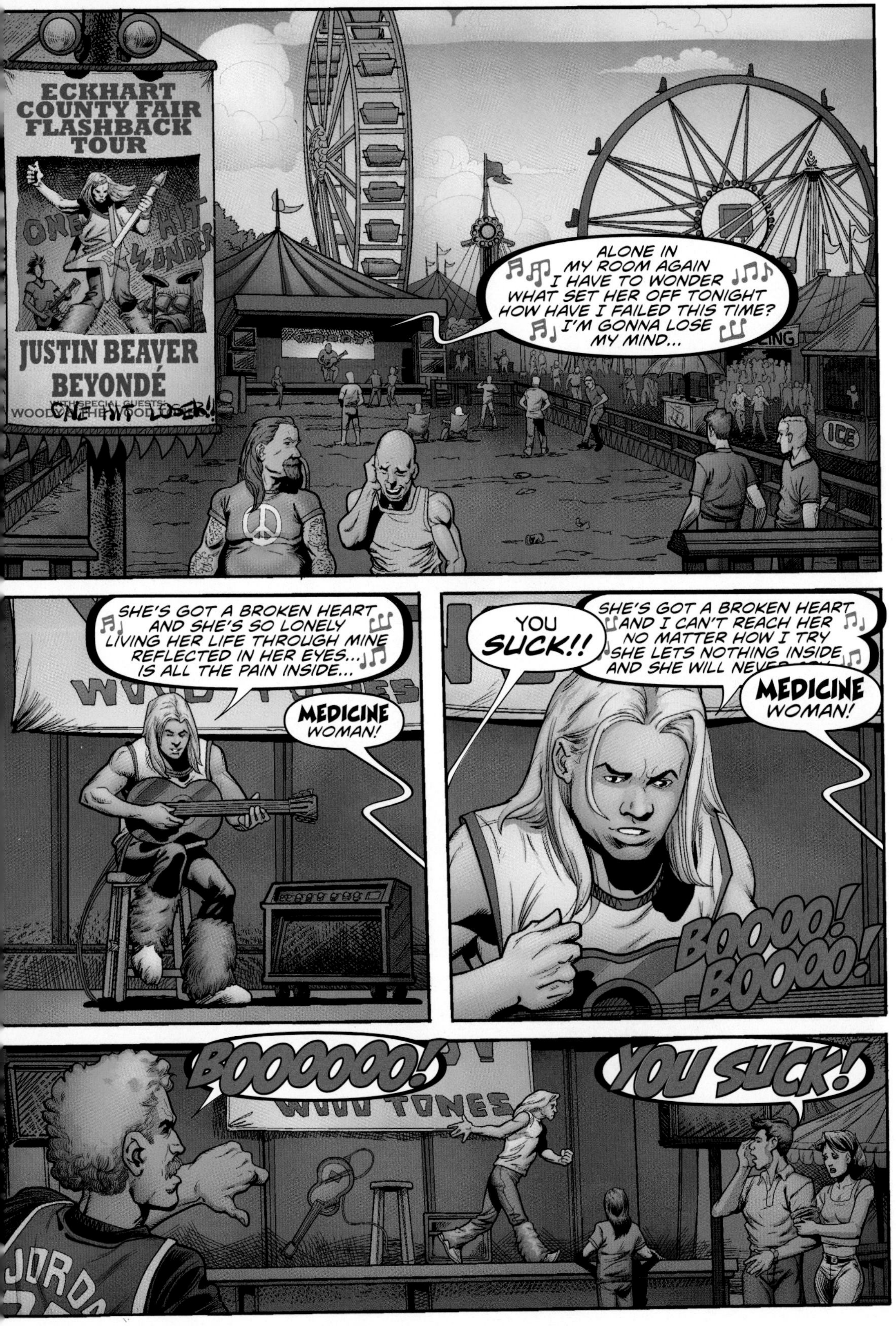

ECKHART COUNTY FAIR FLASHBACK TOUR
ONE HIT WONDER
JUSTIN BEAVER
BEYONDÉ
ONE HIT LOSER!
ALONE IN MY ROOM AGAIN I HAVE TO WONDER WHAT SET HER OFF TONIGHT HOW HAVE I FAILED THIS TIME? I'M GONNA LOSE MY MIND...
ICE
SHE'S GOT A BROKEN HEART AND SHE'S SO LONELY LIVING HER LIFE THROUGH MINE REFLECTED IN HER EYES... IS ALL THE PAIN INSIDE...
MEDICINE WOMAN!
YOU SUCK!!
SHE'S GOT A BROKEN HEART AND I CAN'T REACH HER NO MATTER HOW I TRY SHE LETS NOTHING INSIDE AND SHE WILL NEVE
MEDICINE WOMAN!
BOOOO! BOOOO!
BOOOOOO!
YOU SUCK!
WOOD TONES
JORDA

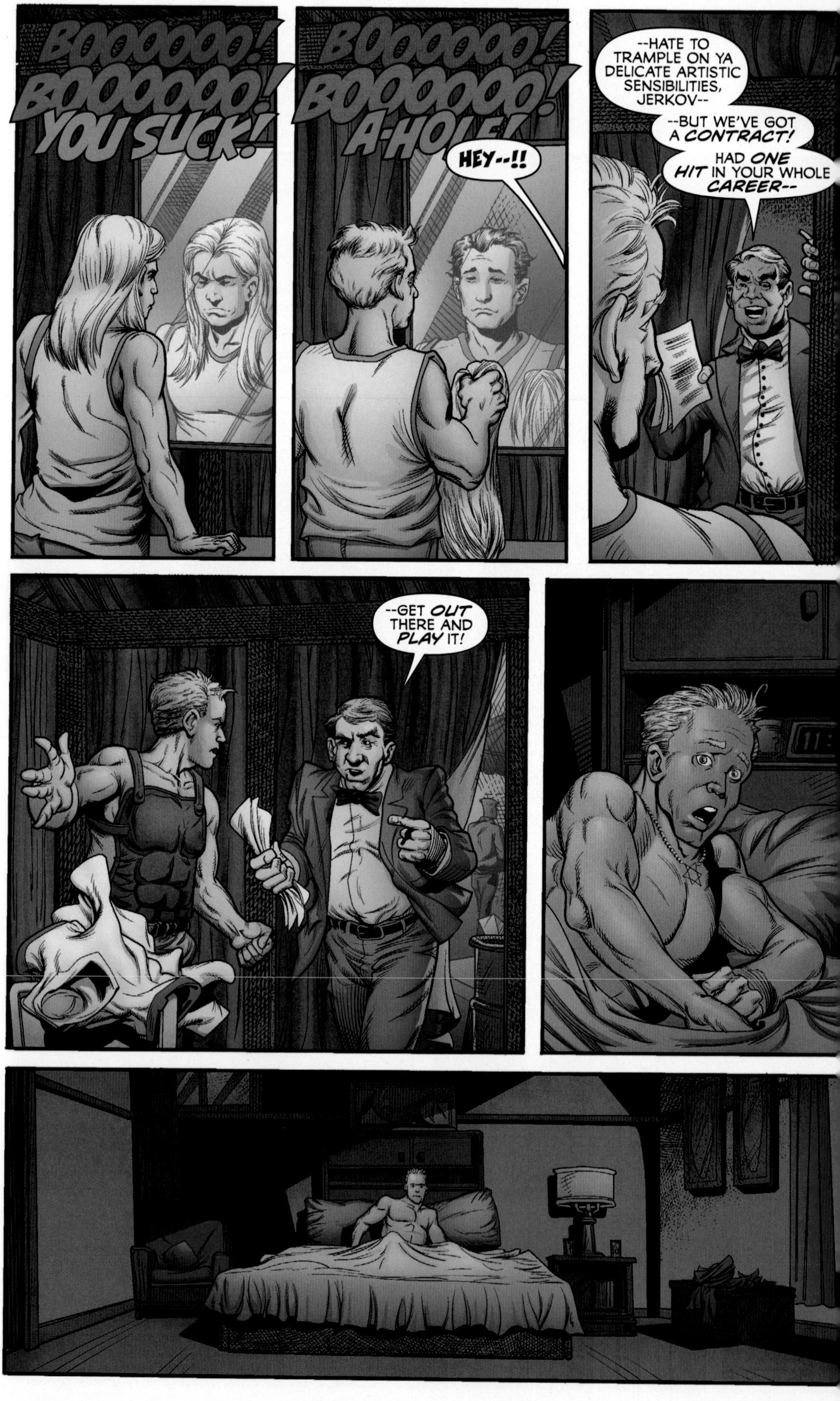
BOOOOOO! BOOOOOO! YOU SUCK!!
BOOOOOO! BOOOOOO! A-HOLE!
HEY--!!
--HATE TO TRAMPLE ON YA DELICATE ARTISTIC SENSIBILITIES, JERKOV--
--BUT WE'VE GOT A CONTRACT!
HAD ONE HIT IN YOUR WHOLE CAREER--
--GET OUT THERE AND PLAY IT!

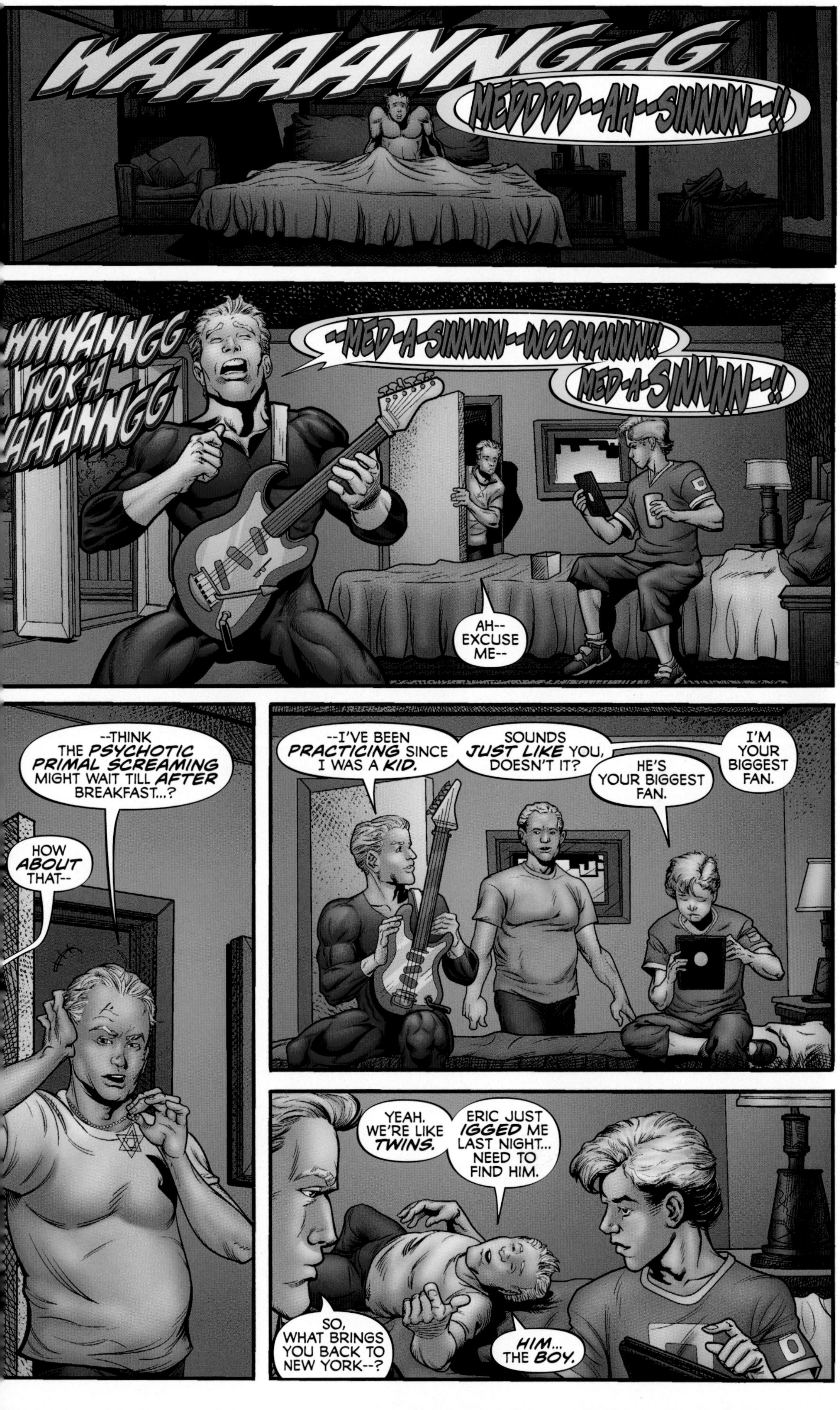
WAAAANNGGG
MEDDDD--AH--SINNNN--!!
HWWANNGG WOK-A WAAANNGG
--MED-A-SINNNN--WOOMANNN!!
MED-A-SINNNN--!!
AH-- EXCUSE ME--
--THINK THE PSYCHOTIC PRIMAL SCREAMING MIGHT WAIT TILL AFTER BREAKFAST...?
HOW ABOUT THAT--
--I'VE BEEN PRACTICING SINCE I WAS A KID.
SOUNDS JUST LIKE YOU, DOESN'T IT?
I'M YOUR BIGGEST FAN.
HE'S YOUR BIGGEST FAN.
YEAH. WE'RE LIKE TWINS.
ERIC JUST IGGED ME LAST NIGHT... NEED TO FIND HIM.
SO, WHAT BRINGS YOU BACK TO NEW YORK--?
HIM... THE BOY.

"The Boy"

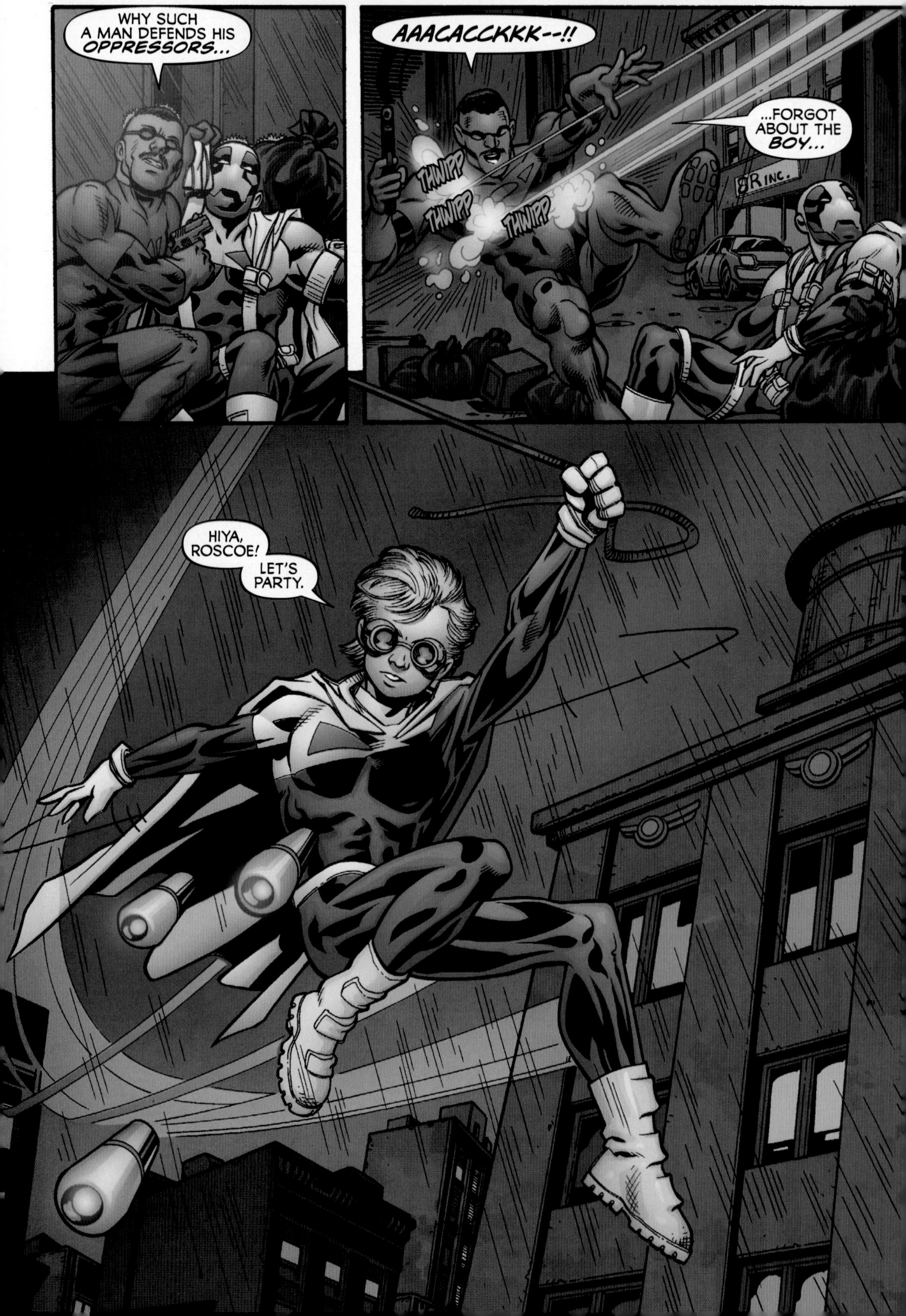
WHY SUCH A MAN DEFENDS HIS OPPRESSORS...
AAACACCKKK--!!
...FORGOT ABOUT THE BOY...
THWIPP
THWIPP
THWIPP
HIYA, ROSCOE!
LET'S PARTY.

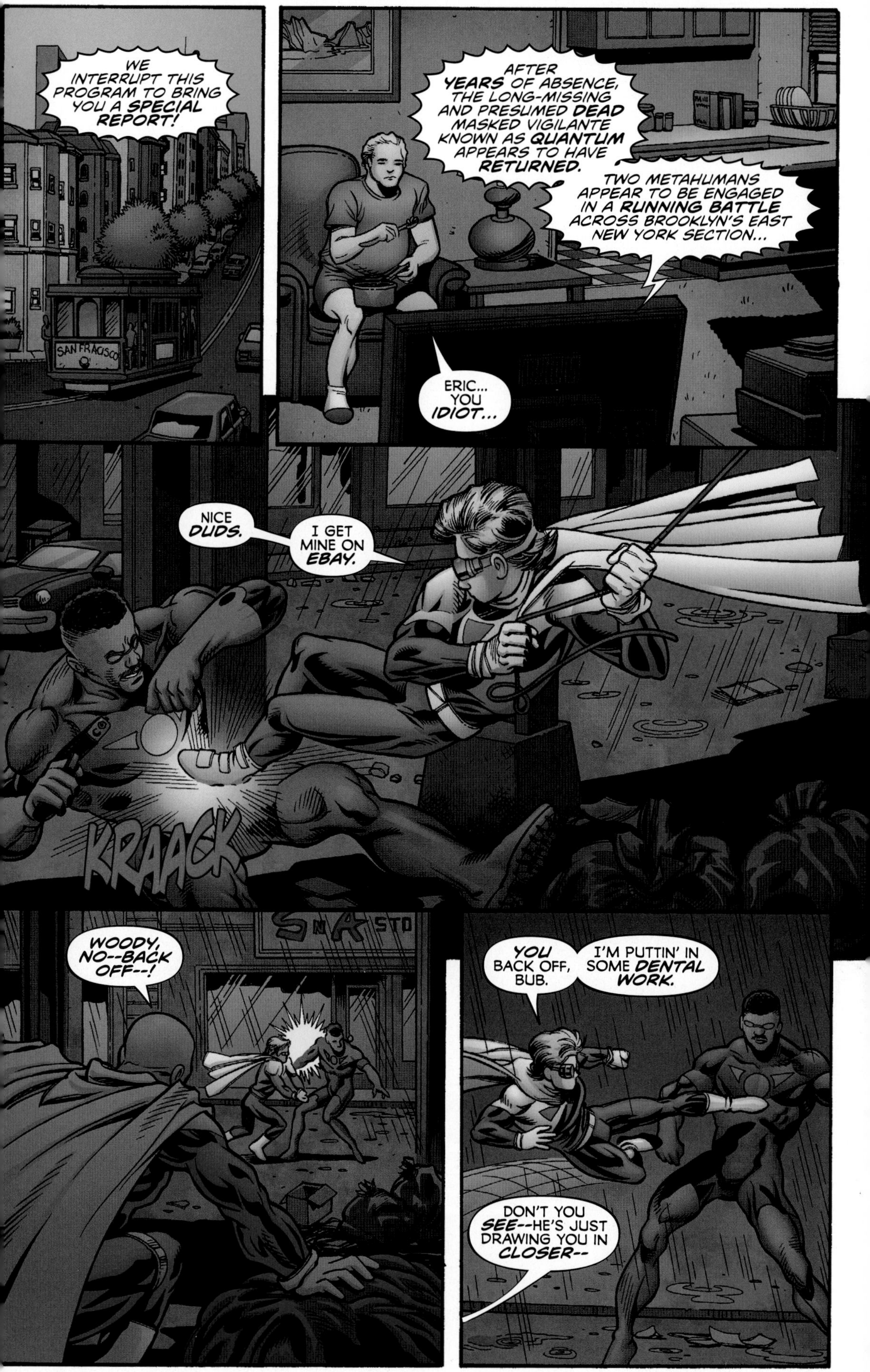
WE INTERRUPT THIS PROGRAM TO BRING YOU A SPECIAL REPORT!
AFTER YEARS OF ABSENCE, THE LONG-MISSING AND PRESUMED DEAD MASKED VIGILANTE KNOWN AS QUANTUM APPEARS TO HAVE RETURNED.
TWO METAHUMANS APPEAR TO BE ENGAGED IN A RUNNING BATTLE ACROSS BROOKLYN'S EAST NEW YORK SECTION...
ERIC... YOU IDIOT...
SAN FRANCISCO
NICE DUDS.
I GET MINE ON EBAY.
KRAACK
WOODY, NO--BACK OFF--!
YOU BACK OFF, BUB.
I'M PUTTIN' IN SOME DENTAL WORK.
DON'T YOU SEE--HE'S JUST DRAWING YOU IN CLOSER--

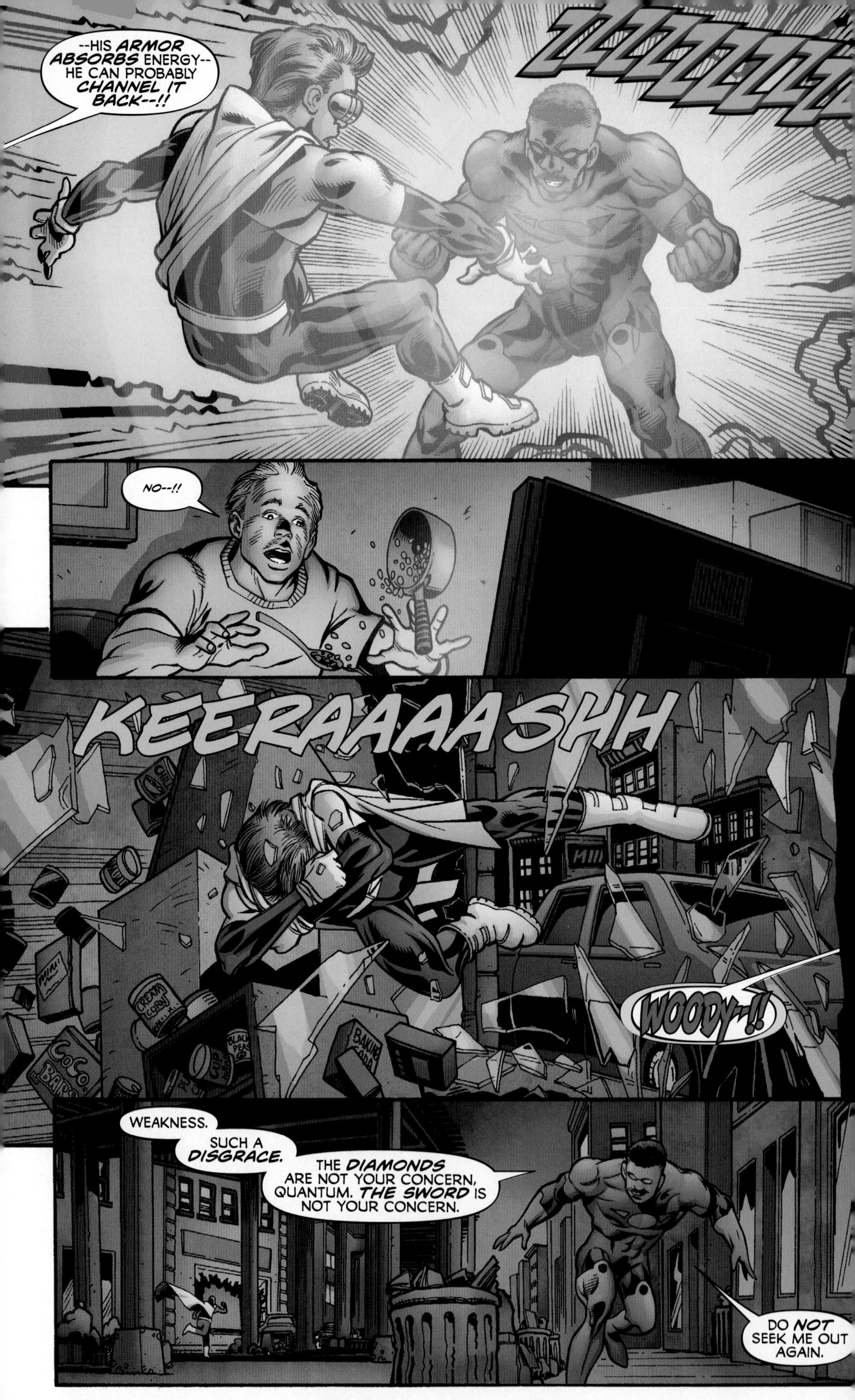
--HIS ARMOR ABSORBS ENERGY-- HE CAN PROBABLY CHANNEL IT BACK--!!
ZZZZZZZT
NO--!!
KEERAAAAASHH
WOODY--!!
WEAKNESS.
SUCH A DISGRACE.
THE DIAMONDS ARE NOT YOUR CONCERN, QUANTUM. THE SWORD IS NOT YOUR CONCERN.
DO NOT SEEK ME OUT AGAIN.

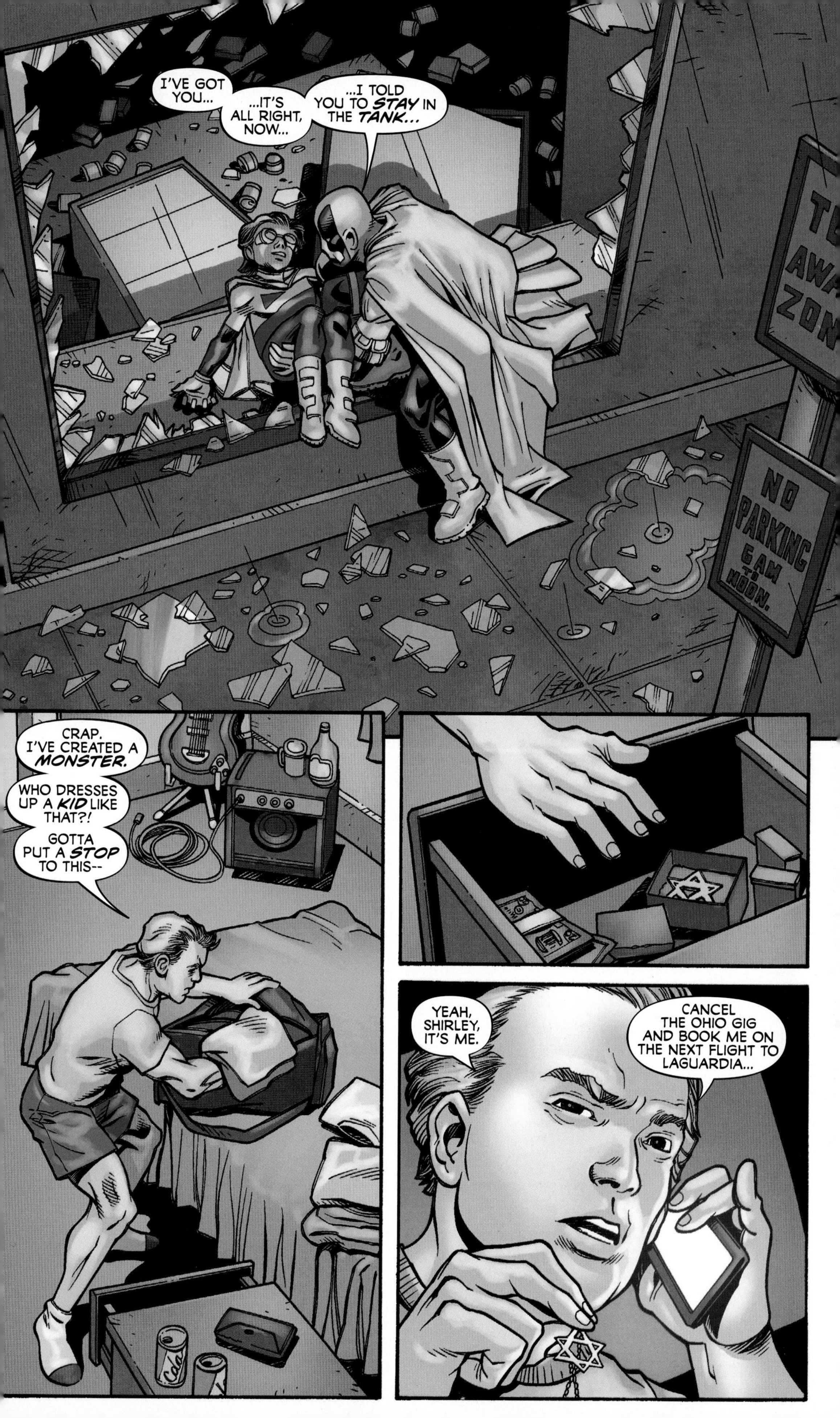

I'VE GOT YOU...
...IT'S ALL RIGHT, NOW...
...I TOLD YOU TO *STAY* IN THE *TANK...*
NO PARKING 6 AM TO NOON.
CRAP. I'VE CREATED A *MONSTER.*
WHO DRESSES UP A *KID* LIKE THAT?!
GOTTA PUT A *STOP* TO THIS--
YEAH, SHIRLEY, IT'S ME.
CANCEL THE OHIO GIG AND BOOK ME ON THE NEXT FLIGHT TO LAGUARDIA...

"Decisions"

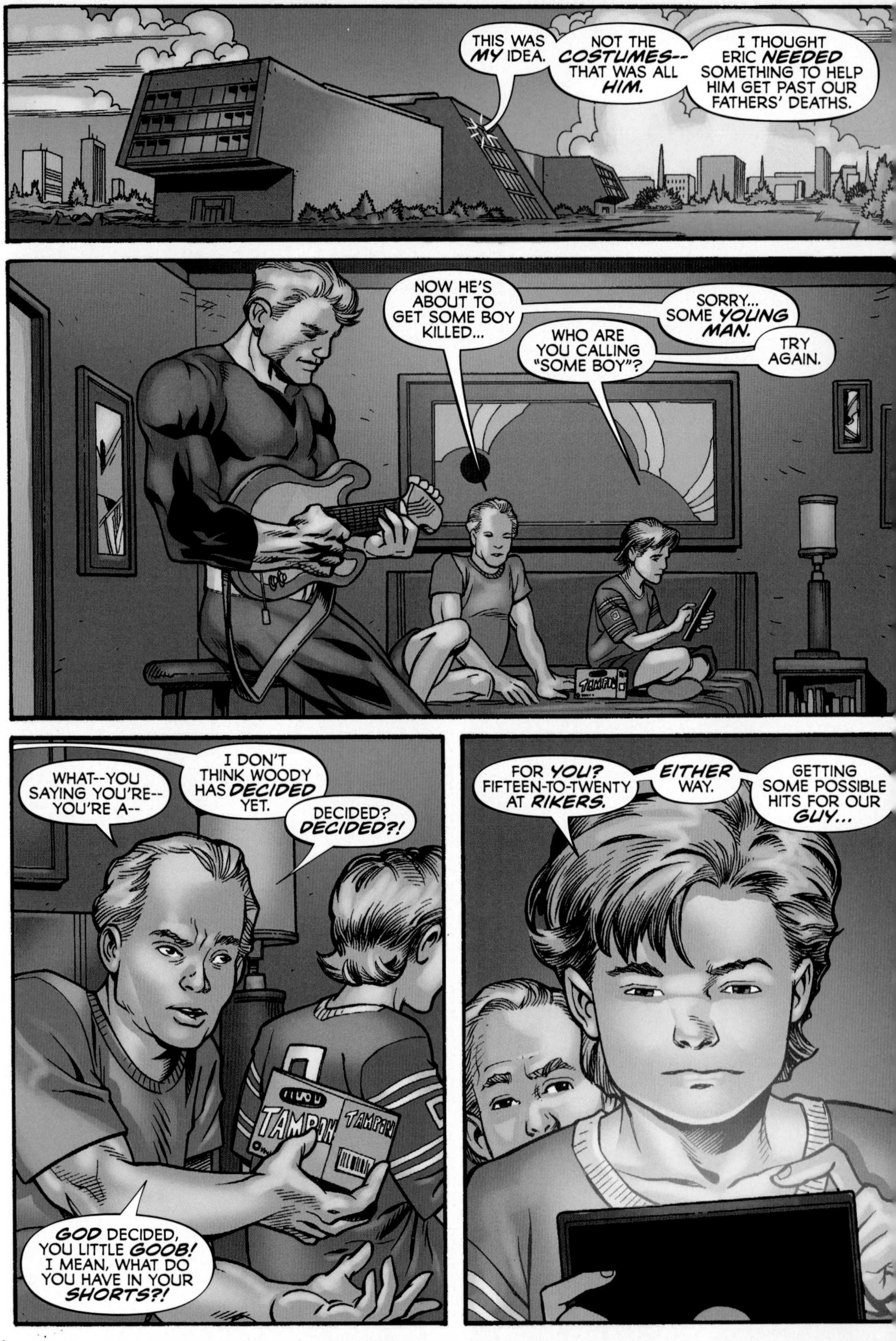
THIS WAS *MY* IDEA.
NOT THE *COSTUMES*-- THAT WAS ALL *HIM.*
I THOUGHT ERIC *NEEDED* SOMETHING TO HELP HIM GET PAST OUR FATHERS' DEATHS.
NOW HE'S ABOUT TO GET SOME BOY KILLED...
SORRY... SOME *YOUNG MAN.*
WHO ARE YOU CALLING "SOME BOY"?
TRY AGAIN.
WHAT--YOU SAYING YOU'RE-- YOU'RE A--
I DON'T THINK WOODY HAS *DECIDED* YET.
DECIDED? *DECIDED?!*
GOD DECIDED, YOU LITTLE *GOOB!* I MEAN, WHAT DO YOU HAVE IN YOUR *SHORTS?!*
FOR *YOU?* FIFTEEN-TO-TWENTY AT *RIKERS.*
EITHER WAY.
GETTING SOME POSSIBLE HITS FOR OUR *GUY...*

DIAMONDS? FINE ART? WHAT'S NEXT-- FABERGÉ EGGS--?

A LOT OF COUNTRIES NO LONGER STORE THEIR *MOST SECRET* DATA ON *SERVERS,* WHICH CAN BE *HACKED.*

THEY'RE USING UNLIKELY RESOURCE DEPOSITS--

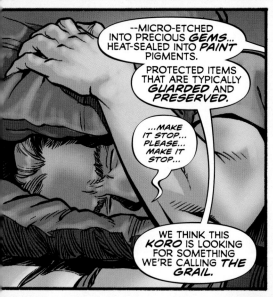

--MICRO-ETCHED INTO PRECIOUS *GEMS...* HEAT-SEALED INTO *PAINT* PIGMENTS.

PROTECTED ITEMS THAT ARE TYPICALLY *GUARDED* AND *PRESERVED.*

...MAKE IT STOP... PLEASE... MAKE IT STOP...

WE THINK THIS *KORO* IS LOOKING FOR SOMETHING WE'RE CALLING *THE GRAIL.*

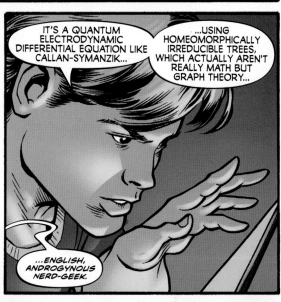

IT'S A QUANTUM ELECTRODYNAMIC DIFFERENTIAL EQUATION LIKE CALLAN-SYMANZIK...

...USING HOMEOMORPHICALLY IRREDUCIBLE TREES, WHICH ACTUALLY AREN'T REALLY MATH BUT GRAPH THEORY...

...ENGLISH, ANDROGYNOUS NERD-GEEK.

...A LIFE EQUATION. A *RECIPE* FOR *FAKE PEOPLE,* EINSTEIN. SYNTHETIC HUMANS-- SUPER-SOLDIERS.

THAT'S WHAT *KORO* IS: AN ARTIFICIAL LIFE FORM.

AND YOU KNOW THAT *HOW?*

BECAUSE THAT'S WHAT *I* AM.

tab

IT'S HOW WE *TRACK* KORO:

CRUISE LIKELY AZERBAIJANI RESOURCE DEPOSITS--THE *DIAMOND EXCHANGE*--THE ART EXHIBIT--

--SEE IF I GET A *HIT* OFF THE PLACE.

NO. STOP. CEASE AND *DESIST*--

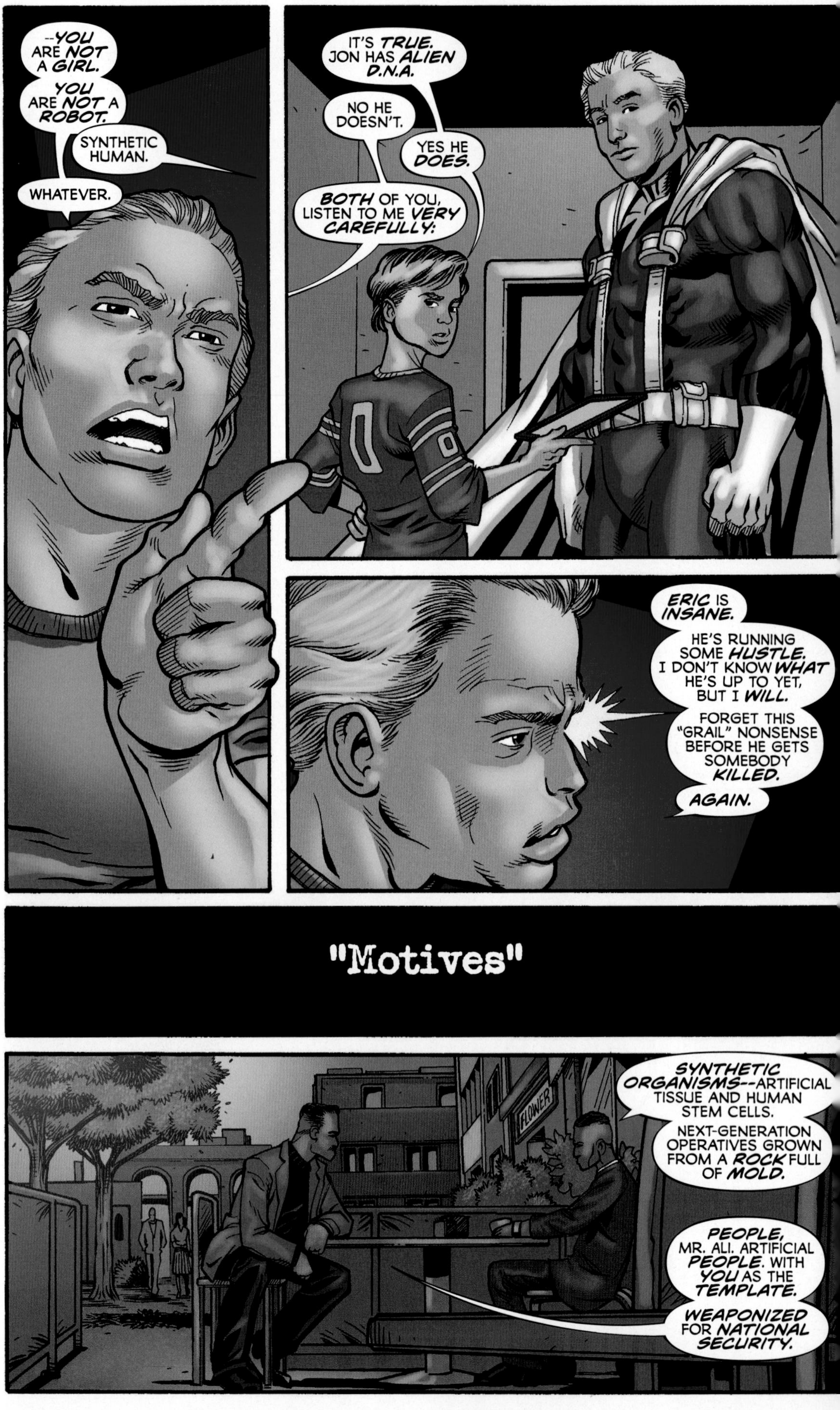
--YOU ARE NOT A GIRL.
YOU ARE NOT A ROBOT.
SYNTHETIC HUMAN.
WHATEVER.
IT'S TRUE. JON HAS ALIEN D.N.A.
NO HE DOESN'T.
YES HE DOES.
BOTH OF YOU, LISTEN TO ME VERY CAREFULLY:
ERIC IS INSANE.
HE'S RUNNING SOME HUSTLE. I DON'T KNOW WHAT HE'S UP TO YET, BUT I WILL.
FORGET THIS "GRAIL" NONSENSE BEFORE HE GETS SOMEBODY KILLED.
AGAIN.
"Motives"
FLOWER
SYNTHETIC ORGANISMS--ARTIFICIAL TISSUE AND HUMAN STEM CELLS.
NEXT-GENERATION OPERATIVES GROWN FROM A ROCK FULL OF MOLD.
PEOPLE, MR. ALI. ARTIFICIAL PEOPLE. WITH YOU AS THE TEMPLATE.
WEAPONIZED FOR NATIONAL SECURITY.

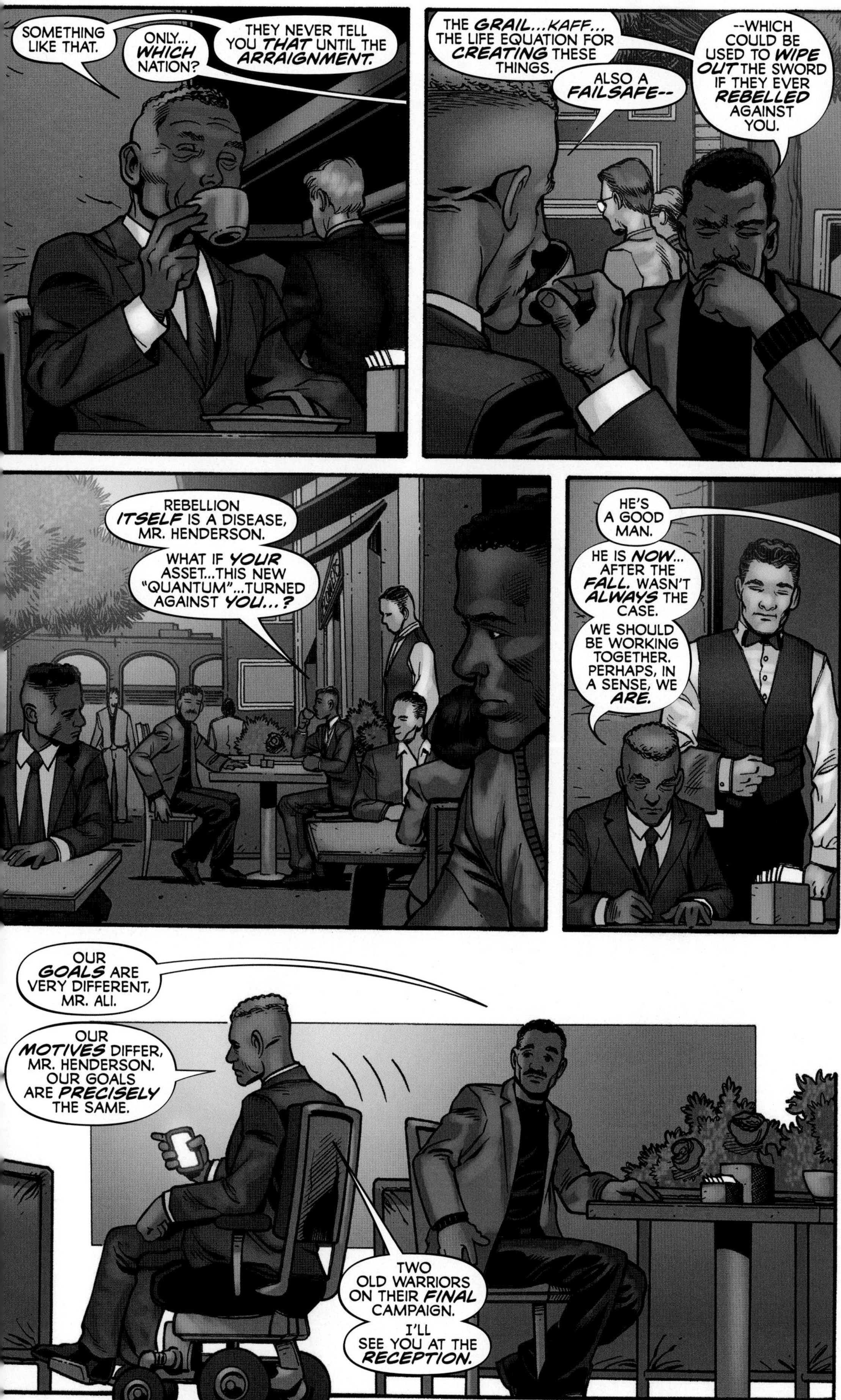
SOMETHING LIKE THAT.
THEY NEVER TELL YOU THAT UNTIL THE ARRAIGNMENT.
ONLY... WHICH NATION?
THE GRAIL...KAFF... THE LIFE EQUATION FOR CREATING THESE THINGS.
--WHICH COULD BE USED TO WIPE OUT THE SWORD IF THEY EVER REBELLED AGAINST YOU.
ALSO A FAILSAFE--
REBELLION ITSELF IS A DISEASE, MR. HENDERSON.
WHAT IF YOUR ASSET...THIS NEW "QUANTUM"...TURNED AGAINST YOU...?
HE'S A GOOD MAN.
HE IS NOW... AFTER THE FALL. WASN'T ALWAYS THE CASE.
WE SHOULD BE WORKING TOGETHER. PERHAPS, IN A SENSE, WE ARE.
OUR GOALS ARE VERY DIFFERENT, MR. ALI.
OUR MOTIVES DIFFER, MR. HENDERSON. OUR GOALS ARE PRECISELY THE SAME.
TWO OLD WARRIORS ON THEIR FINAL CAMPAIGN.
I'LL SEE YOU AT THE RECEPTION.

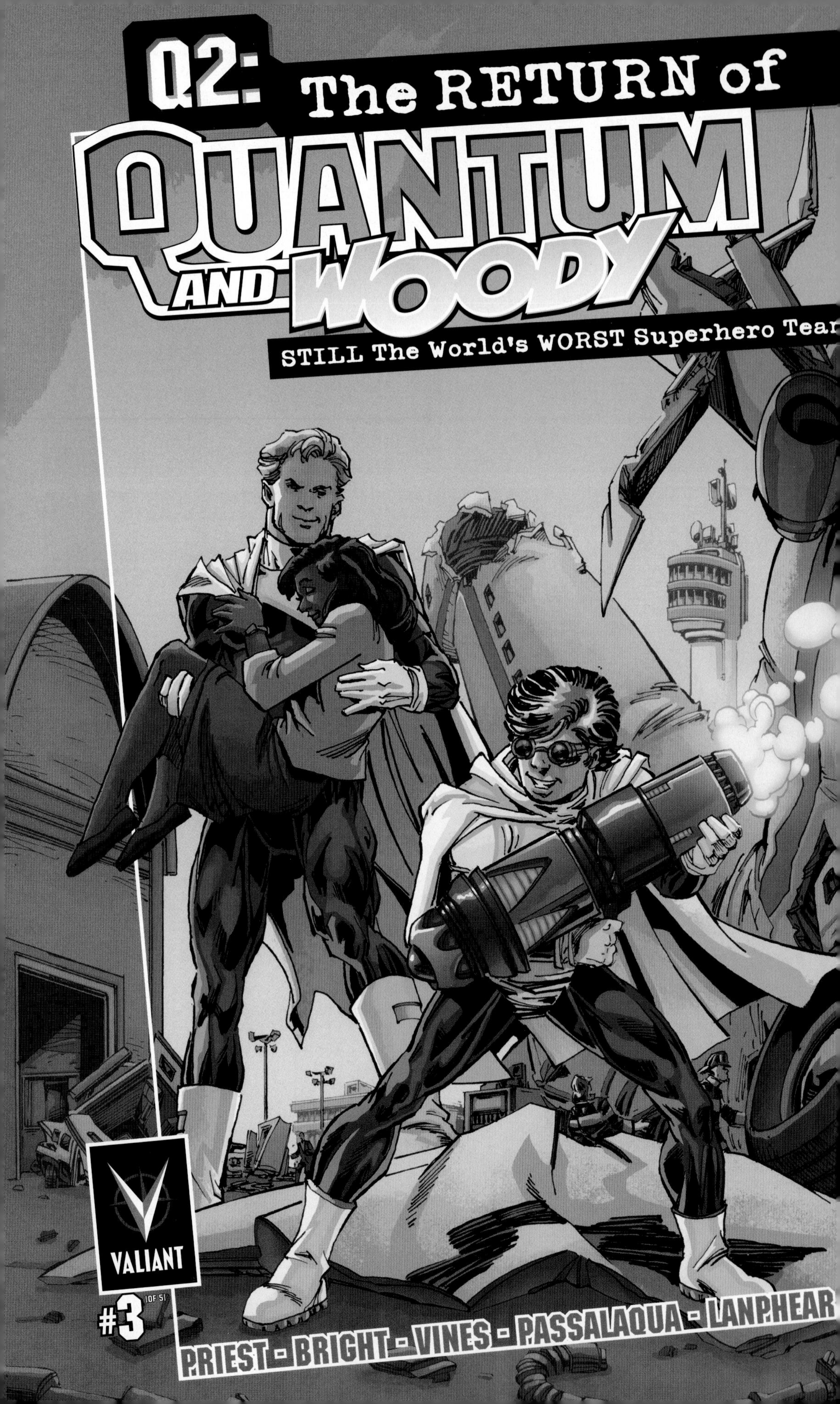

Q2: The RETURN of
QUANTUM AND WOODY
STILL The World's WORST Superhero Tea
VALIANT
#3 (OF 5)
PRIEST - BRIGHT - VINES - PASSALAQUA - LANPHEAR

"The Banjo"

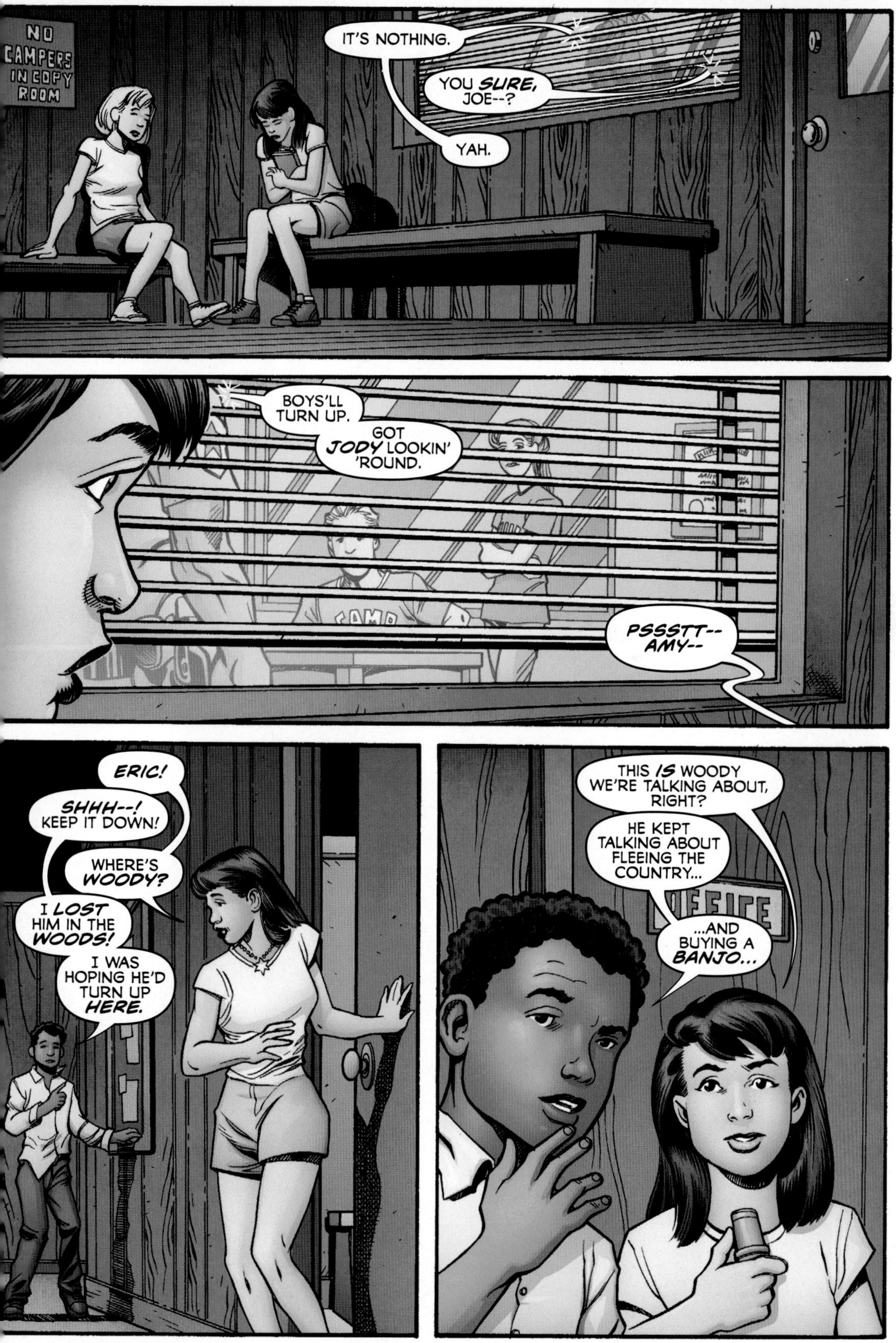

NO CAMPERS IN COPY ROOM
IT'S NOTHING.
YOU *SURE,* JOE--?
YAH.
BOYS'LL TURN UP.
GOT *JODY* LOOKIN' 'ROUND.
PSSSTT-- AMY--
ERIC!
SHHH--! KEEP IT DOWN!
WHERE'S *WOODY?*
I *LOST* HIM IN THE *WOODS!*
I WAS HOPING HE'D TURN UP *HERE.*
THIS *IS* WOODY WE'RE TALKING ABOUT, RIGHT?
HE KEPT TALKING ABOUT FLEEING THE COUNTRY...
...AND BUYING A *BANJO...*

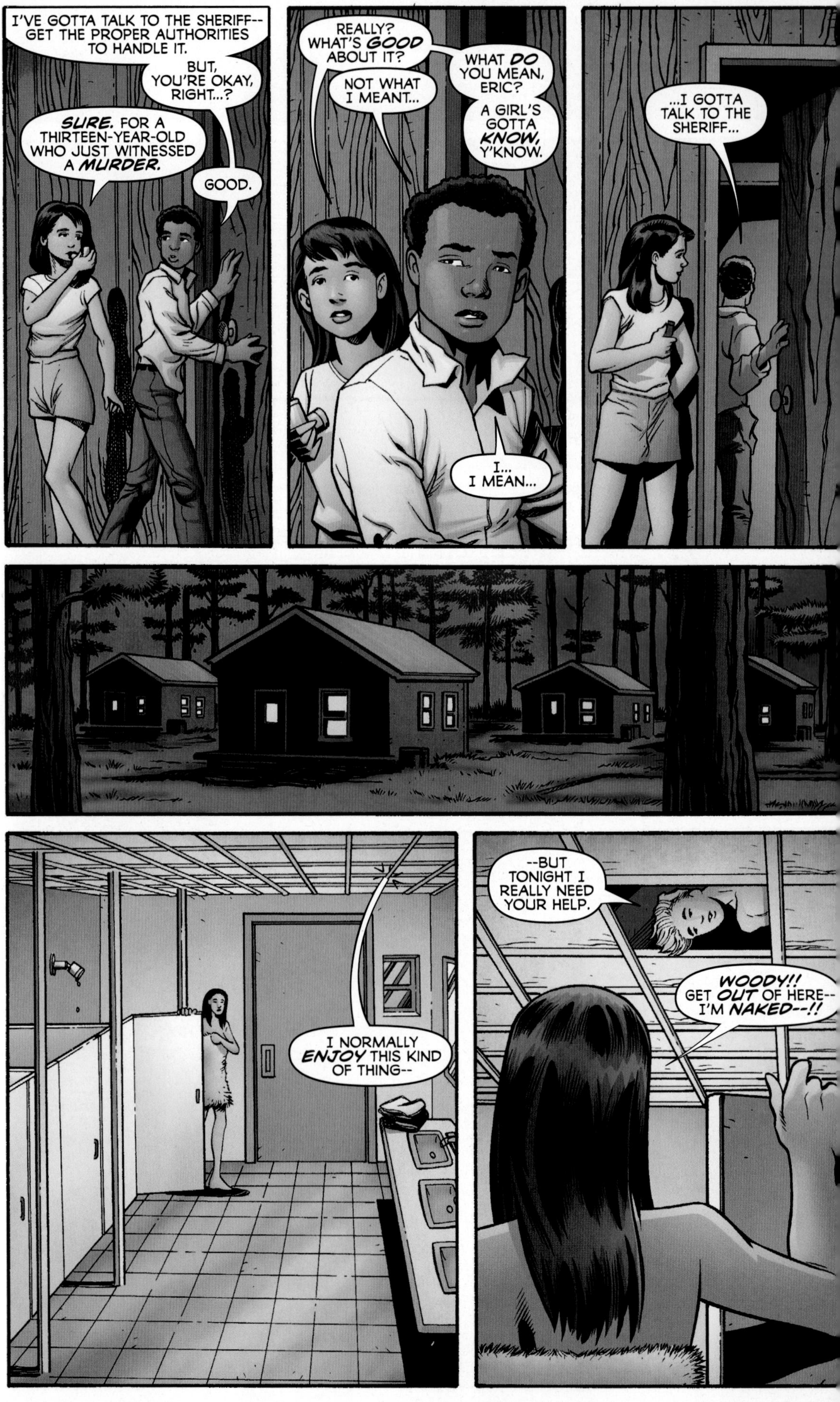

I'VE GOTTA TALK TO THE SHERIFF-- GET THE PROPER AUTHORITIES TO HANDLE IT.
BUT, YOU'RE OKAY, RIGHT...?
SURE. FOR A THIRTEEN-YEAR-OLD WHO JUST WITNESSED A MURDER.
GOOD.
REALLY? WHAT'S GOOD ABOUT IT?
NOT WHAT I MEANT...
WHAT DO YOU MEAN, ERIC?
A GIRL'S GOTTA KNOW, Y'KNOW.
I... I MEAN...
...I GOTTA TALK TO THE SHERIFF...
I NORMALLY ENJOY THIS KIND OF THING--
--BUT TONIGHT I REALLY NEED YOUR HELP.
WOODY!! GET OUT OF HERE-- I'M NAKED--!!

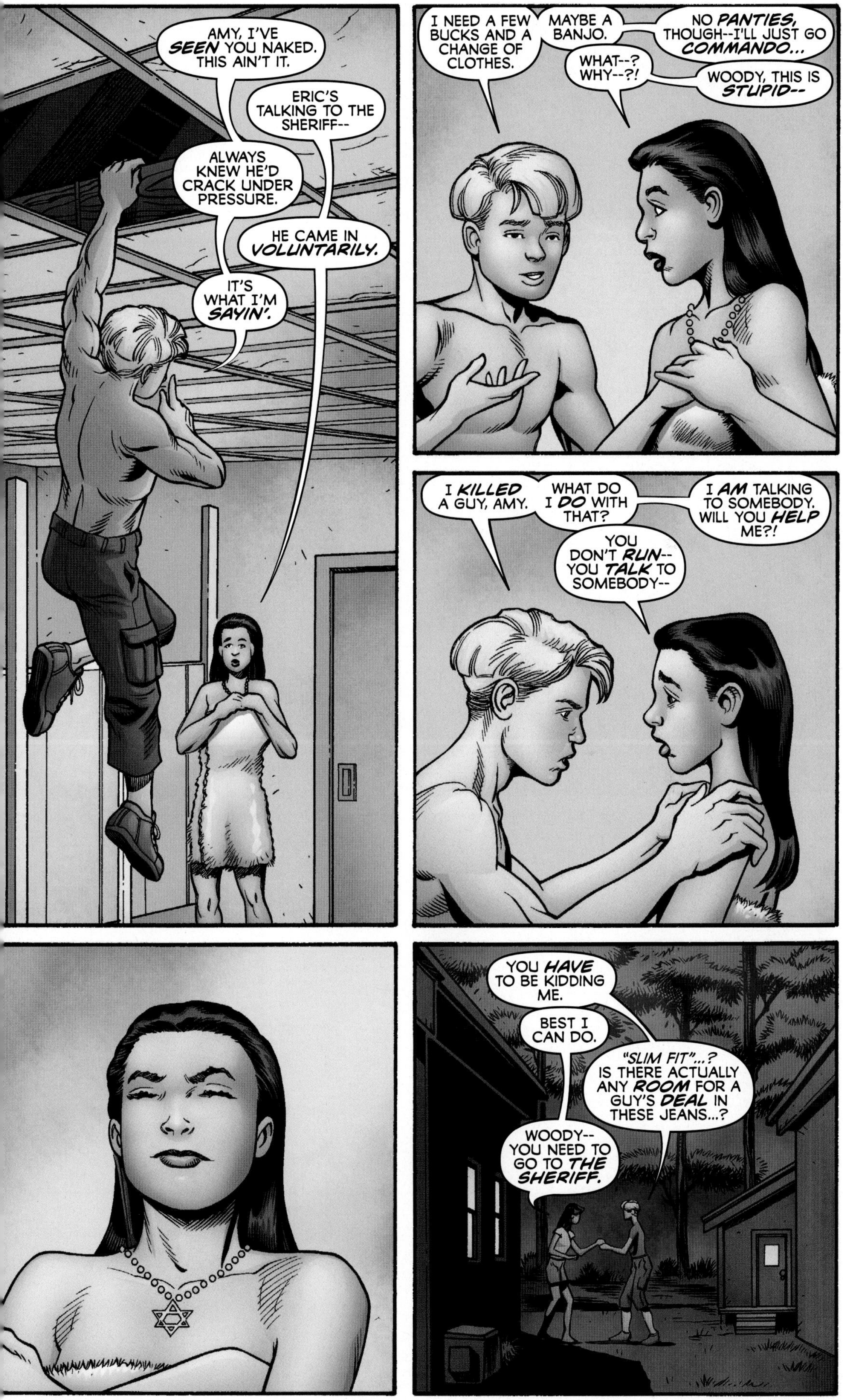
AMY, I'VE *SEEN* YOU NAKED. THIS AIN'T IT.
ERIC'S TALKING TO THE SHERIFF--
ALWAYS KNEW HE'D CRACK UNDER PRESSURE.
HE CAME IN *VOLUNTARILY.*
IT'S WHAT I'M *SAYIN'.*
I NEED A FEW BUCKS AND A CHANGE OF CLOTHES.
MAYBE A BANJO.
NO *PANTIES,* THOUGH--I'LL JUST GO *COMMANDO...*
WHAT--? WHY--?!
WOODY, THIS IS *STUPID--*
I *KILLED* A GUY, AMY.
WHAT DO I *DO* WITH THAT?
YOU DON'T *RUN*-- YOU *TALK* TO SOMEBODY--
I *AM* TALKING TO SOMEBODY. WILL YOU *HELP* ME?!
YOU *HAVE* TO BE KIDDING ME.
BEST I CAN DO.
"*SLIM FIT*"...? IS THERE ACTUALLY ANY *ROOM* FOR A GUY'S *DEAL* IN THESE JEANS...?
WOODY-- YOU NEED TO GO TO *THE SHERIFF.*

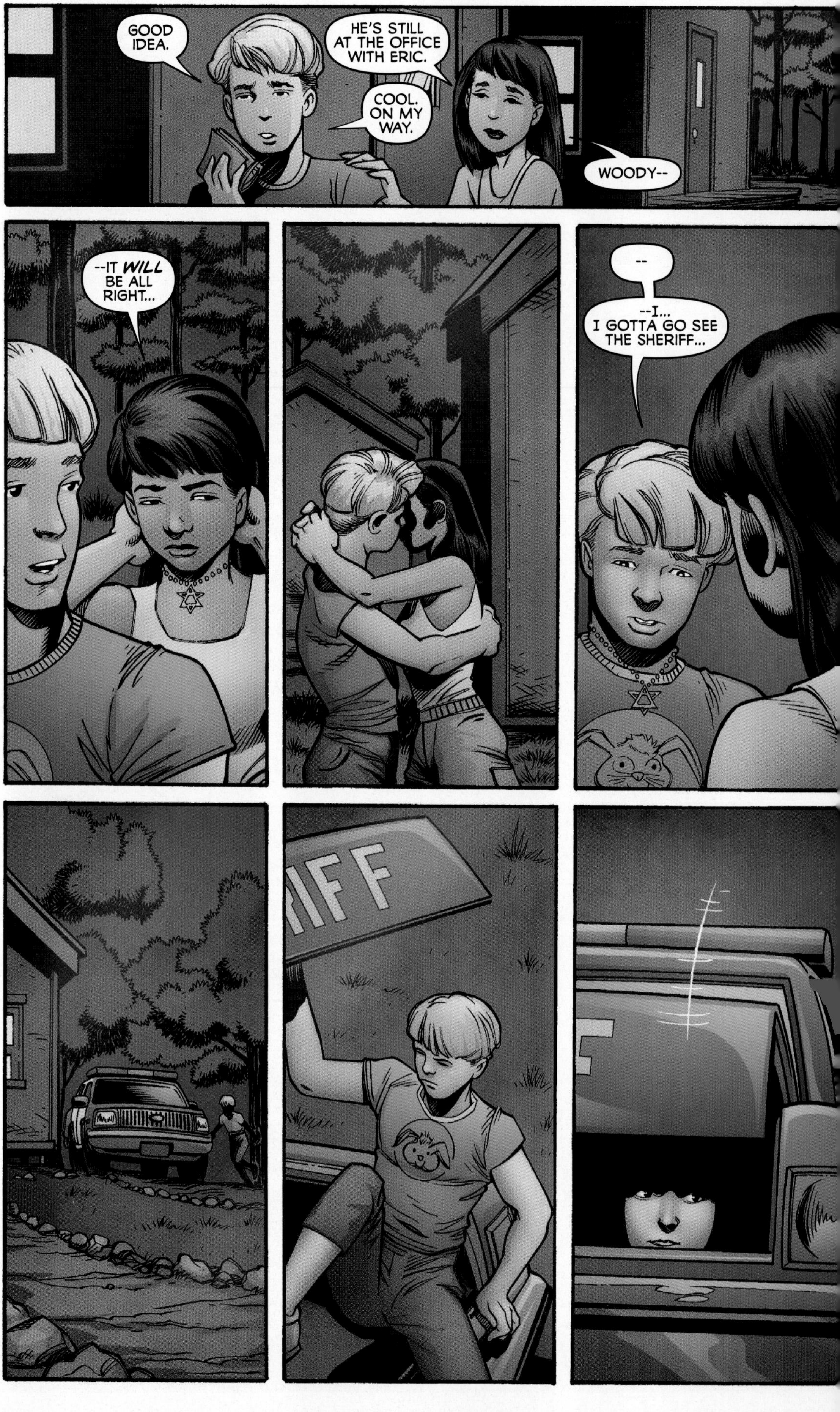
GOOD IDEA.
HE'S STILL AT THE OFFICE WITH ERIC.
COOL. ON MY WAY.
WOODY--
--IT *WILL* BE ALL RIGHT...
--
--I... I GOTTA GO SEE THE SHERIFF...
IFF

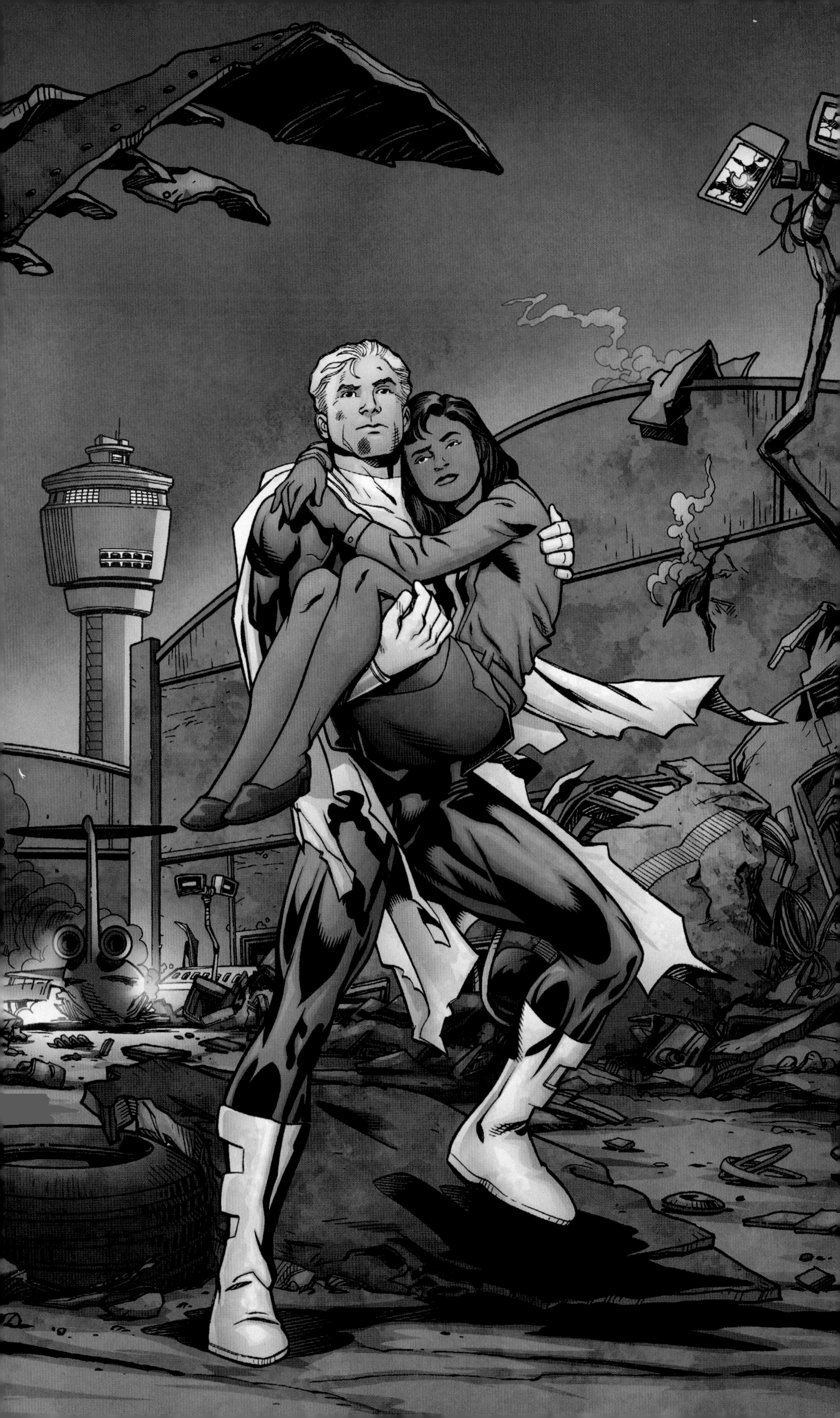

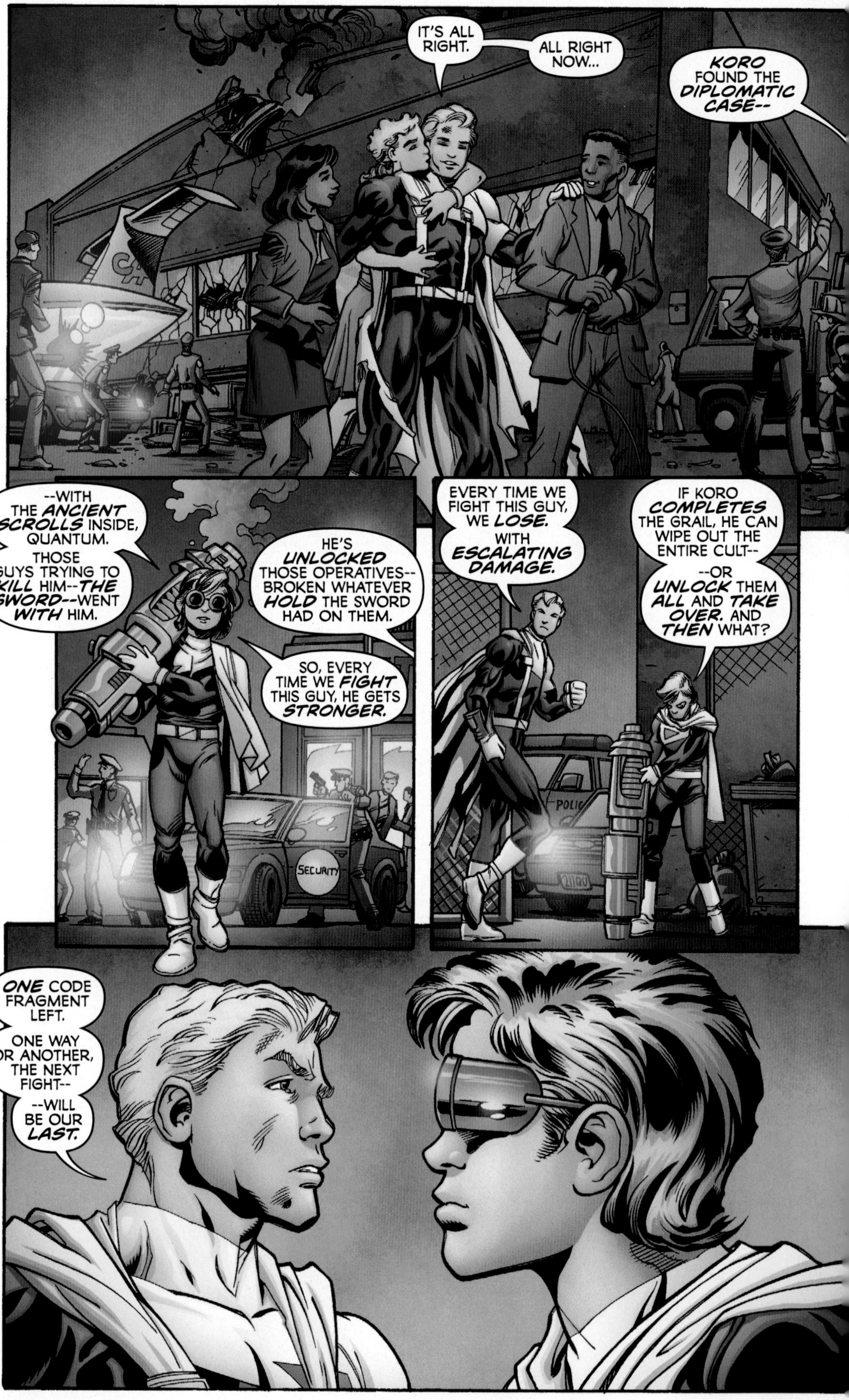
IT'S ALL RIGHT.
ALL RIGHT NOW...
KORO FOUND THE DIPLOMATIC CASE--
--WITH THE ANCIENT SCROLLS INSIDE, QUANTUM.
THOSE GUYS TRYING TO KILL HIM--THE SWORD--WENT WITH HIM.
HE'S UNLOCKED THOSE OPERATIVES--BROKEN WHATEVER HOLD THE SWORD HAD ON THEM.
SO, EVERY TIME WE FIGHT THIS GUY, HE GETS STRONGER.
SECURITY
EVERY TIME WE FIGHT THIS GUY, WE LOSE.
WITH ESCALATING DAMAGE.
IF KORO COMPLETES THE GRAIL, HE CAN WIPE OUT THE ENTIRE CULT--
--OR UNLOCK THEM ALL AND TAKE OVER. AND THEN WHAT?
ONE CODE FRAGMENT LEFT.
ONE WAY OR ANOTHER, THE NEXT FIGHT--
--WILL BE OUR LAST.

"Secrets"

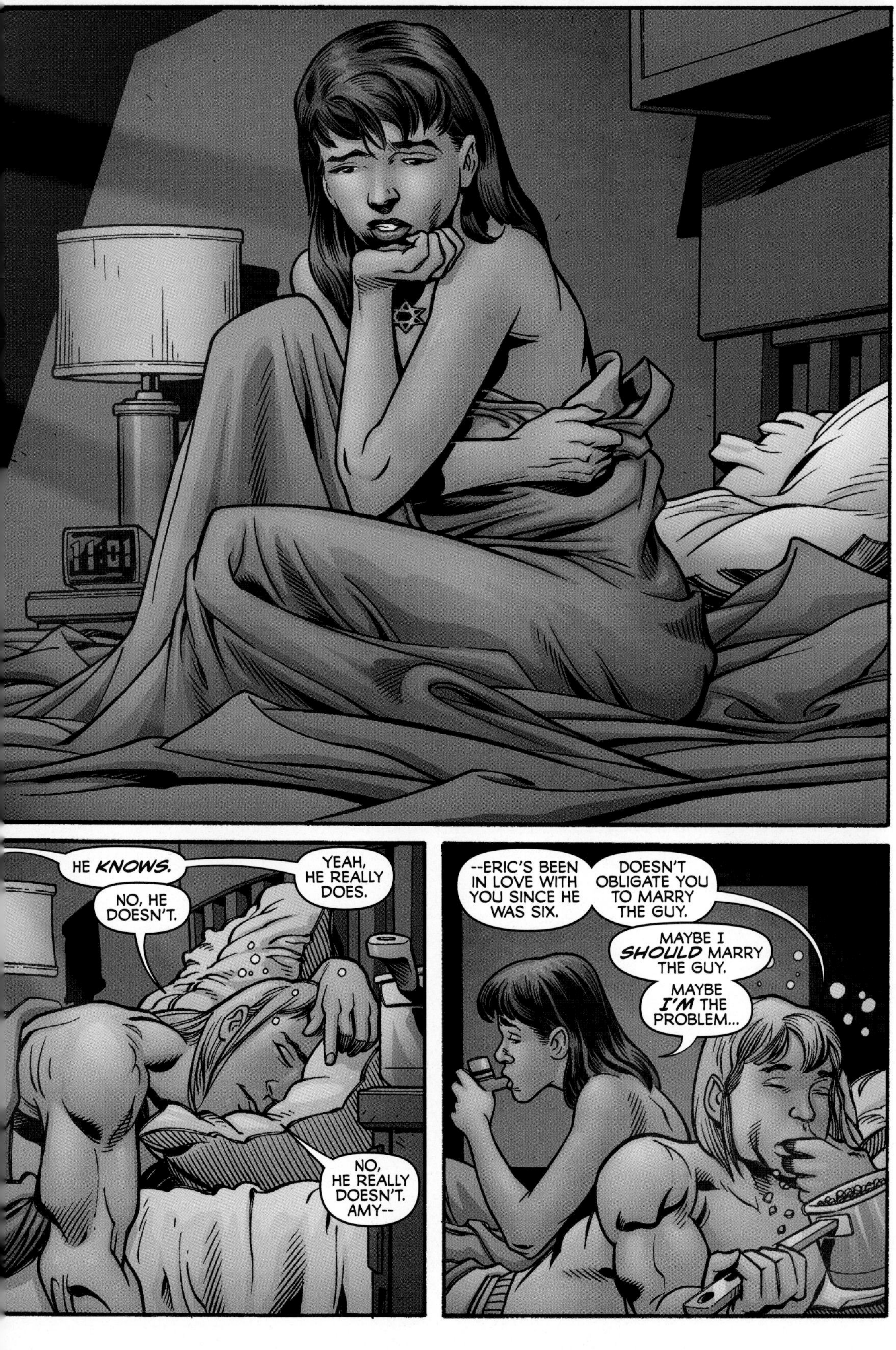
11:01
HE *KNOWS.*
NO, HE DOESN'T.
YEAH, HE REALLY DOES.
NO, HE REALLY DOESN'T. AMY--
--ERIC'S BEEN IN LOVE WITH YOU SINCE HE WAS SIX.
DOESN'T OBLIGATE YOU TO MARRY THE GUY.
MAYBE I *SHOULD* MARRY THE GUY.
MAYBE *I'M* THE PROBLEM...

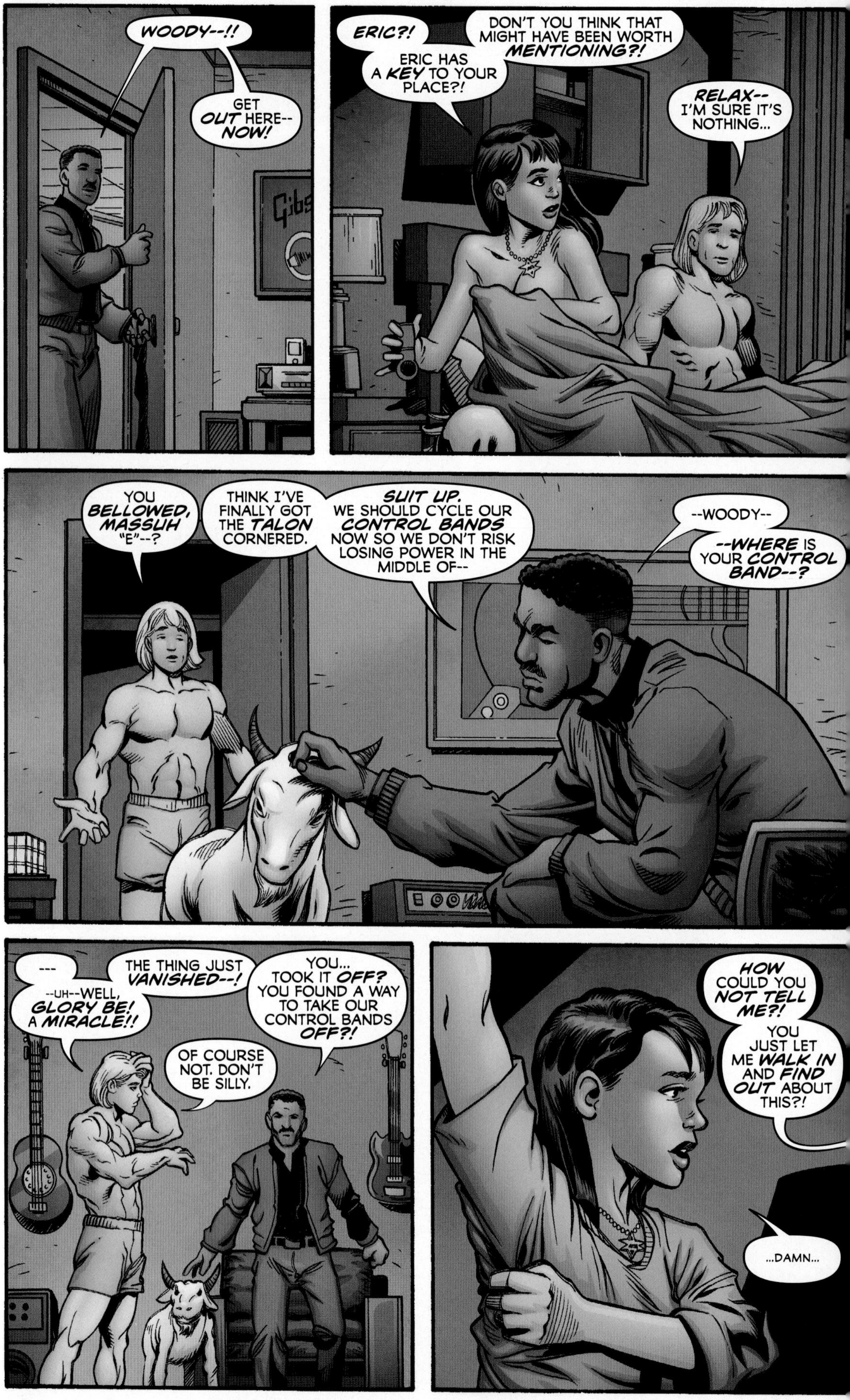
WOODY--!!
GET OUT HERE-- NOW!
ERIC?!
DON'T YOU THINK THAT MIGHT HAVE BEEN WORTH MENTIONING?!
ERIC HAS A KEY TO YOUR PLACE?!
RELAX-- I'M SURE IT'S NOTHING...
YOU BELLOWED, MASSUH "E"--?
THINK I'VE FINALLY GOT THE TALON CORNERED.
SUIT UP. WE SHOULD CYCLE OUR CONTROL BANDS NOW SO WE DON'T RISK LOSING POWER IN THE MIDDLE OF--
--WOODY--
--WHERE IS YOUR CONTROL BAND--?

THE THING JUST VANISHED--!
--UH--WELL, GLORY BE! A MIRACLE!!
YOU... TOOK IT OFF? YOU FOUND A WAY TO TAKE OUR CONTROL BANDS OFF?!
OF COURSE NOT. DON'T BE SILLY.
HOW COULD YOU NOT TELL ME?!
YOU JUST LET ME WALK IN AND FIND OUT ABOUT THIS?!
...DAMN...

HOW--?! E.M. BURST? NANOTECH...? OSCILLATING FIELD PARTICLE ACCELERATOR--?

A *PAPER CLIP*--?!

ERIC-- STOP IT--

ACTUALLY, THERE'S THIS LITTLE *PIN HOLE*... SEE, YOU TAKE A PAPER CLIP... GOTTA *JIGGLE* IT...

I CAN *EXPLAIN*--

ERIC--

--*ERIC*--!!

ERIC-- WHEEZE--!

ERIC-- *WAIT*--!!

WHEEZE--!! WHEEZE--!!

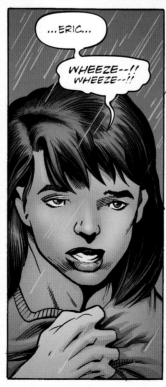

...ERIC...

WHEEZE--!! WHEEZE--!!

"Partners"

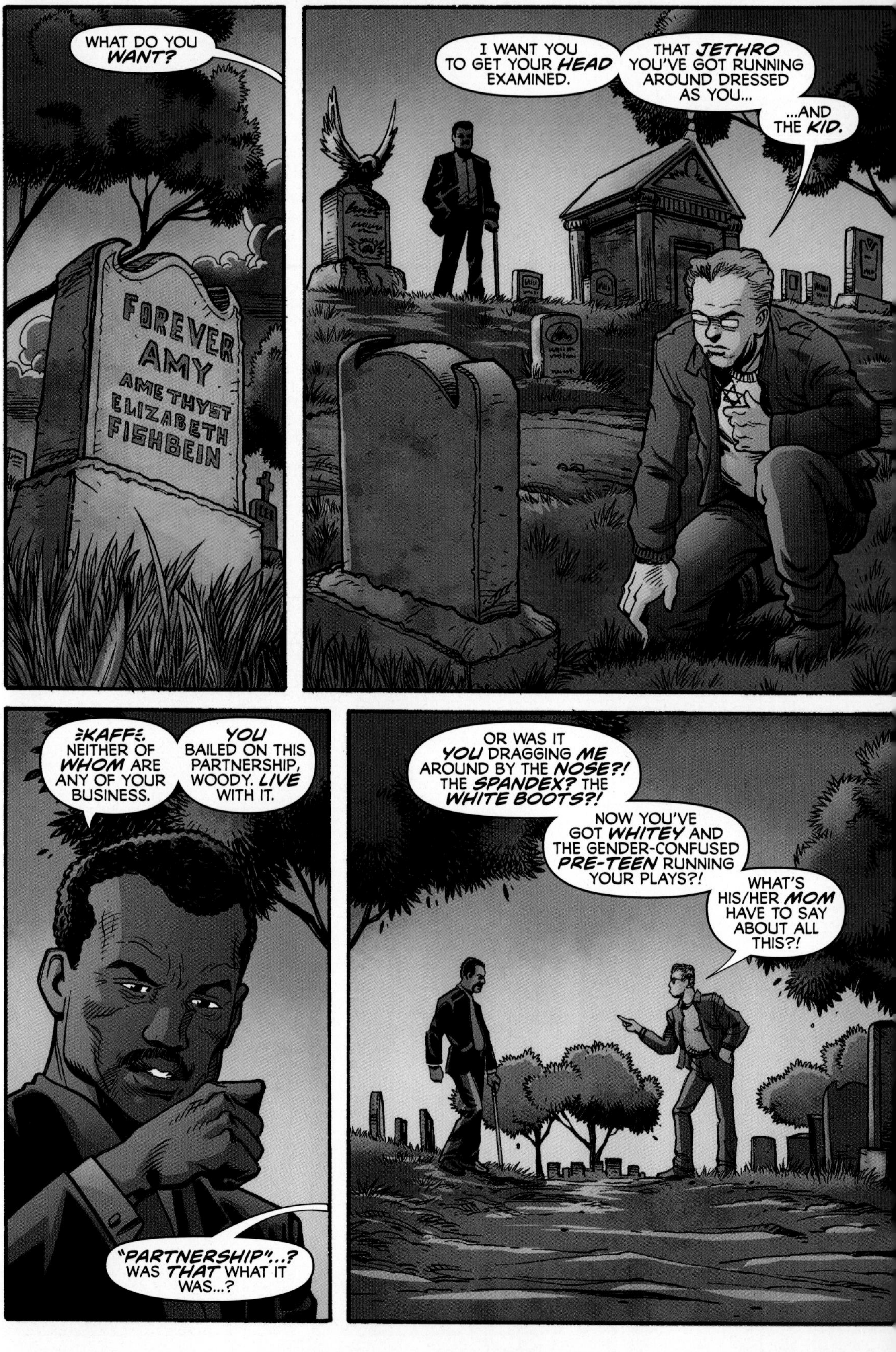

FOREVER AMY AMETHYST ELIZABETH FISHBEIN
WHAT DO YOU WANT?
I WANT YOU TO GET YOUR HEAD EXAMINED.
THAT JETHRO YOU'VE GOT RUNNING AROUND DRESSED AS YOU...
...AND THE KID.
:KAFF:. NEITHER OF WHOM ARE ANY OF YOUR BUSINESS.
YOU BAILED ON THIS PARTNERSHIP, WOODY. LIVE WITH IT.
"PARTNERSHIP"...? WAS THAT WHAT IT WAS...?
OR WAS IT YOU DRAGGING ME AROUND BY THE NOSE?! THE SPANDEX? THE WHITE BOOTS?!
NOW YOU'VE GOT WHITEY AND THE GENDER-CONFUSED PRE-TEEN RUNNING YOUR PLAYS?!
WHAT'S HIS/HER MOM HAVE TO SAY ABOUT ALL THIS?!

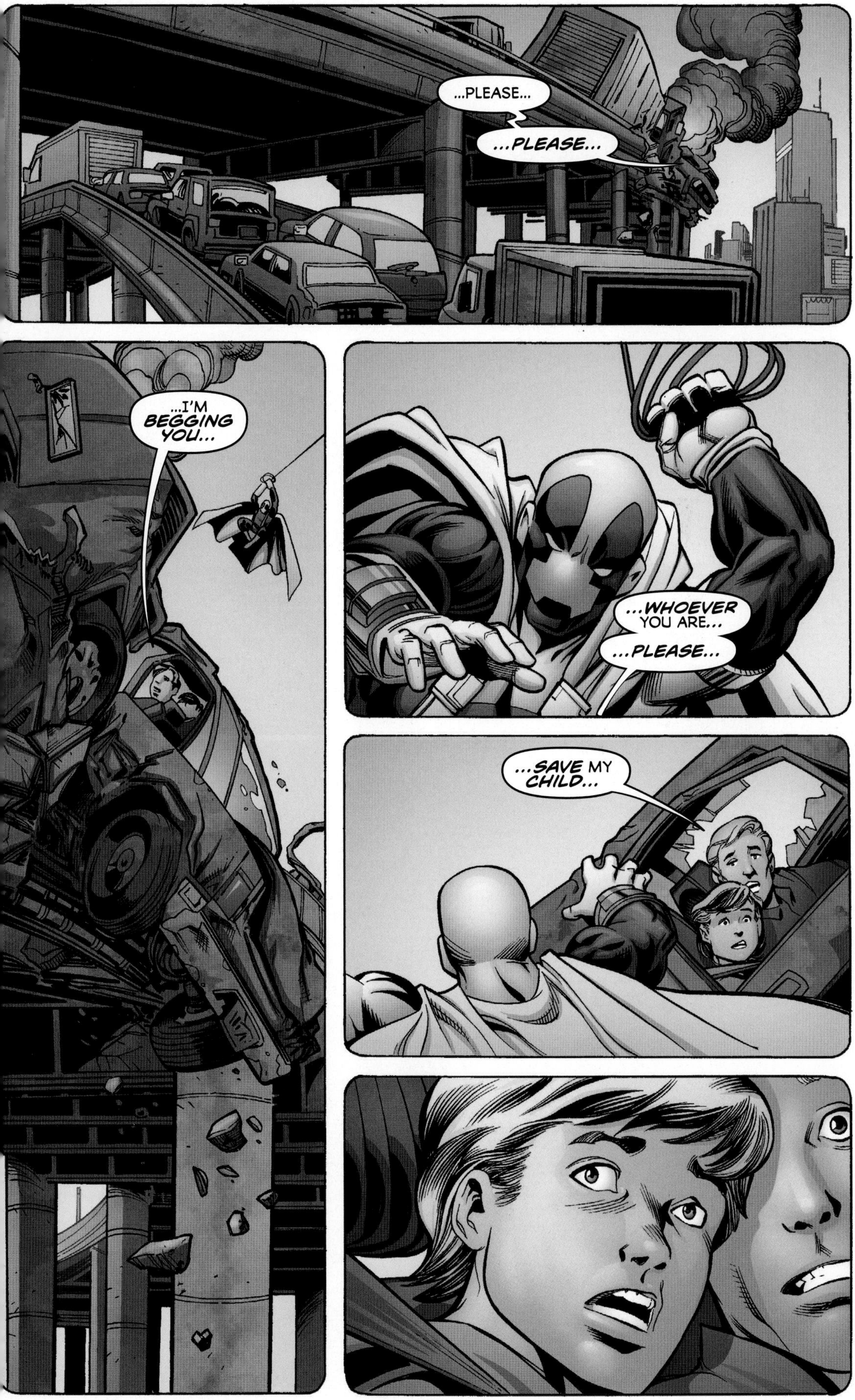

...PLEASE...
...PLEASE...
...I'M BEGGING YOU...
...WHOEVER YOU ARE...
...PLEASE...
...SAVE MY CHILD...

THE FATHER *LET* GO.

NO CHILD SHOULD *EVER* LOSE A PARENT... ≩KAFF≩

THE WAY *WE* DID, RIGHT? THAT'S THE PSYCHO THINKING--YOU *IDENTIFYING* WITH THIS KID?

AND NOW THIS LITTLE *BOY* THINKS HE'S A LITTLE *GIRL*...

...OR... VICE VERSA...

IT'S A *PHASE.* IT'LL *PASS.*

NO, IT *WON'T.* THAT'S WHAT I THOUGHT ABOUT *YOU.* ABOUT THIS WHOLE "QUANTUM" BUSINESS!

KICK SOME ASS UNTIL ERIC GETS OVER HIMSELF.

YOU ARE WHO YOU *ARE.*

BUT *YOU'VE* GONE TOO FAR.

A *NEW* "QUANTUM AND WOODY," ONLY WITH *OTHER PEOPLE?* WHOSE *STUPID IDEA* WAS *THAT?!*

AND THIS "GRAIL" *KORO* IS AFTER...

...*GOMER* AND *SCRAPPY-DOO* THINK YOU'RE TRYING TO KEEP IT OUT OF THE *WRONG HANDS,* BUT I *KNOW* YOU, ERIC--

--"ALIEN D.N.A.," SYNTHETIC PEOPLE--

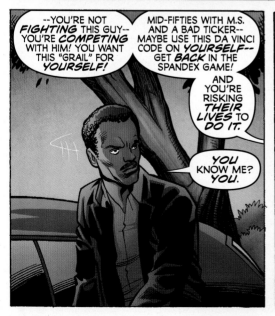

--YOU'RE NOT *FIGHTING* THIS GUY-- YOU'RE *COMPETING* WITH HIM! YOU WANT THIS "GRAIL" FOR *YOURSELF!*

MID-FIFTIES WITH M.S. AND A BAD TICKER-- MAYBE USE THIS *DA VINCI CODE* ON *YOURSELF*-- GET *BACK* IN THE SPANDEX GAME!

AND YOU'RE RISKING *THEIR* LIVES TO DO IT.

YOU KNOW ME? *YOU.*

WAIT AND SEE.

...SIR...

...THE *YACHT* REMAINS OUR BEST GUESS FOR WHERE THE FINAL PIECE OF THE GRAIL IS.

THE YACHT *BLUEPRINTS* ARE ON YOUR DESK.

R&D SAYS THEY'LL NEED A COUPLE OF DAYS TO FABRICATE A NEW *CONTROL BAND* FOR JON--

I TOLD THEM NOT TO *BOTHER.*

--SIR--?!

IT'S OVER. LET THE SWORD KEEP THE DAMNED GRAIL.

WOODY'S RIGHT. ≥KAFF≤ I *HAVE* LOST MY MIND...

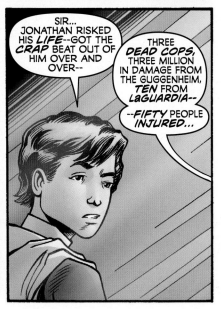

SIR... JONATHAN RISKED HIS *LIFE*--GOT THE *CRAP* BEAT OUT OF HIM OVER AND OVER--

THREE *DEAD COPS,* THREE MILLION IN DAMAGE FROM THE GUGGENHEIM, *TEN* FROM LaGUARDIA--

--*FIFTY* PEOPLE INJURED...

"We Are"

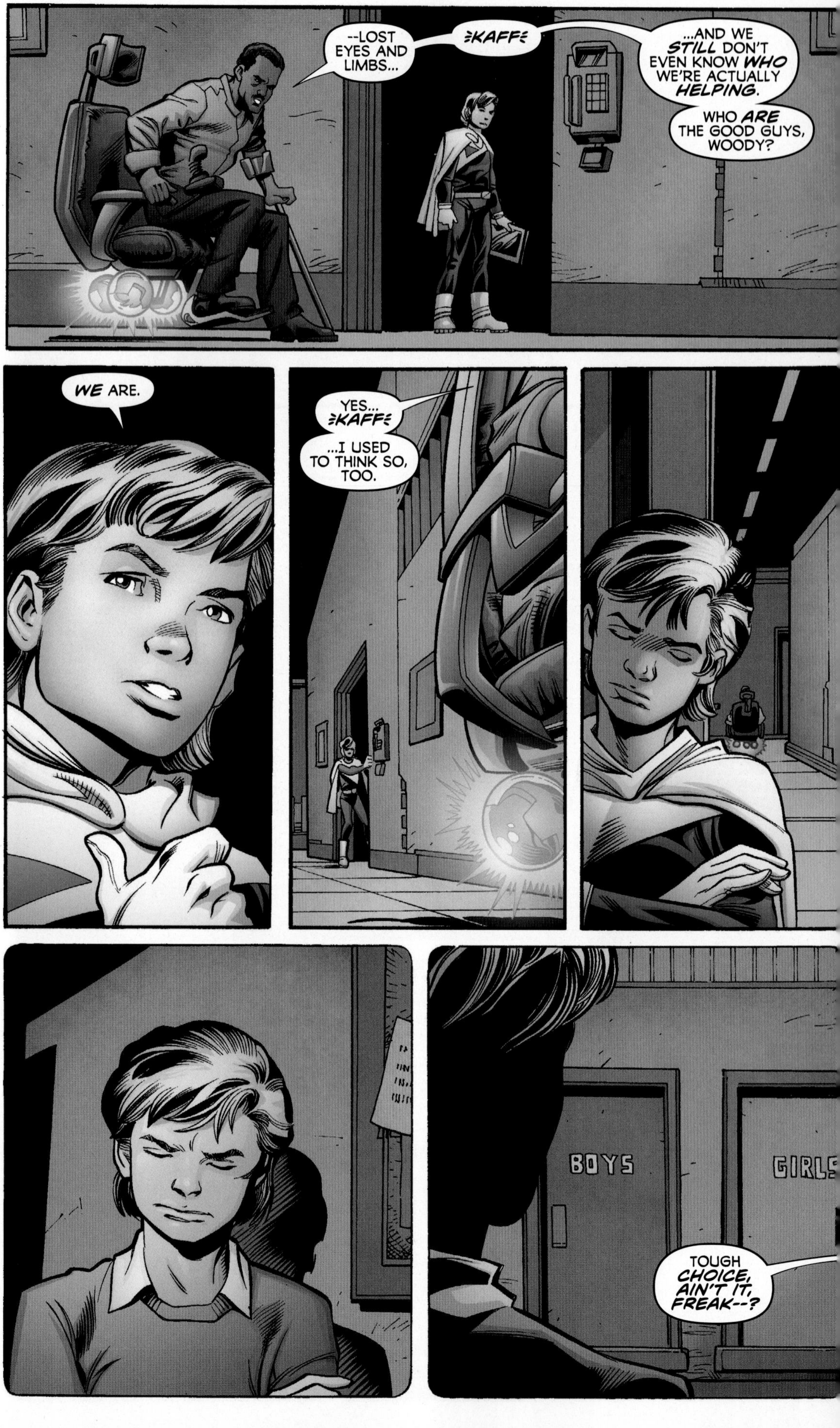
--LOST EYES AND LIMBS...
KAFF
...AND WE STILL DON'T EVEN KNOW WHO WE'RE ACTUALLY HELPING.
WHO ARE THE GOOD GUYS, WOODY?
WE ARE.
YES... KAFF
...I USED TO THINK SO, TOO.
BOYS
GIRLS
TOUGH CHOICE, AIN'T IT, FREAK--?

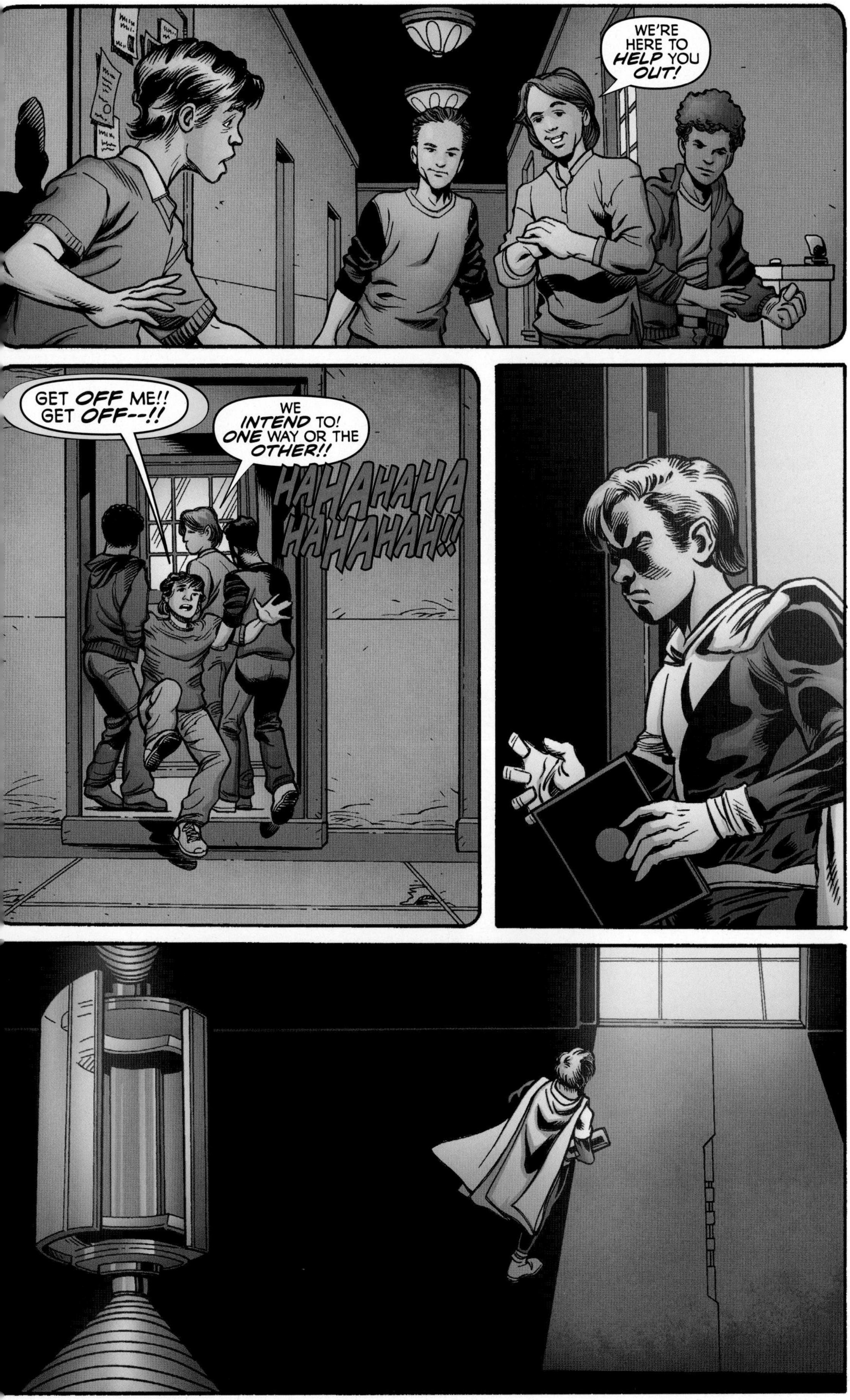
WE'RE HERE TO HELP YOU OUT!
GET OFF ME!! GET OFF--!!
WE INTEND TO! ONE WAY OR THE OTHER!!
HAHAHAHA HAHAHAH!!

"Riptide"

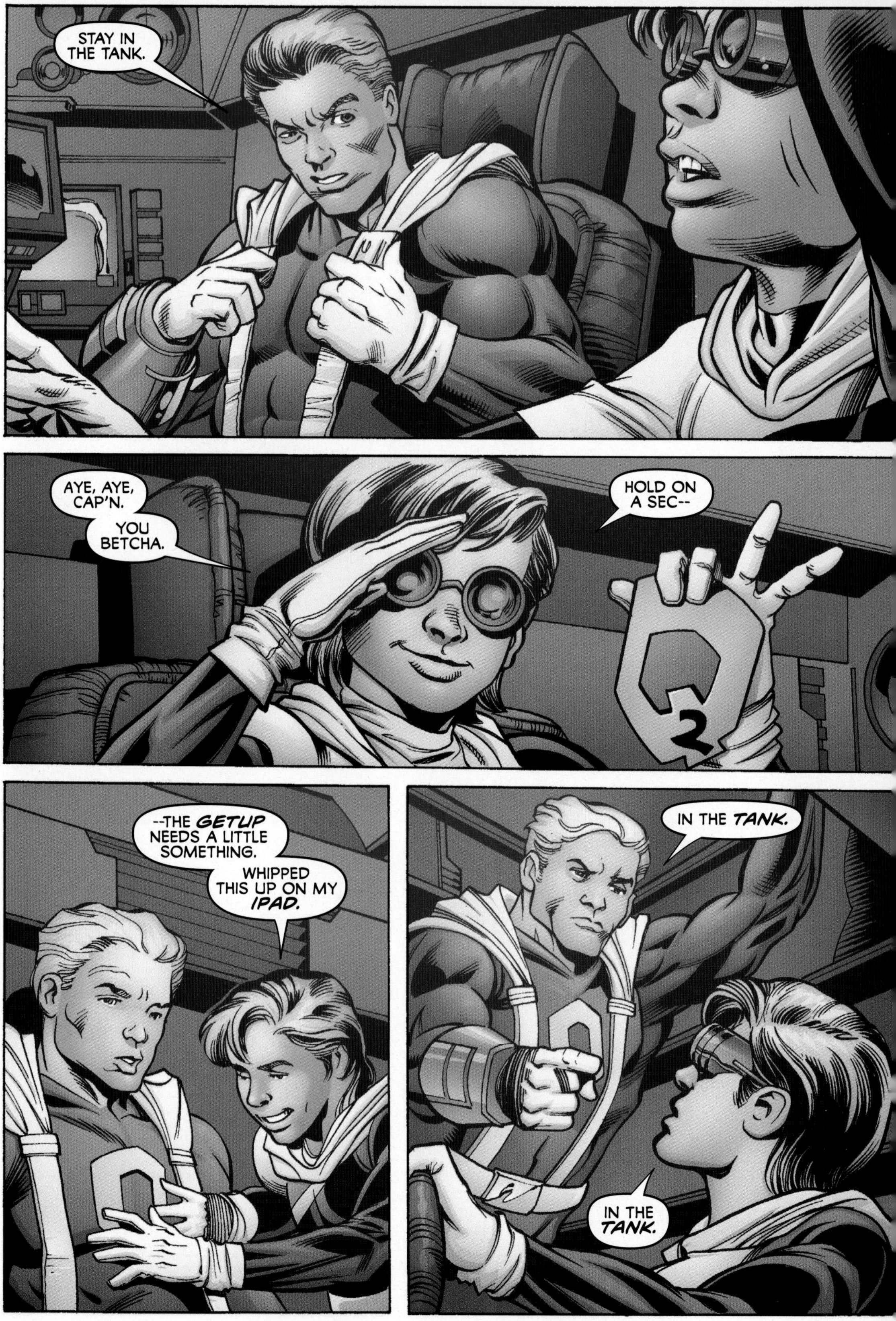
STAY IN THE TANK.
AYE, AYE, CAP'N.
YOU BETCHA.
HOLD ON A SEC--
--THE GETUP NEEDS A LITTLE SOMETHING.
WHIPPED THIS UP ON MY IPAD.
IN THE TANK.
IN THE TANK.

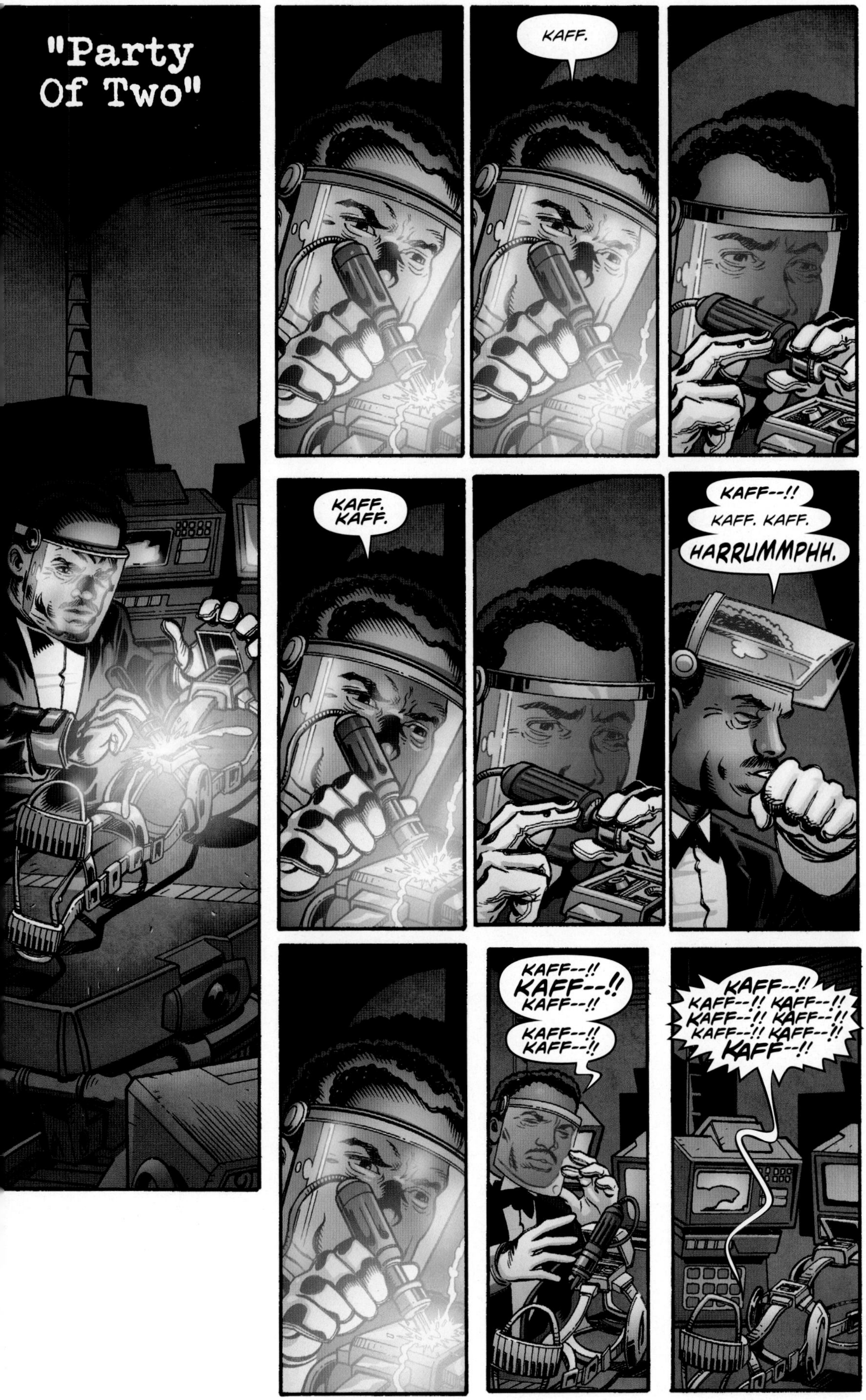

"Party Of Two"
KAFF.
KAFF. KAFF.
KAFF--!!
KAFF. KAFF.
HARRUMMPHH.
KAFF--!! KAFF--!! KAFF--!!
KAFF--!! KAFF--!!
KAFF--!! KAFF--!! KAFF--!! KAFF--!! KAFF--!! KAFF--!! KAFF--!! KAFF--!!

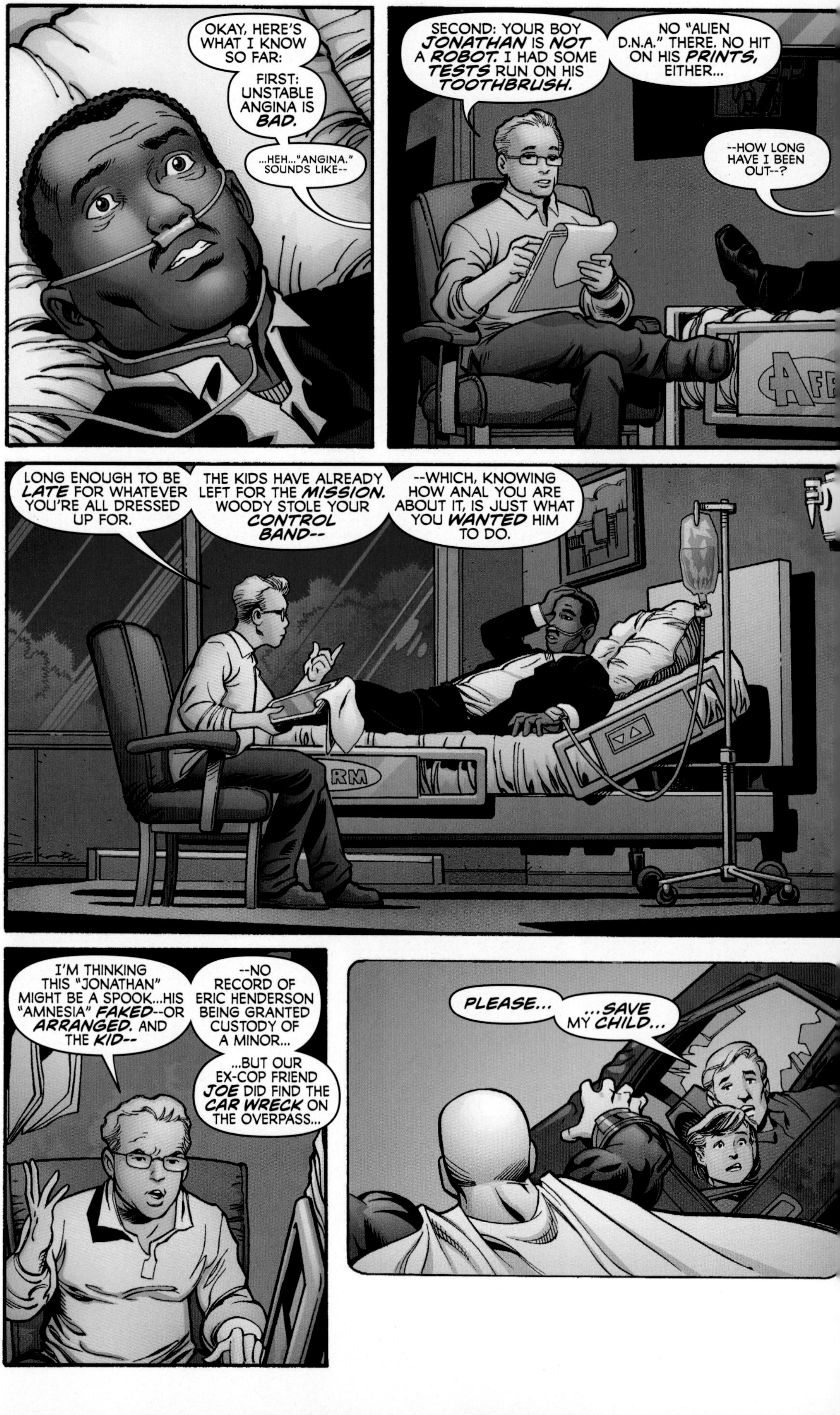
OKAY, HERE'S WHAT I KNOW SO FAR:
FIRST: UNSTABLE ANGINA IS BAD.
...HEH..."ANGINA." SOUNDS LIKE--
SECOND: YOUR BOY JONATHAN IS NOT A ROBOT. I HAD SOME TESTS RUN ON HIS TOOTHBRUSH.
NO "ALIEN D.N.A." THERE. NO HIT ON HIS PRINTS, EITHER...
--HOW LONG HAVE I BEEN OUT--?
LONG ENOUGH TO BE LATE FOR WHATEVER YOU'RE ALL DRESSED UP FOR.
THE KIDS HAVE ALREADY LEFT FOR THE MISSION. WOODY STOLE YOUR CONTROL BAND--
--WHICH, KNOWING HOW ANAL YOU ARE ABOUT IT, IS JUST WHAT YOU WANTED HIM TO DO.
I'M THINKING THIS "JONATHAN" MIGHT BE A SPOOK...HIS "AMNESIA" FAKED--OR ARRANGED. AND THE KID--
--NO RECORD OF ERIC HENDERSON BEING GRANTED CUSTODY OF A MINOR...
...BUT OUR EX-COP FRIEND JOE DID FIND THE CAR WRECK ON THE OVERPASS...
PLEASE...
...SAVE MY CHILD...

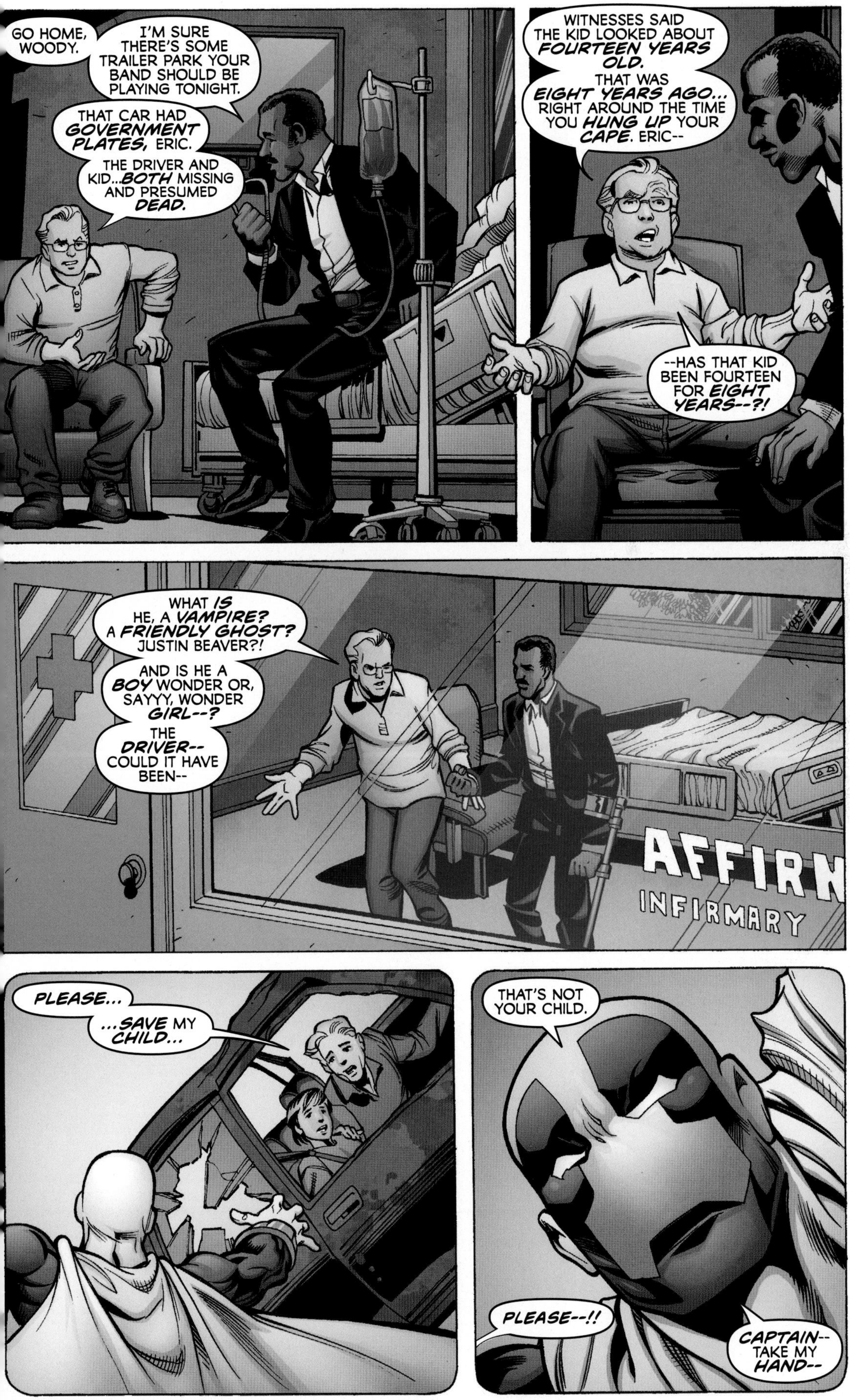
GO HOME, WOODY.
I'M SURE THERE'S SOME TRAILER PARK YOUR BAND SHOULD BE PLAYING TONIGHT.
THAT CAR HAD GOVERNMENT PLATES, ERIC.
THE DRIVER AND KID...BOTH MISSING AND PRESUMED DEAD.
WITNESSES SAID THE KID LOOKED ABOUT FOURTEEN YEARS OLD.
THAT WAS EIGHT YEARS AGO... RIGHT AROUND THE TIME YOU HUNG UP YOUR CAPE. ERIC--
--HAS THAT KID BEEN FOURTEEN FOR EIGHT YEARS--?!
WHAT IS HE, A VAMPIRE? A FRIENDLY GHOST? JUSTIN BEAVER?!
AND IS HE A BOY WONDER OR, SAYYY, WONDER GIRL--?
THE DRIVER-- COULD IT HAVE BEEN--
AFFIRM
INFIRMARY
PLEASE...
...SAVE MY CHILD...
THAT'S NOT YOUR CHILD.
PLEASE--!!
CAPTAIN-- TAKE MY HAND--

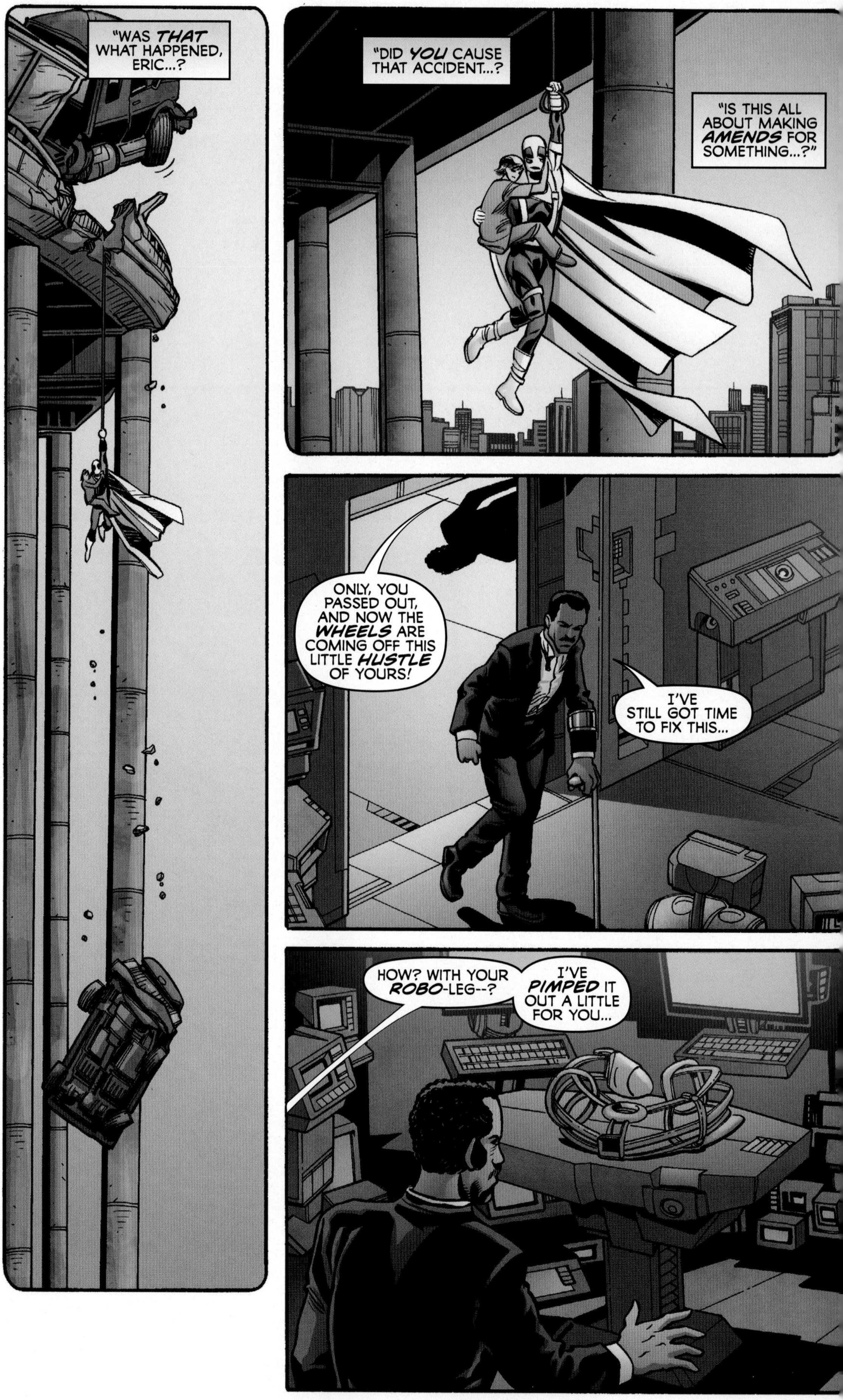
"WAS THAT WHAT HAPPENED, ERIC...?
"DID YOU CAUSE THAT ACCIDENT...?
"IS THIS ALL ABOUT MAKING AMENDS FOR SOMETHING...?"
ONLY, YOU PASSED OUT, AND NOW THE WHEELS ARE COMING OFF THIS LITTLE HUSTLE OF YOURS!
I'VE STILL GOT TIME TO FIX THIS...
HOW? WITH YOUR ROBO-LEG--?
I'VE PIMPED IT OUT A LITTLE FOR YOU...

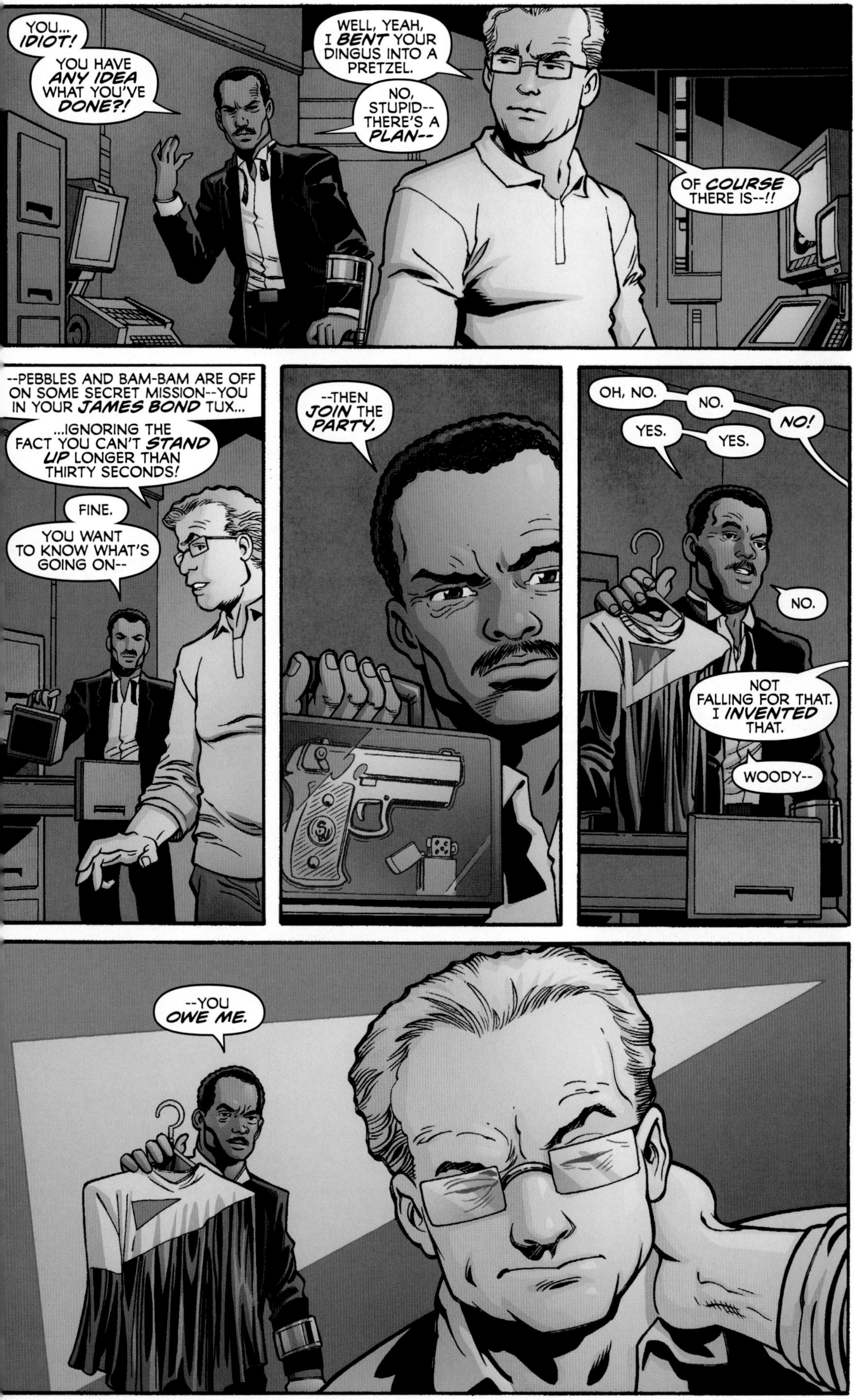
YOU... IDIOT!
YOU HAVE ANY IDEA WHAT YOU'VE DONE?!
WELL, YEAH, I BENT YOUR DINGUS INTO A PRETZEL.
NO, STUPID-- THERE'S A PLAN--
OF COURSE THERE IS--!!
--PEBBLES AND BAM-BAM ARE OFF ON SOME SECRET MISSION--YOU IN YOUR JAMES BOND TUX...
...IGNORING THE FACT YOU CAN'T STAND UP LONGER THAN THIRTY SECONDS!
FINE.
YOU WANT TO KNOW WHAT'S GOING ON--
--THEN JOIN THE PARTY.
OH, NO.
NO.
NO!
YES.
YES.
NO.
NOT FALLING FOR THAT. I INVENTED THAT.
WOODY--
--YOU OWE ME.

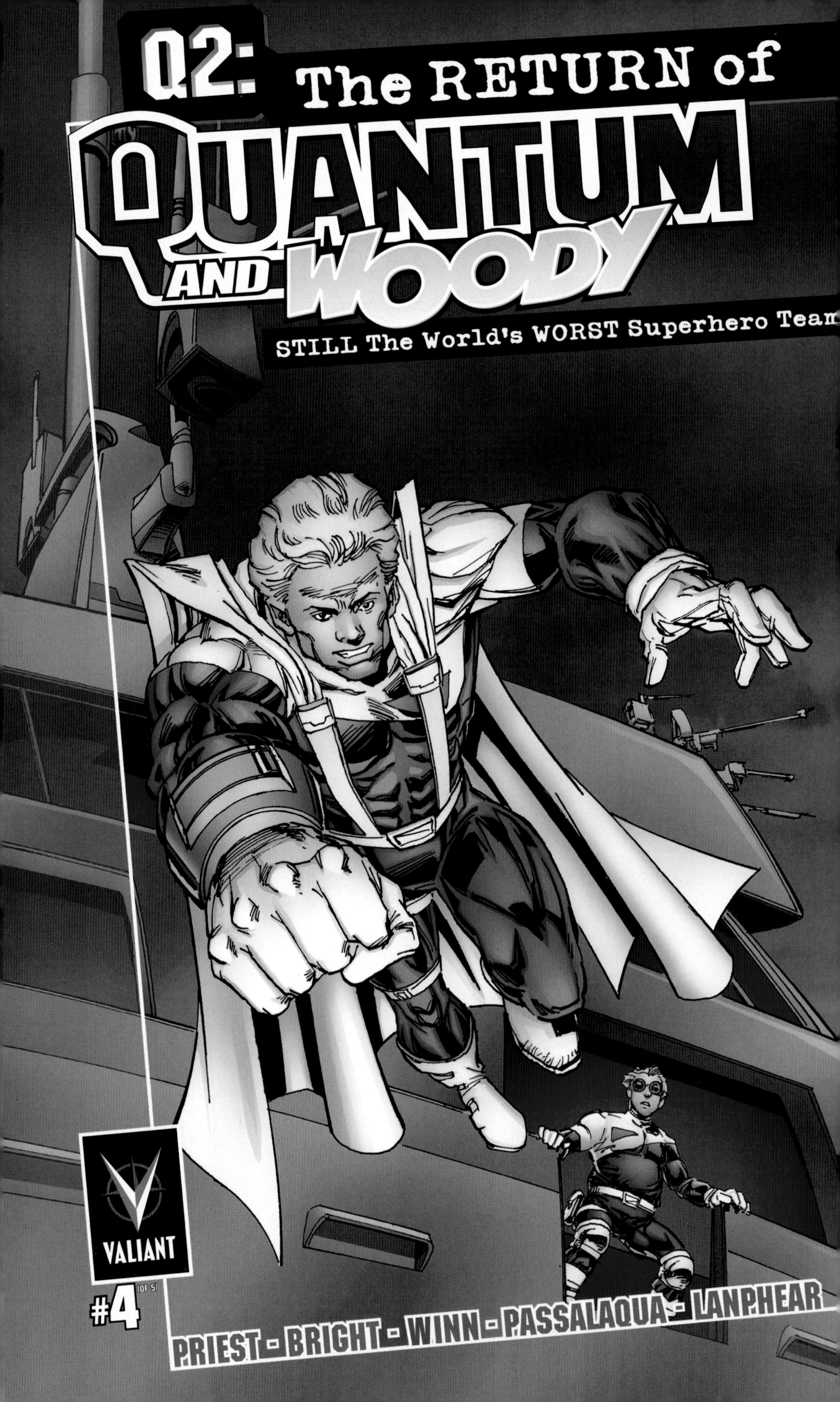

Q2: The RETURN of
QUANTUM AND WOODY
STILL The World's WORST Superhero Team
VALIANT
#4 [OF 5]
PRIEST - BRIGHT - WINN - PASSALAQUA - LANPHEAR

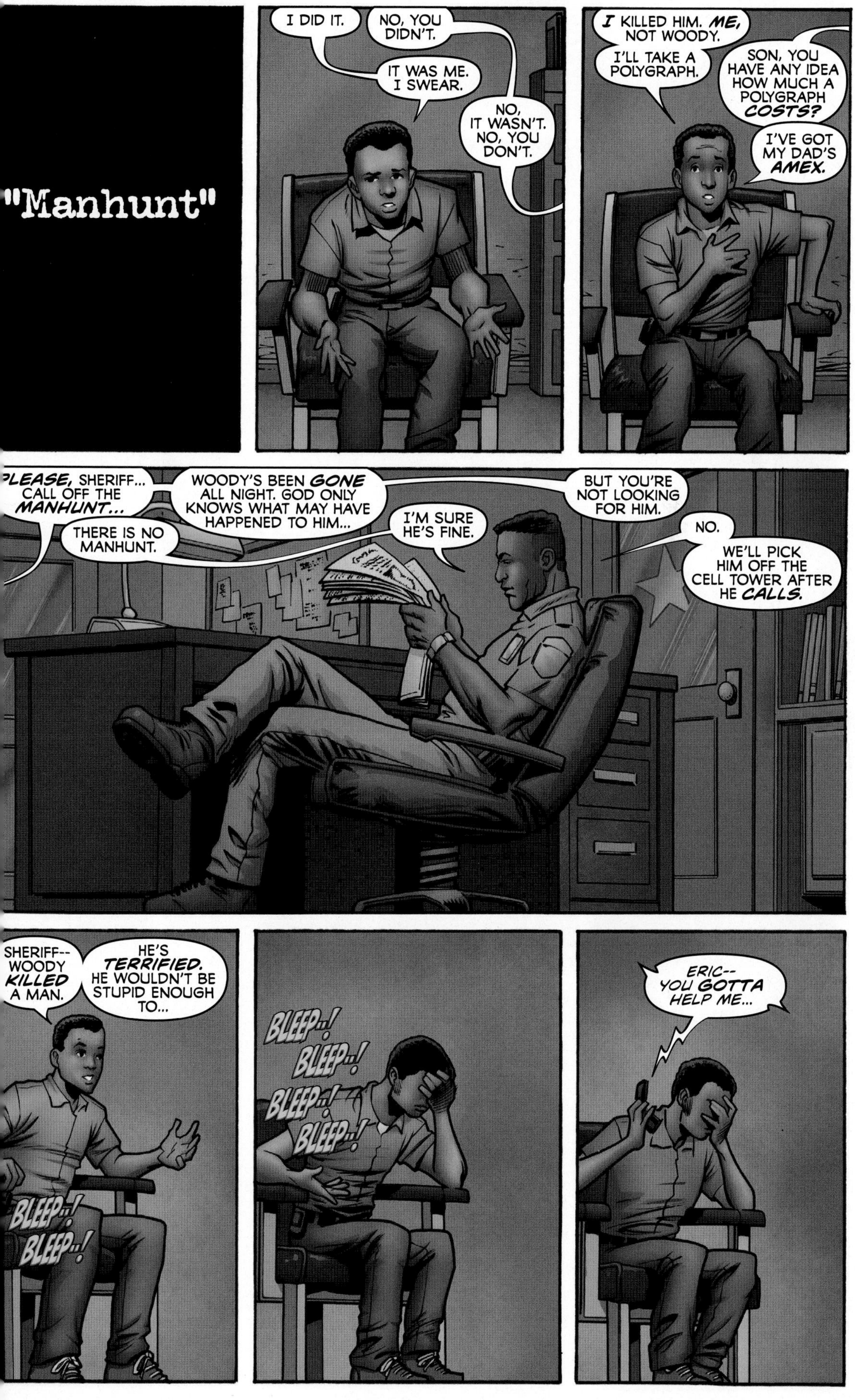
"Manhunt"
I DID IT.
NO, YOU DIDN'T.
IT WAS ME. I SWEAR.
NO, IT WASN'T. NO, YOU DON'T.
I KILLED HIM. ME, NOT WOODY.
I'LL TAKE A POLYGRAPH.
SON, YOU HAVE ANY IDEA HOW MUCH A POLYGRAPH COSTS?
I'VE GOT MY DAD'S AMEX.
PLEASE, SHERIFF... CALL OFF THE MANHUNT...
THERE IS NO MANHUNT.
WOODY'S BEEN GONE ALL NIGHT. GOD ONLY KNOWS WHAT MAY HAVE HAPPENED TO HIM...
I'M SURE HE'S FINE.
BUT YOU'RE NOT LOOKING FOR HIM.
NO.
WE'LL PICK HIM OFF THE CELL TOWER AFTER HE CALLS.
SHERIFF-- WOODY KILLED A MAN.
HE'S TERRIFIED. HE WOULDN'T BE STUPID ENOUGH TO...
BLEEP..! BLEEP..!
BLEEP..! BLEEP..! BLEEP..! BLEEP..!
ERIC-- YOU GOTTA HELP ME...

"The Privilege of Purpose"

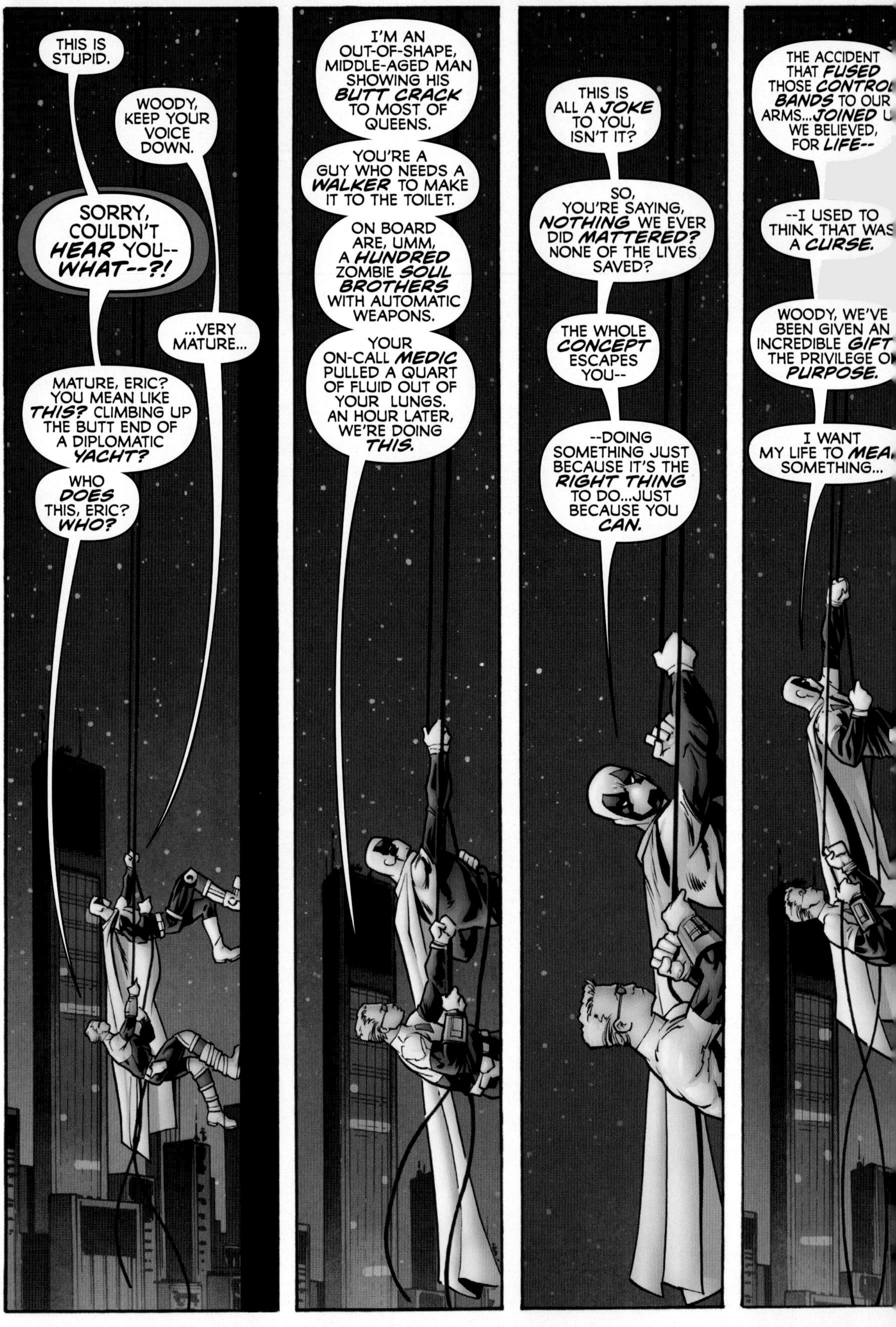
THIS IS STUPID.
WOODY, KEEP YOUR VOICE DOWN.
SORRY, COULDN'T HEAR YOU-- WHAT--?!
...VERY MATURE...
MATURE, ERIC? YOU MEAN LIKE THIS? CLIMBING UP THE BUTT END OF A DIPLOMATIC YACHT?
WHO DOES THIS, ERIC? WHO?
I'M AN OUT-OF-SHAPE, MIDDLE-AGED MAN SHOWING HIS BUTT CRACK TO MOST OF QUEENS.
YOU'RE A GUY WHO NEEDS A WALKER TO MAKE IT TO THE TOILET.
ON BOARD ARE, UMM, A HUNDRED ZOMBIE SOUL BROTHERS WITH AUTOMATIC WEAPONS.
YOUR ON-CALL MEDIC PULLED A QUART OF FLUID OUT OF YOUR LUNGS. AN HOUR LATER, WE'RE DOING THIS.
THIS IS ALL A JOKE TO YOU, ISN'T IT?
SO, YOU'RE SAYING, NOTHING WE EVER DID MATTERED? NONE OF THE LIVES SAVED?
THE WHOLE CONCEPT ESCAPES YOU--
--DOING SOMETHING JUST BECAUSE IT'S THE RIGHT THING TO DO...JUST BECAUSE YOU CAN.
THE ACCIDENT THAT FUSED THOSE CONTRO BANDS TO OUR ARMS...JOINED U WE BELIEVED, FOR LIFE--
--I USED TO THINK THAT WAS A CURSE.
WOODY, WE'VE BEEN GIVEN AN INCREDIBLE GIFT THE PRIVILEGE O PURPOSE.
I WANT MY LIFE TO MEA SOMETHING...

NICE SPEECH, BUT NO SALE.
YOU ARE UP TO SOMETHING. I'M GONNA FIGURE IT OUT.
THE KID I GREW UP WITH WAS A NERVOUS, EGGHEAD, NERDY INTROVERT.
THE BITTER OLD MAN I'VE FOUND HERE IS A SCHEMING, MANIPULATIVE LIAR.
NOW THAT'S PROGRESS.
YOU EVER THINK MAYBE IT'S YOU--?
MAYBE IF YOU WERE LESS THE FIFTY-YEAR-OLD TEENAGER AND TOOK... WELL... SOMETHING IN YOUR LIFE MORE SERIOUSLY--
--THEN I MIGHT BETTER AFFORD TO BE LESS OF A LIAR.
THAT'S WHAT I MEAN BY "MANIPULATIVE."
I'M RESPONSIBLE FOR YOUR GASLIGHTING THAT MUPPET INTO BELIEVING HE'S SOME KIND OF ROBOT...
...AND GOD ONLY KNOWS WHAT THE DEAL IS WITH YOU AND THAT PINT-SIZED WOODY...
DON'T KID YOURSELF, ERIC. THIS IS ALL YOU.
YOU TAKE THE ATRIUM WHILE I CONTINUE UP TO THE PROMENADE AND SWOOP DOWN--
SEE-- THIS IS WHAT I MEAN--
"SWOOP DOWN"? WHO THE HELL DOES THAT, ERIC?! WHO "SWOOPS"?!
ENOUGH WITH THE SWOOPING, ALREADY.
--?!
WHAT ARE YOU DOING--?!
WHAT'S IT LOOK LIKE I'M DOING?
WE'LL LIKELY FACE A DOZEN SUPER-POWERED, HEAVILY ARMED PROFESSIONAL KILLERS. BETTER TO GO WHILE I HAVE THE CHANCE.
BECAUSE IT'S THE RIGHT THING TO DO.
BECAUSE I CAN.

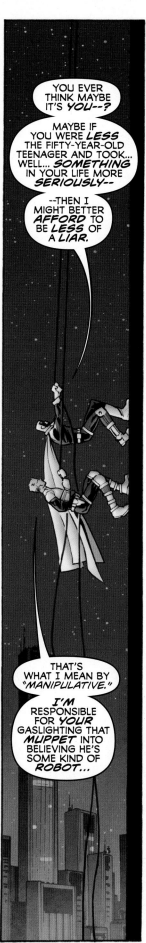

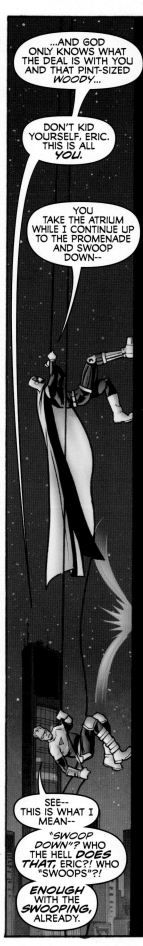

"Vive La France"

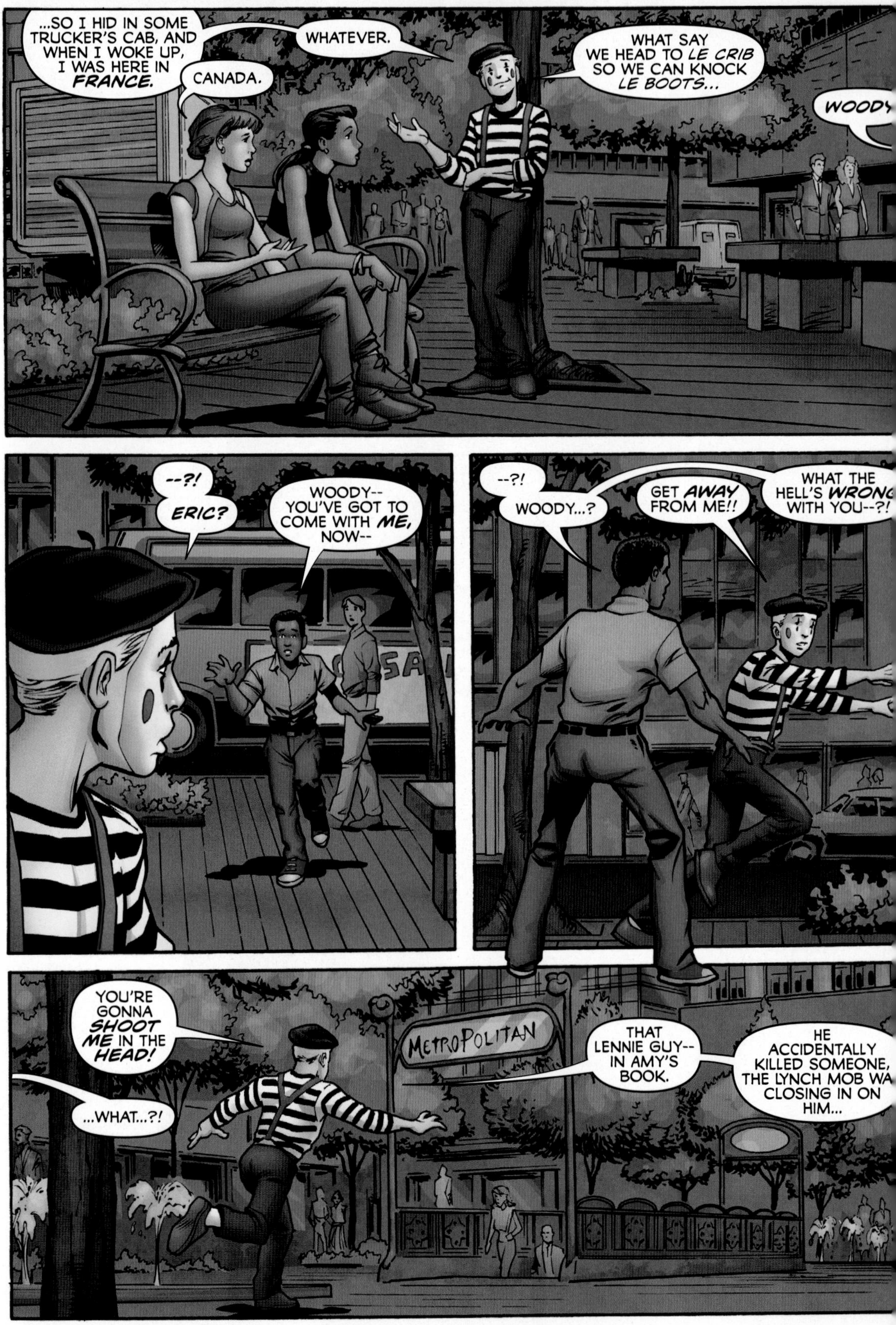
...SO I HID IN SOME TRUCKER'S CAB, AND WHEN I WOKE UP, I WAS HERE IN FRANCE.
CANADA.
WHATEVER.
WHAT SAY WE HEAD TO LE CRIB SO WE CAN KNOCK LE BOOTS...
WOODY
--?!
ERIC?
WOODY-- YOU'VE GOT TO COME WITH ME, NOW--
--?!
WOODY...?
GET AWAY FROM ME!!
WHAT THE HELL'S WRONG WITH YOU--?!
YOU'RE GONNA SHOOT ME IN THE HEAD!
...WHAT...?!
METROPOLITAN
THAT LENNIE GUY-- IN AMY'S BOOK.
HE ACCIDENTALLY KILLED SOMEONE, THE LYNCH MOB WA CLOSING IN ON HIM...

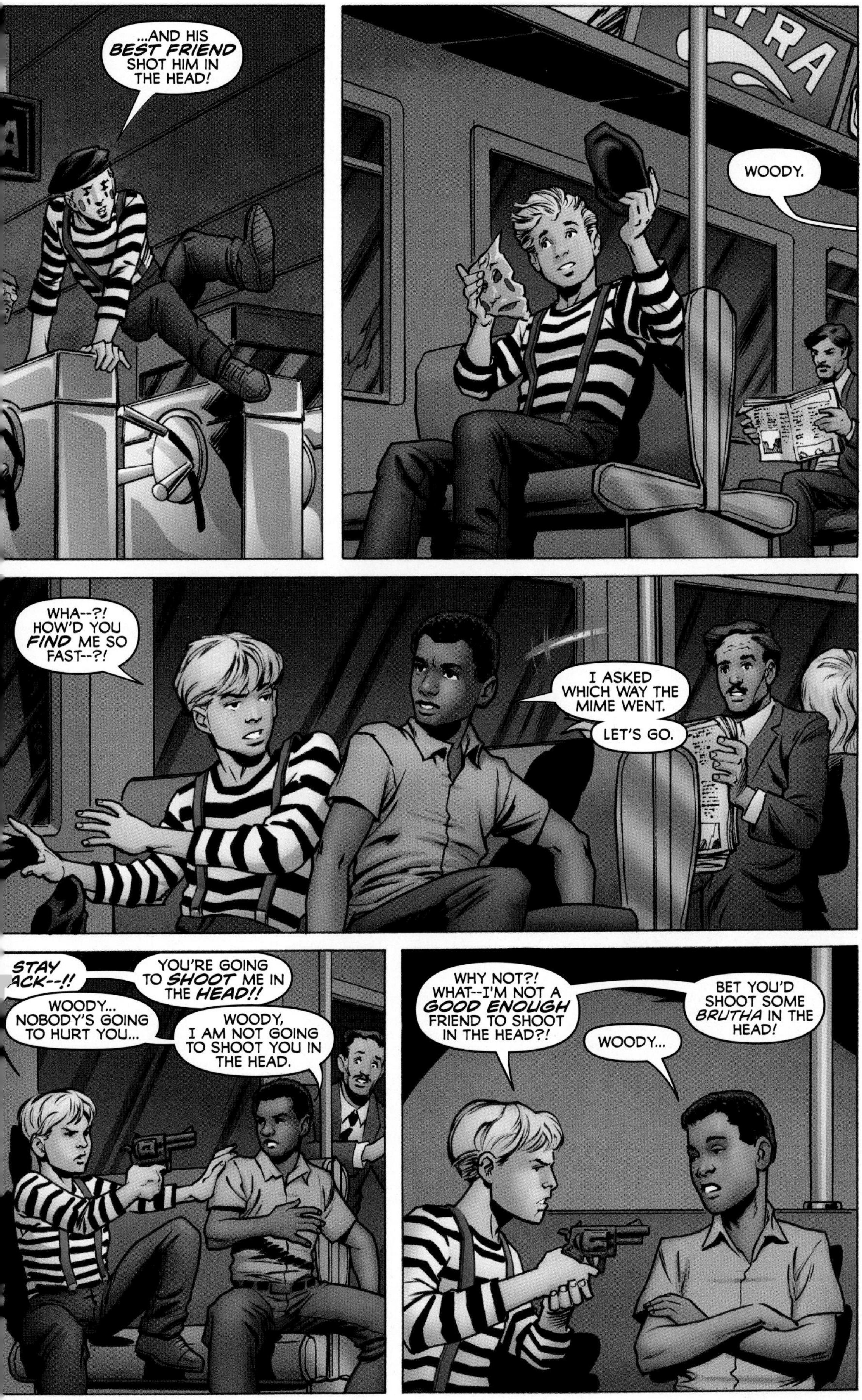

...AND HIS *BEST FRIEND* SHOT HIM IN THE HEAD!
WOODY.
WHA--?! HOW'D YOU *FIND* ME SO FAST--?!
I ASKED WHICH WAY THE MIME WENT.
LET'S GO.
STAY ACK--!!
YOU'RE GOING TO *SHOOT* ME IN THE *HEAD!!*
WOODY... NOBODY'S GOING TO HURT YOU...
WOODY, I AM NOT GOING TO SHOOT YOU IN THE HEAD.
WHY NOT?! WHAT--I'M NOT A *GOOD ENOUGH* FRIEND TO SHOOT IN THE HEAD?!
BET YOU'D SHOOT SOME *BRUTHA* IN THE HEAD!
WOODY...

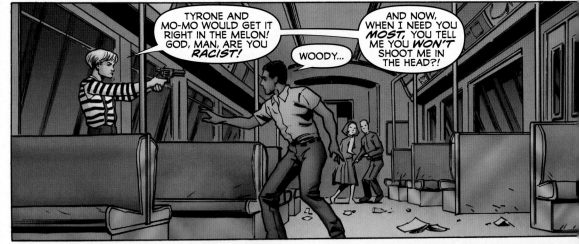

TYRONE AND MO-MO WOULD GET IT RIGHT IN THE MELON! GOD, MAN, ARE YOU *RACIST!*

WOODY...

AND NOW, WHEN I NEED YOU *MOST,* YOU TELL ME YOU *WON'T* SHOOT ME IN THE HEAD?!

-- --ALL RIGHT, WOODY. I'LL SHOOT YOU IN THE HEAD.

DAMN STRAIGHT.

DON'T MOVE--!!

PUT THE *GUN DOWN--!!*

IT'S ALL RIGHT, OFFICER-- WOODY'S JUST--

PUT IT *DOWN!!*

HEY, WHY DON'T YOU TWO *RELAX--* HIT *LE DONUT SHOPPE...?*

WOODY-- DON'T *WAVE* THAT THING AROUND--

GET *DOWN--!!*

BLAAMM

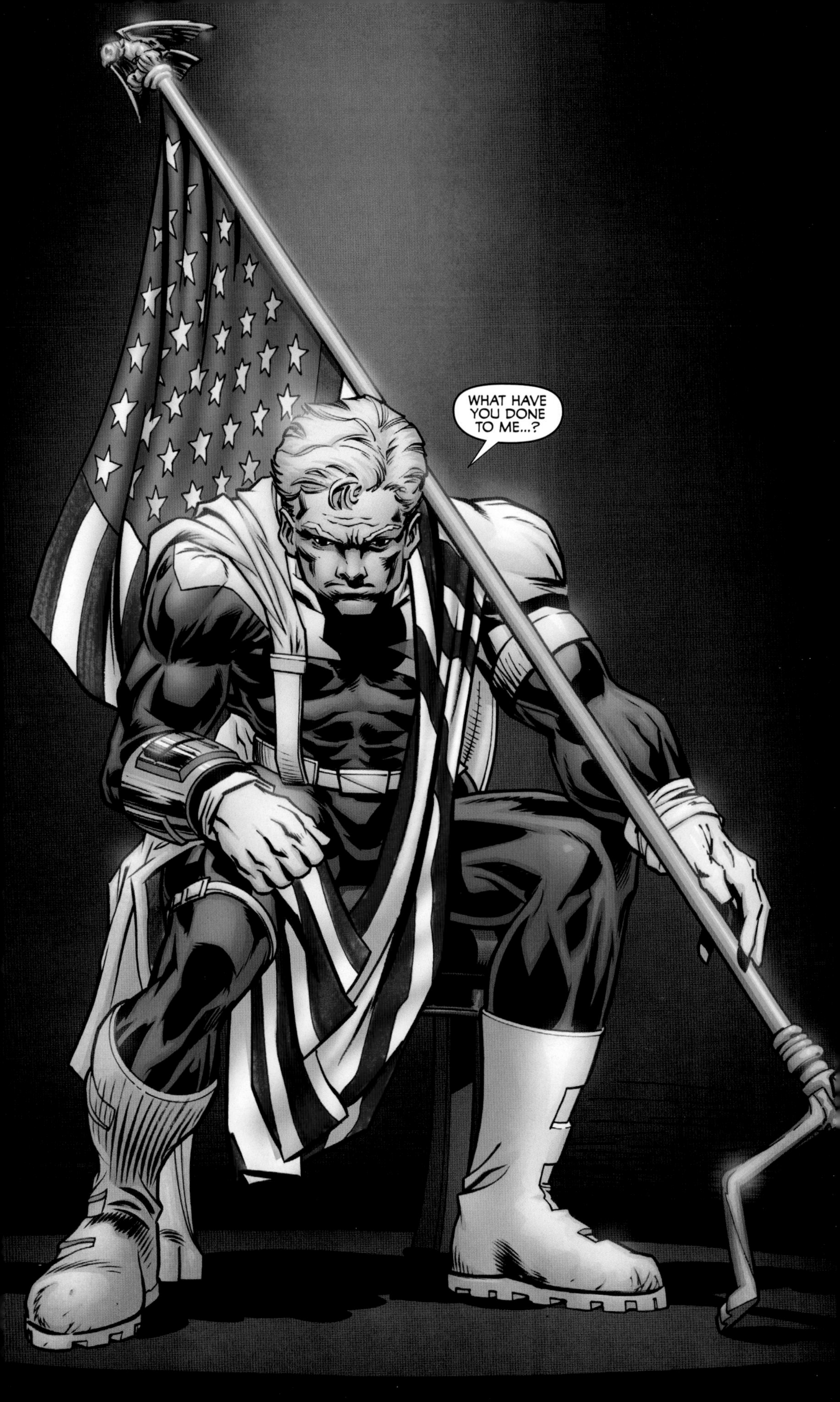
WHAT HAVE YOU DONE TO ME...?

"Klack"

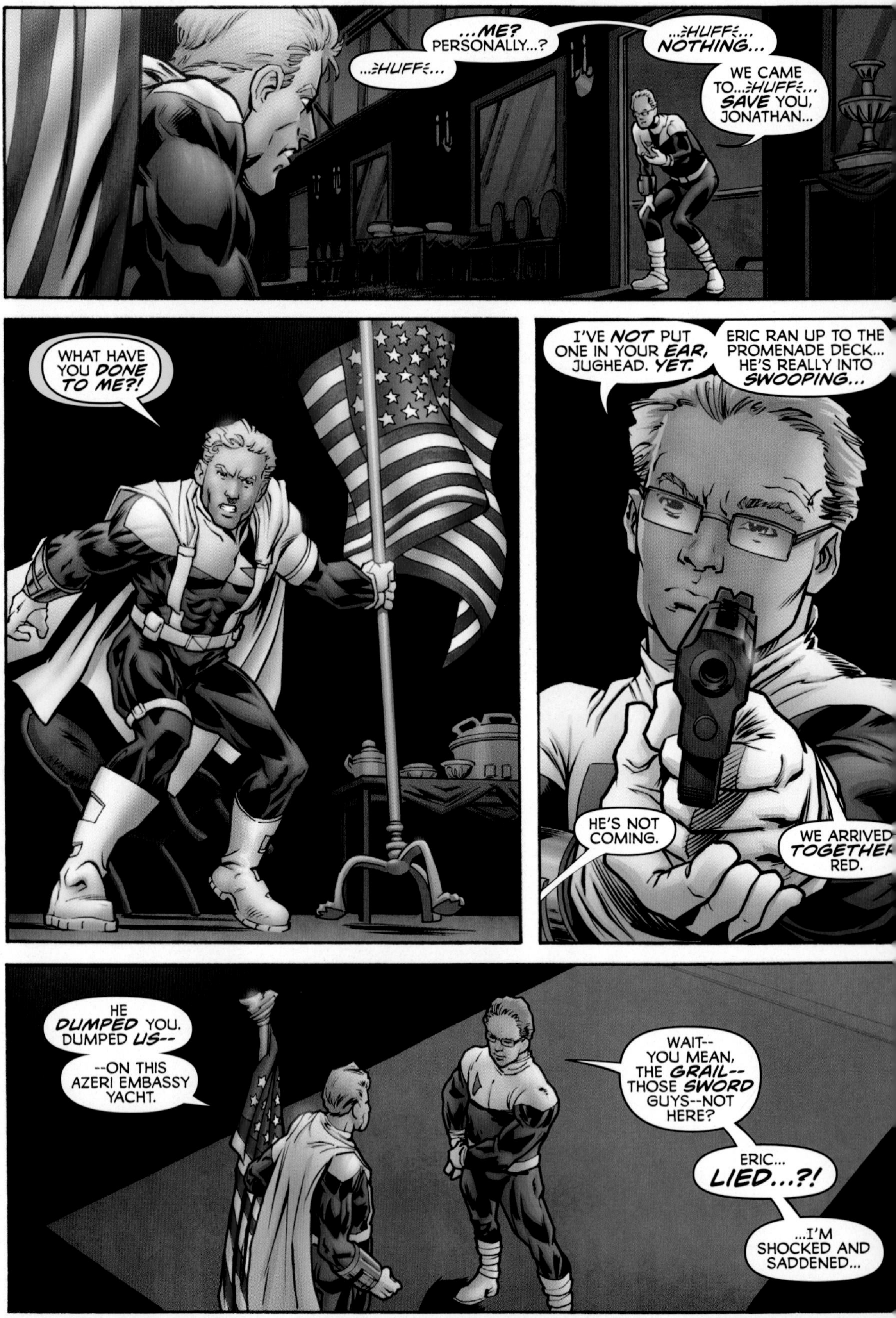

...HUFF...
...ME? PERSONALLY...?
...HUFF... NOTHING...
WE CAME TO...HUFF... SAVE YOU, JONATHAN...
WHAT HAVE YOU DONE TO ME?!
I'VE NOT PUT ONE IN YOUR EAR, JUGHEAD. YET.
ERIC RAN UP TO THE PROMENADE DECK... HE'S REALLY INTO SWOOPING...
HE'S NOT COMING.
WE ARRIVED TOGETHER RED.
HE DUMPED YOU. DUMPED US--
--ON THIS AZERI EMBASSY YACHT.
WAIT-- YOU MEAN, THE GRAIL-- THOSE SWORD GUYS--NOT HERE?
ERIC... LIED...?!
...I'M SHOCKED AND SADDENED...

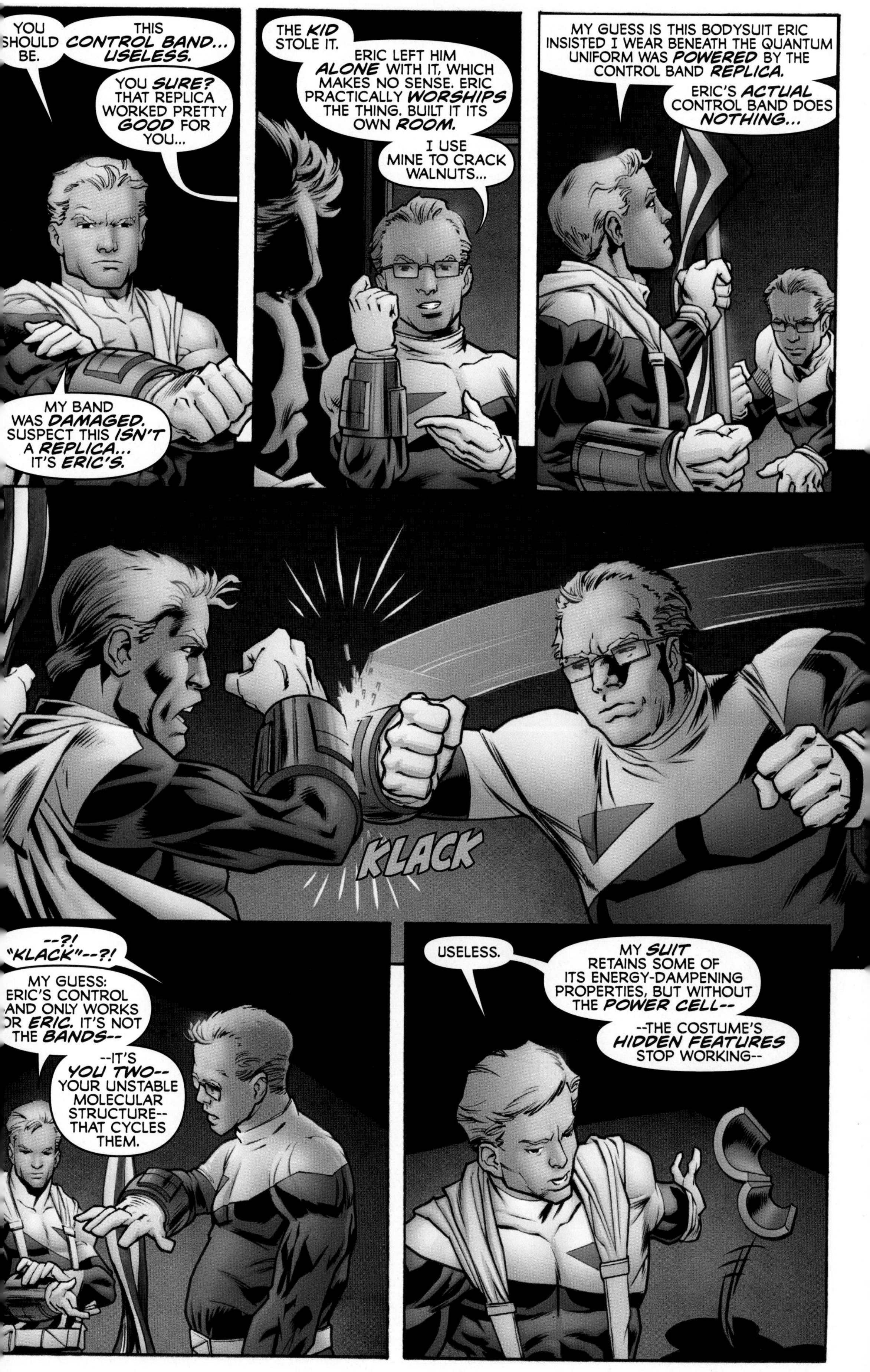

YOU SHOULD BE.
THIS CONTROL BAND... USELESS.
YOU SURE? THAT REPLICA WORKED PRETTY GOOD FOR YOU...
MY BAND WAS DAMAGED. SUSPECT THIS ISN'T A REPLICA... IT'S ERIC'S.
THE KID STOLE IT.
ERIC LEFT HIM ALONE WITH IT, WHICH MAKES NO SENSE. ERIC PRACTICALLY WORSHIPS THE THING. BUILT IT ITS OWN ROOM.
I USE MINE TO CRACK WALNUTS...
MY GUESS IS THIS BODYSUIT ERIC INSISTED I WEAR BENEATH THE QUANTUM UNIFORM WAS POWERED BY THE CONTROL BAND REPLICA.
ERIC'S ACTUAL CONTROL BAND DOES NOTHING...
KLACK
--?! "KLACK"--?!
MY GUESS: ERIC'S CONTROL AND ONLY WORKS R ERIC. IT'S NOT THE BANDS--
--IT'S YOU TWO-- YOUR UNSTABLE MOLECULAR STRUCTURE-- THAT CYCLES THEM.
USELESS.
MY SUIT RETAINS SOME OF ITS ENERGY-DAMPENING PROPERTIES, BUT WITHOUT THE POWER CELL--
--THE COSTUME'S HIDDEN FEATURES STOP WORKING--

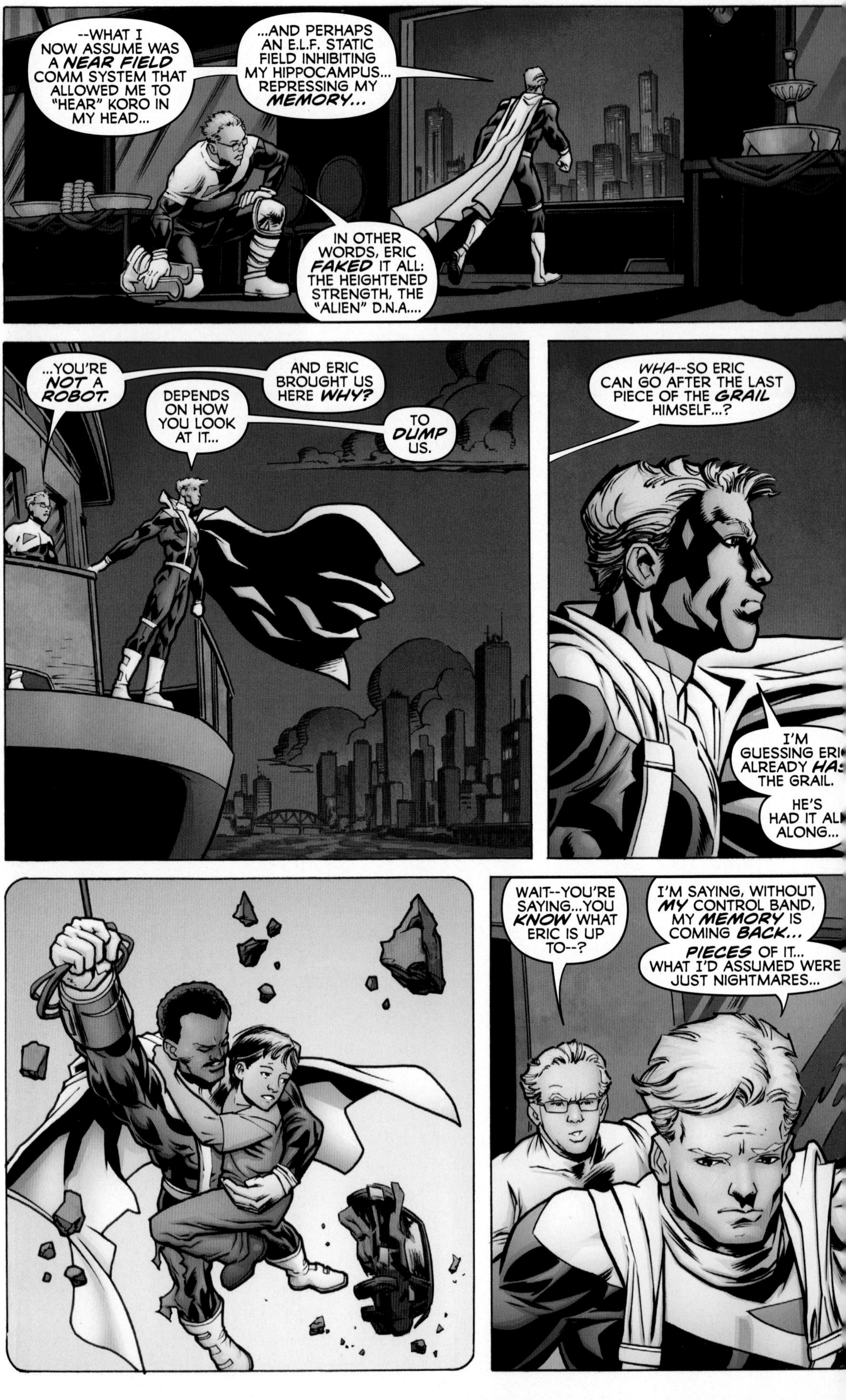
--WHAT I NOW ASSUME WAS A NEAR FIELD COMM SYSTEM THAT ALLOWED ME TO "HEAR" KORO IN MY HEAD...
...AND PERHAPS AN E.L.F. STATIC FIELD INHIBITING MY HIPPOCAMPUS... REPRESSING MY MEMORY...
IN OTHER WORDS, ERIC FAKED IT ALL: THE HEIGHTENED STRENGTH, THE "ALIEN" D.N.A....
...YOU'RE NOT A ROBOT.
AND ERIC BROUGHT US HERE WHY?
DEPENDS ON HOW YOU LOOK AT IT...
TO DUMP US.
WHA--SO ERIC CAN GO AFTER THE LAST PIECE OF THE GRAIL HIMSELF...?
I'M GUESSING ERI ALREADY HA THE GRAIL.
HE'S HAD IT AL ALONG...
WAIT--YOU'RE SAYING...YOU KNOW WHAT ERIC IS UP TO--?
I'M SAYING, WITHOUT MY CONTROL BAND, MY MEMORY IS COMING BACK...
PIECES OF IT... WHAT I'D ASSUMED WERE JUST NIGHTMARES...

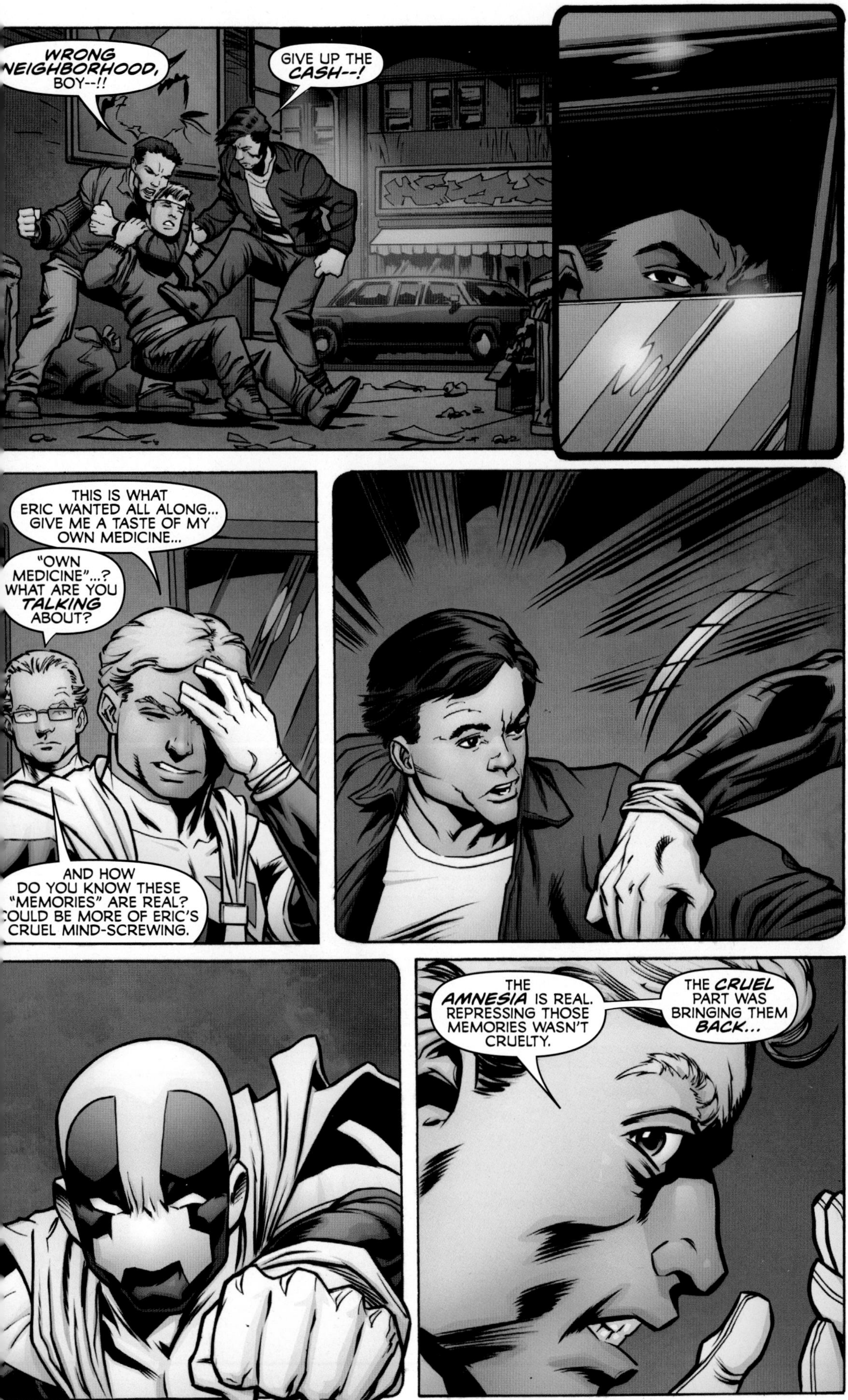
WRONG NEIGHBORHOOD, BOY--!!
GIVE UP THE CASH--!
THIS IS WHAT ERIC WANTED ALL ALONG... GIVE ME A TASTE OF MY OWN MEDICINE...
"OWN MEDICINE"...? WHAT ARE YOU TALKING ABOUT?
AND HOW DO YOU KNOW THESE "MEMORIES" ARE REAL? COULD BE MORE OF ERIC'S CRUEL MIND-SCREWING.
THE AMNESIA IS REAL. REPRESSING THOSE MEMORIES WASN'T CRUELTY.
THE CRUEL PART WAS BRINGING THEM BACK...

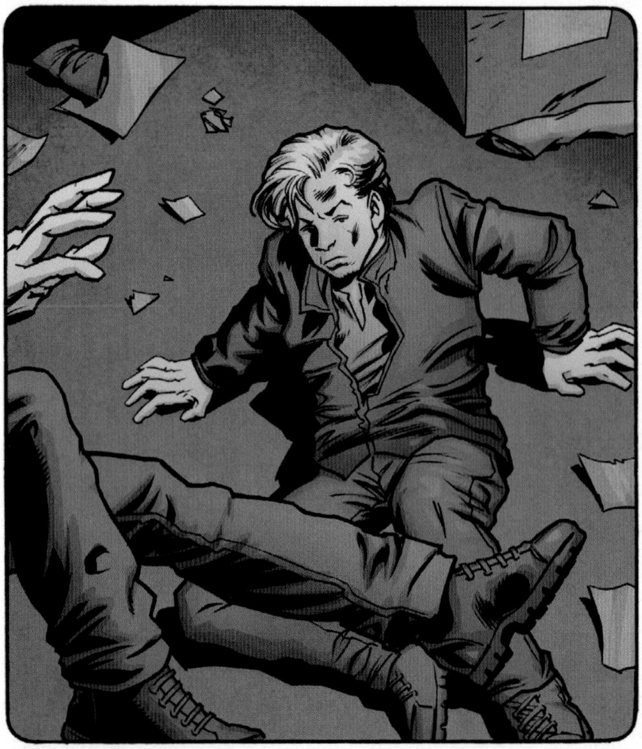

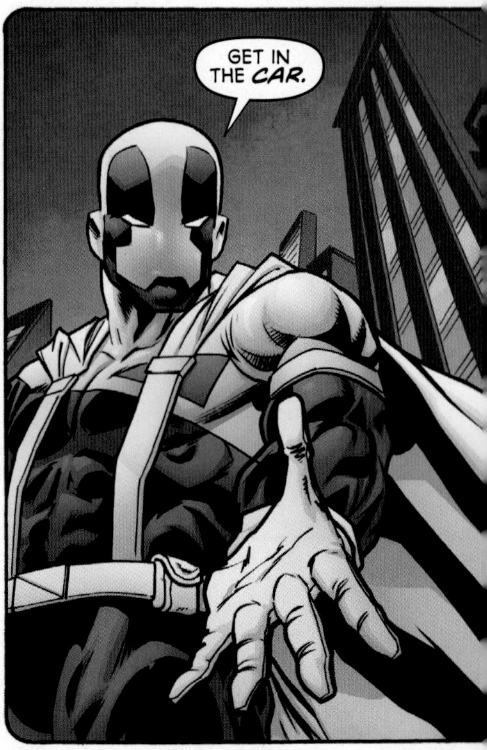
GET IN THE *CAR.*

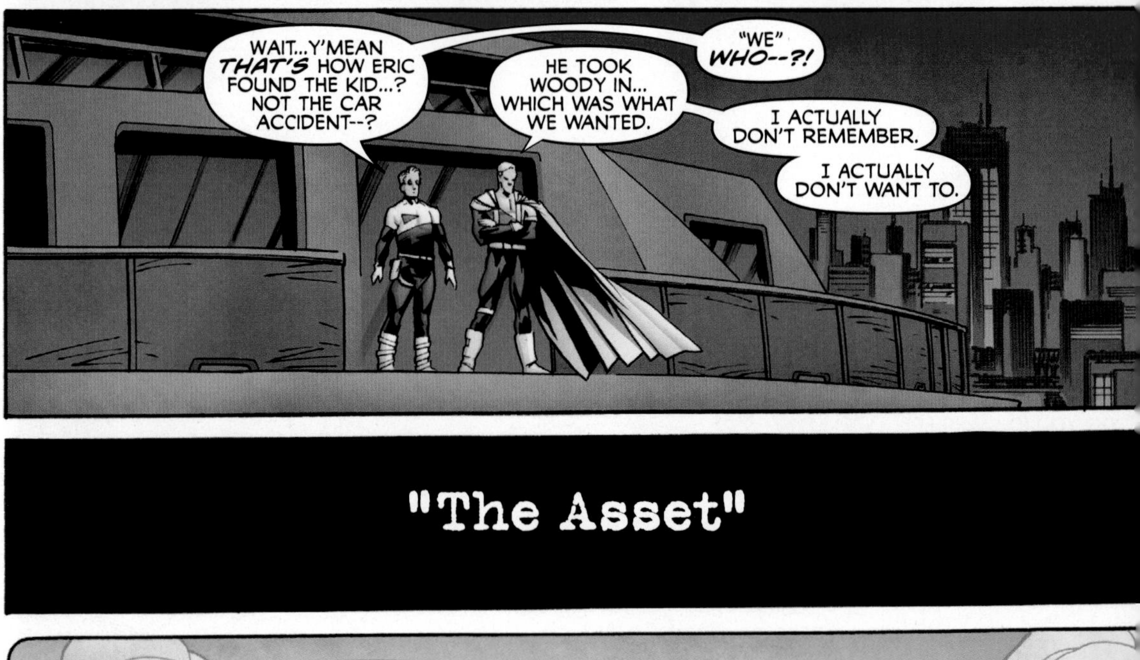
WAIT...Y'MEAN *THAT'S* HOW ERIC FOUND THE KID...? NOT THE CAR ACCIDENT--?
HE TOOK WOODY IN... WHICH WAS WHAT WE WANTED.
"WE" *WHO--?!*
I ACTUALLY DON'T REMEMBER.
I ACTUALLY DON'T WANT TO.

"The Asset"

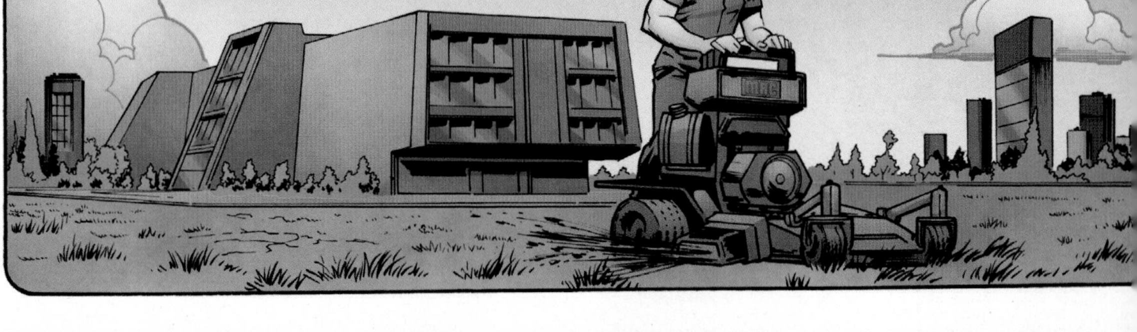
THE *MISSION* IS *OVER,* CAPTAIN.
--?! MR. HENDERSON--?

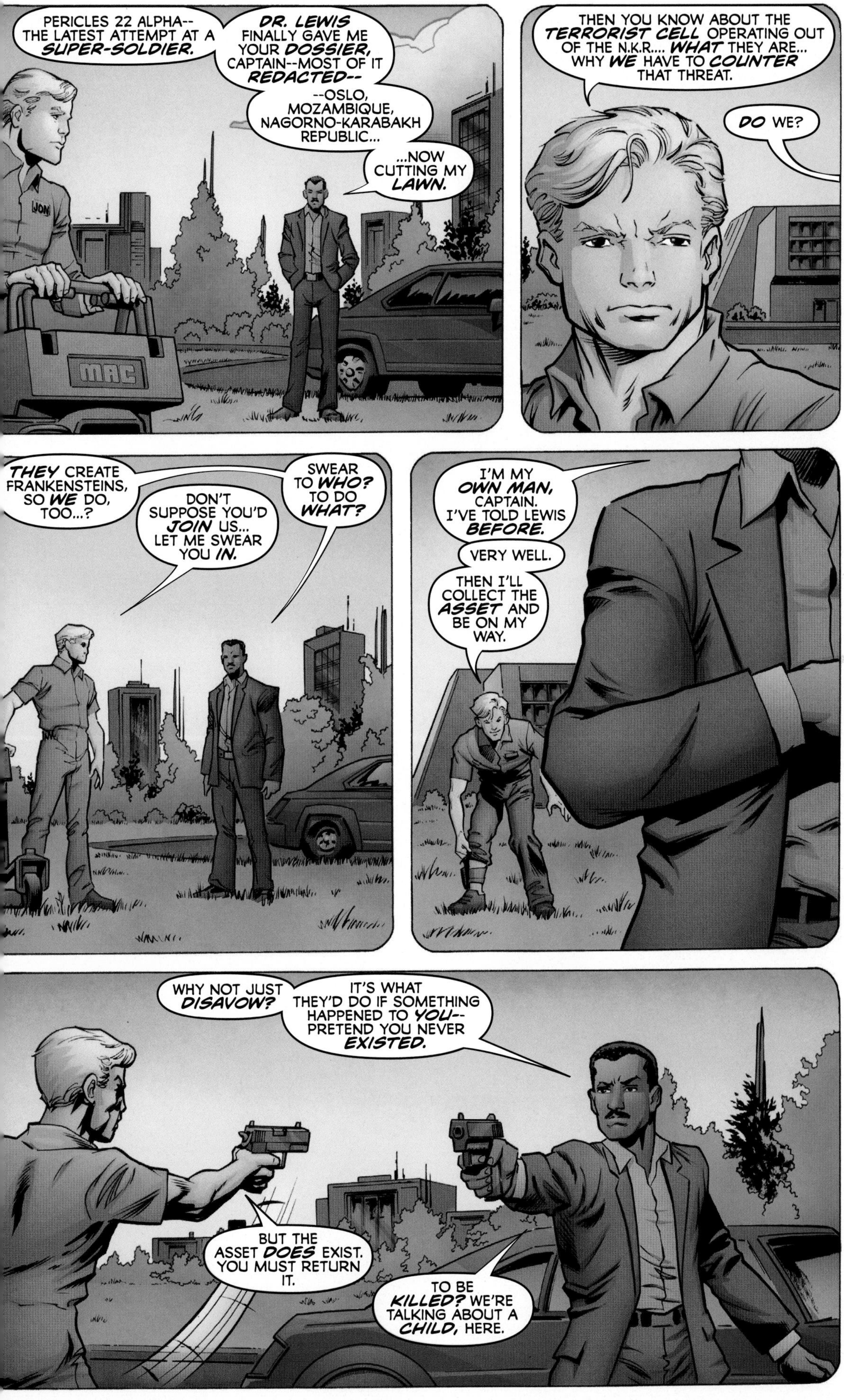

PERICLES 22 ALPHA-- THE LATEST ATTEMPT AT A SUPER-SOLDIER.
DR. LEWIS FINALLY GAVE ME YOUR DOSSIER, CAPTAIN--MOST OF IT REDACTED--
--OSLO, MOZAMBIQUE, NAGORNO-KARABAKH REPUBLIC...
...NOW CUTTING MY LAWN.
JON
MAC
THEN YOU KNOW ABOUT THE TERRORIST CELL OPERATING OUT OF THE N.K.R.... WHAT THEY ARE... WHY WE HAVE TO COUNTER THAT THREAT.
DO WE?
THEY CREATE FRANKENSTEINS, SO WE DO, TOO...?
DON'T SUPPOSE YOU'D JOIN US... LET ME SWEAR YOU IN.
SWEAR TO WHO? TO DO WHAT?
I'M MY OWN MAN, CAPTAIN. I'VE TOLD LEWIS BEFORE.
VERY WELL.
THEN I'LL COLLECT THE ASSET AND BE ON MY WAY.
WHY NOT JUST DISAVOW?
IT'S WHAT THEY'D DO IF SOMETHING HAPPENED TO YOU-- PRETEND YOU NEVER EXISTED.
BUT THE ASSET DOES EXIST. YOU MUST RETURN IT.
TO BE KILLED? WE'RE TALKING ABOUT A CHILD, HERE.

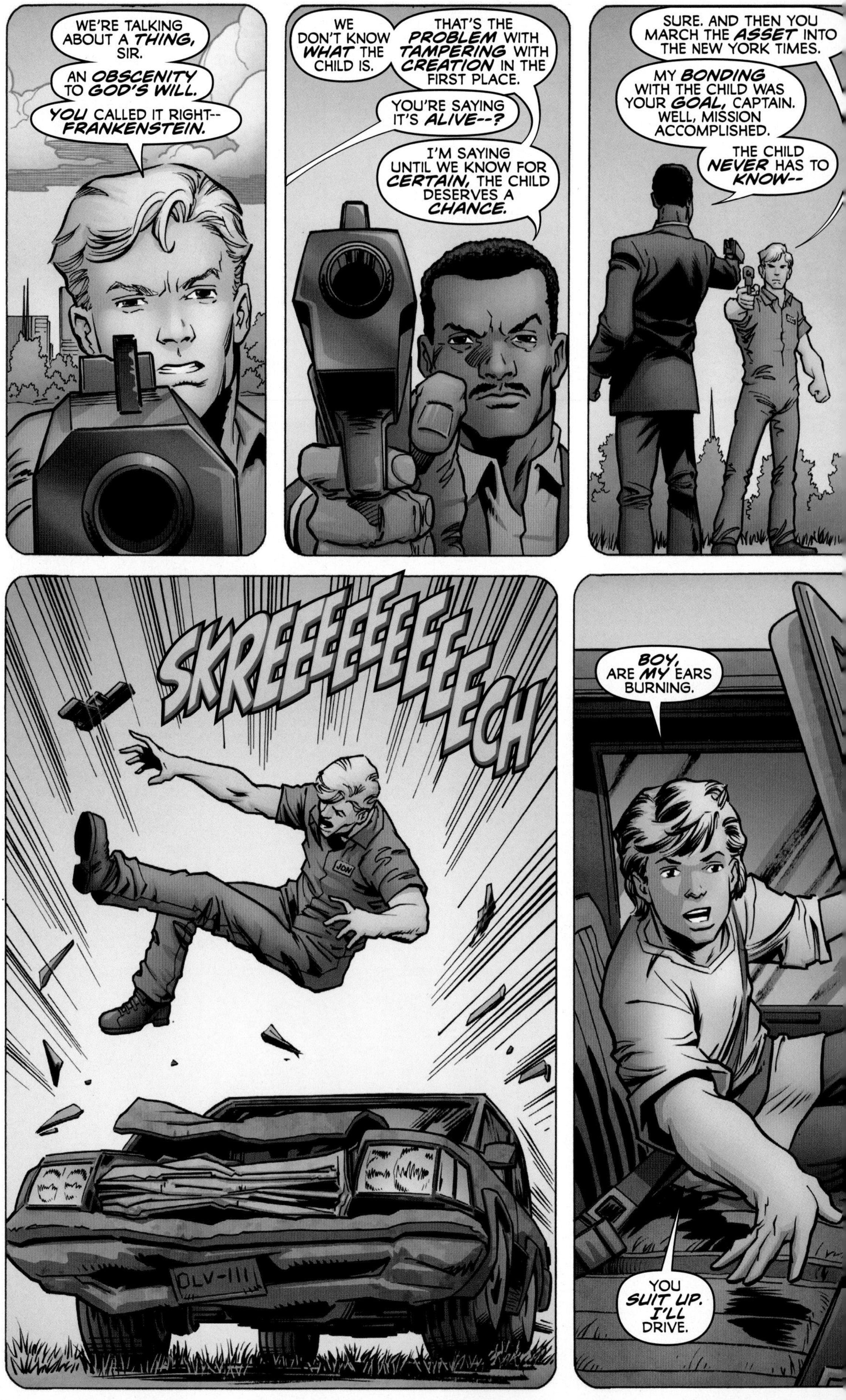

WE'RE TALKING ABOUT A THING, SIR.
AN OBSCENITY TO GOD'S WILL.
YOU CALLED IT RIGHT-- FRANKENSTEIN.
WE DON'T KNOW WHAT THE CHILD IS.
THAT'S THE PROBLEM WITH TAMPERING WITH CREATION IN THE FIRST PLACE.
YOU'RE SAYING IT'S ALIVE--?
I'M SAYING UNTIL WE KNOW FOR CERTAIN, THE CHILD DESERVES A CHANCE.
SURE. AND THEN YOU MARCH THE ASSET INTO THE NEW YORK TIMES.
MY BONDING WITH THE CHILD WAS YOUR GOAL, CAPTAIN. WELL, MISSION ACCOMPLISHED.
THE CHILD NEVER HAS TO KNOW--
SKREEEEEEEEEEECH
JON
OLV-111
BOY, ARE MY EARS BURNING.
YOU SUIT UP. I'LL DRIVE.

"The Constant Gardener"

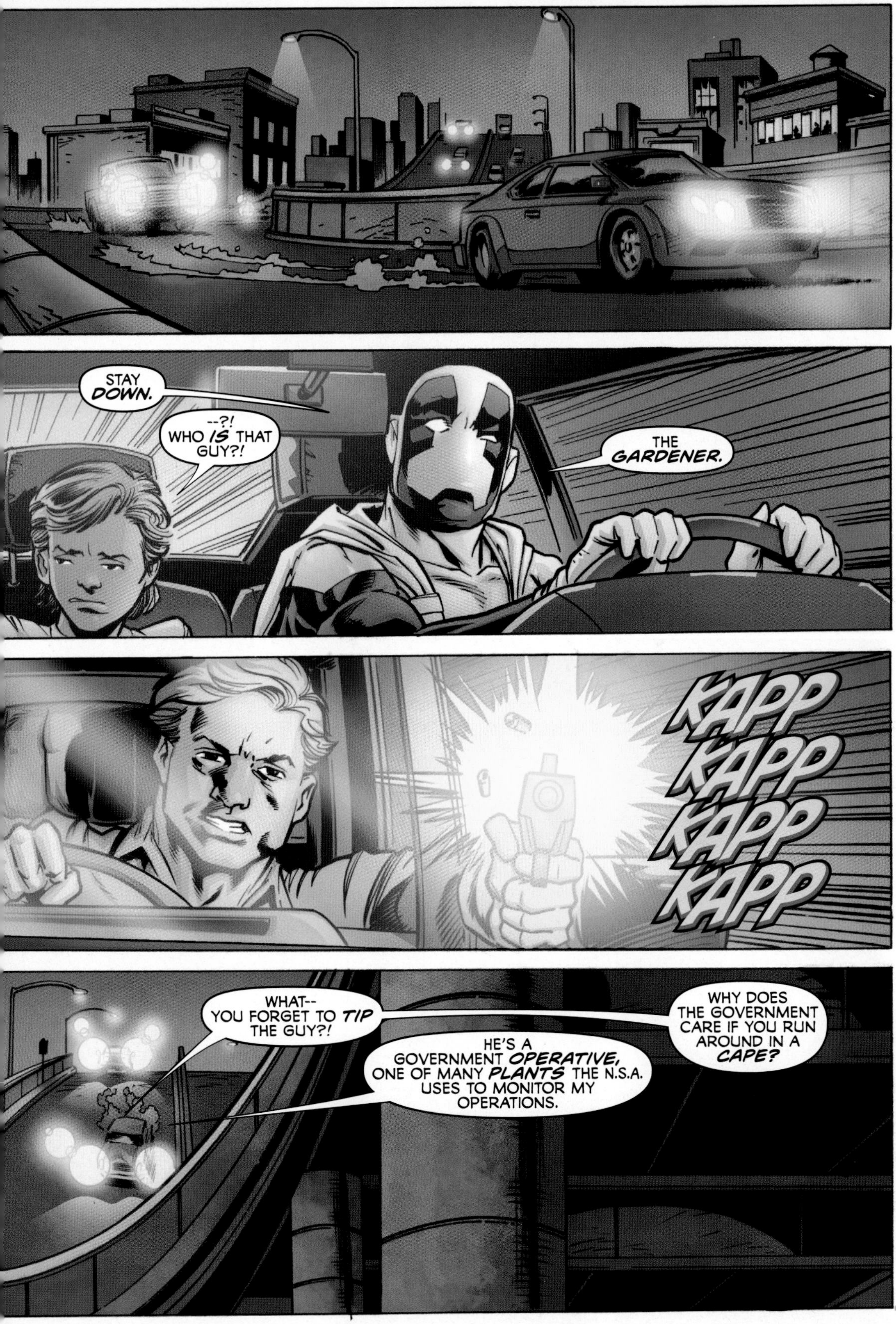
STAY DOWN.
--?! WHO IS THAT GUY?!
THE GARDENER.
KAPP KAPP KAPP KAPP
WHAT-- YOU FORGET TO TIP THE GUY?!
HE'S A GOVERNMENT OPERATIVE, ONE OF MANY PLANTS THE N.S.A. USES TO MONITOR MY OPERATIONS.
WHY DOES THE GOVERNMENT CARE IF YOU RUN AROUND IN A CAPE?

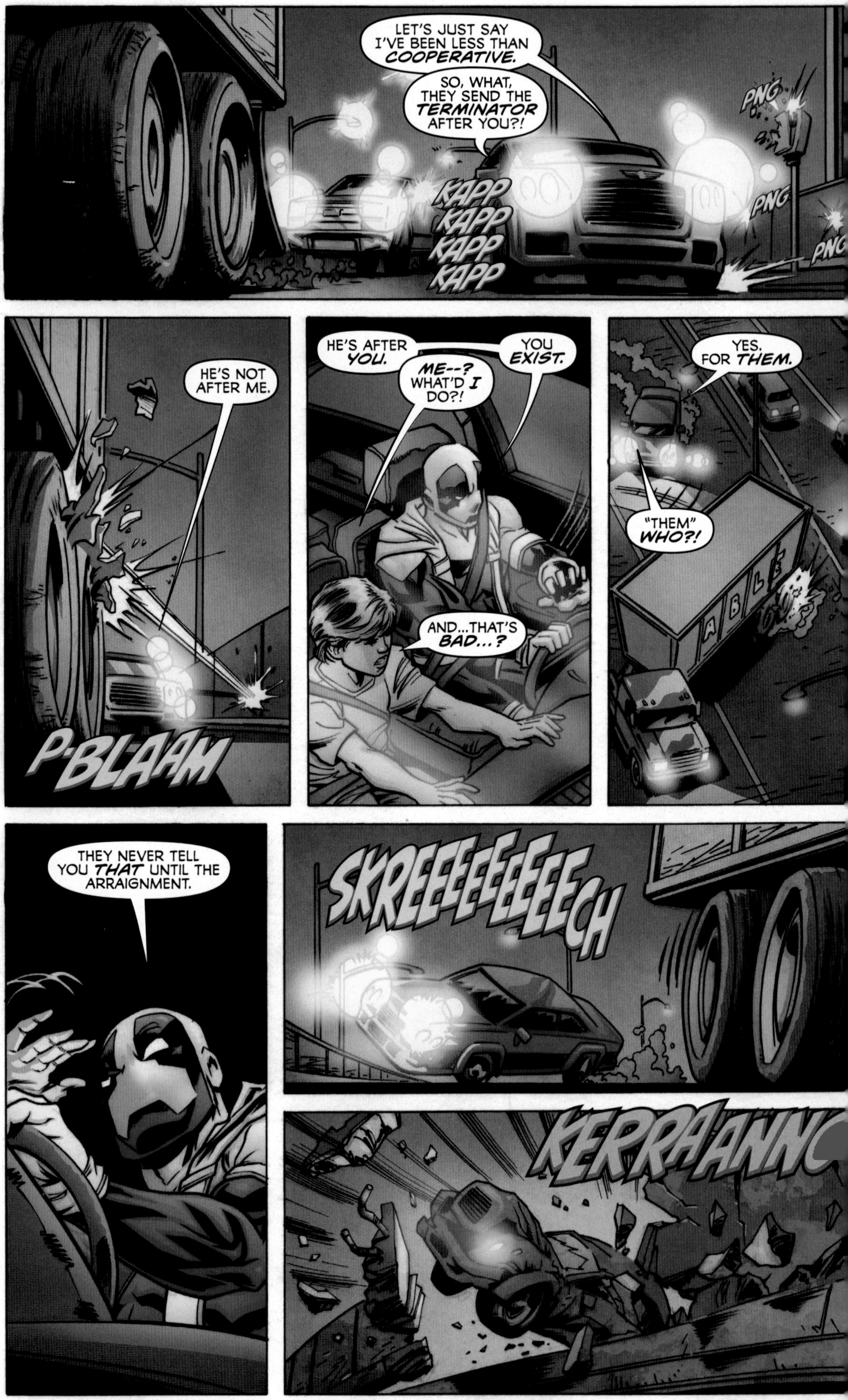

LET'S JUST SAY I'VE BEEN LESS THAN COOPERATIVE.
SO, WHAT, THEY SEND THE TERMINATOR AFTER YOU?!
PNG
KAPP KAPP KAPP KAPP
PNG
PNG
HE'S NOT AFTER ME.
P-BLAAM
HE'S AFTER YOU.
ME--? WHAT'D I DO?!
YOU EXIST.
AND...THAT'S BAD...?
YES. FOR THEM.
"THEM" WHO?!
THEY NEVER TELL YOU THAT UNTIL THE ARRAIGNMENT.
SKREEEEEEEEEECH
KERRAANNG

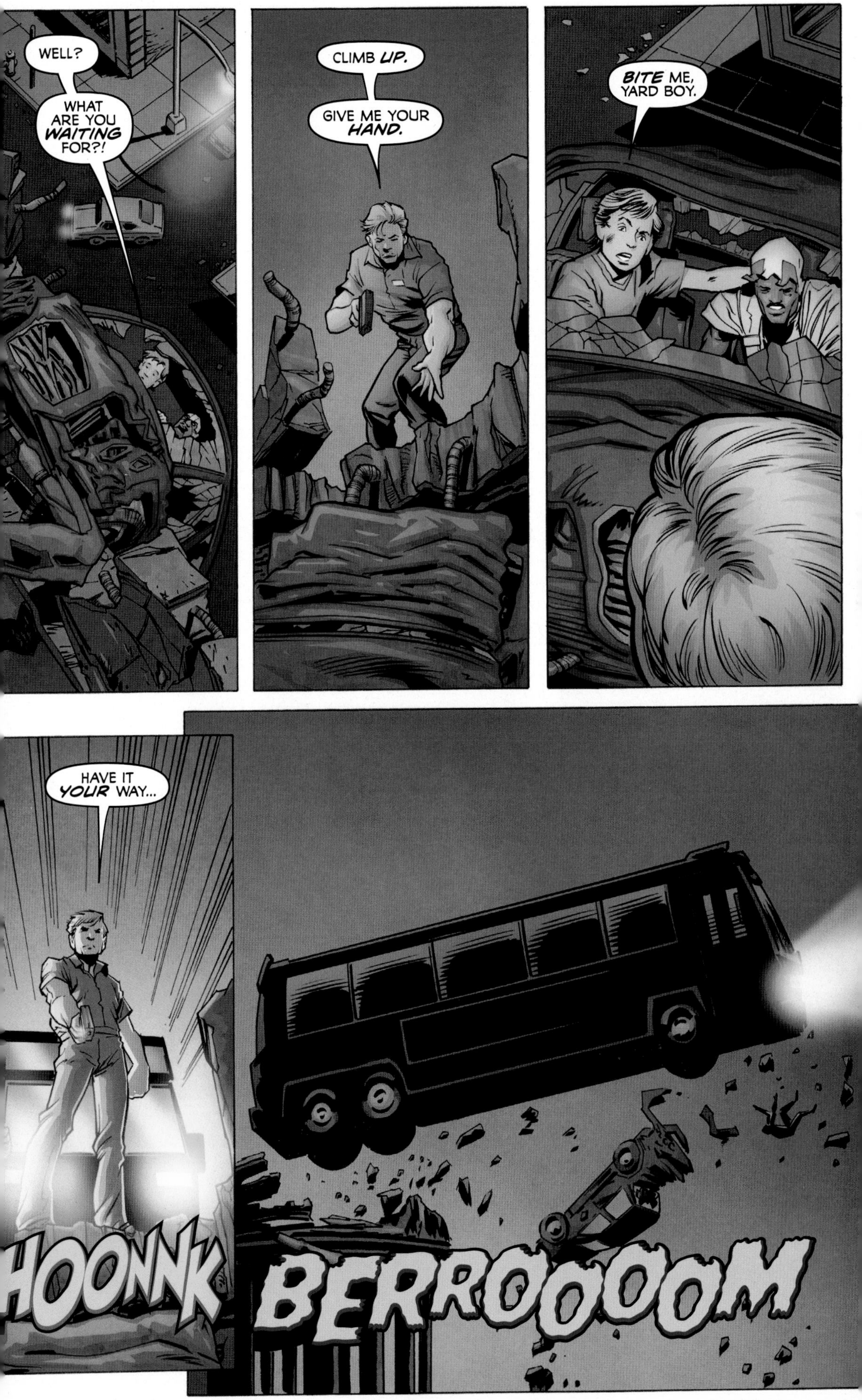

WELL?
WHAT ARE YOU *WAITING* FOR?!
CLIMB *UP.*
GIVE ME YOUR *HAND.*
BITE ME, YARD BOY.
HAVE IT *YOUR* WAY...
HOONNK
BERROOOOM

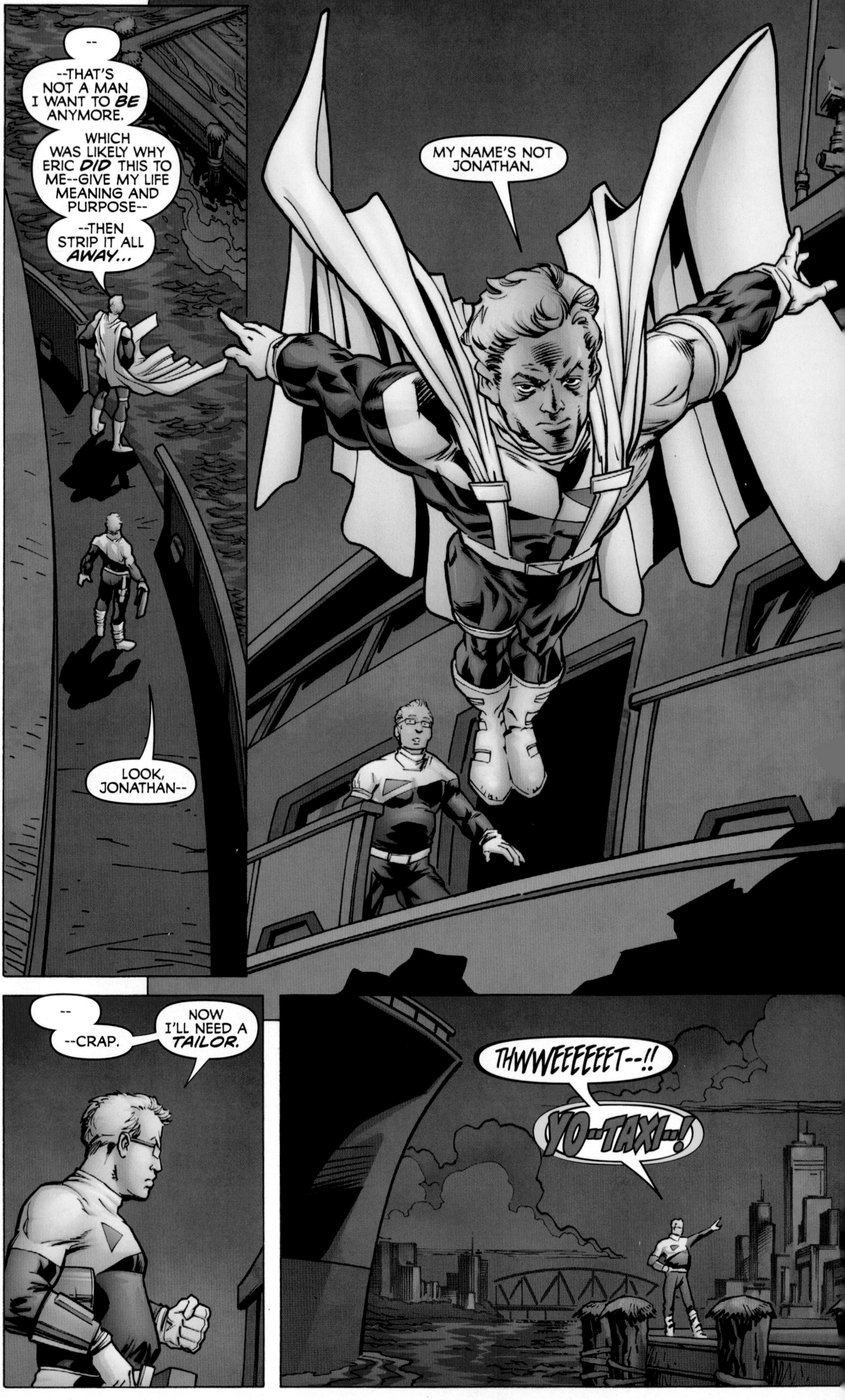
--
--THAT'S NOT A MAN I WANT TO *BE* ANYMORE.
WHICH WAS LIKELY WHY ERIC *DID* THIS TO ME--GIVE MY LIFE MEANING AND PURPOSE--
--THEN STRIP IT ALL *AWAY...*
LOOK, JONATHAN--
MY NAME'S NOT JONATHAN.
--
--CRAP.
NOW I'LL NEED A *TAILOR.*
THWWEEEEEET--!!
YO--TAXI--!

"Night School"

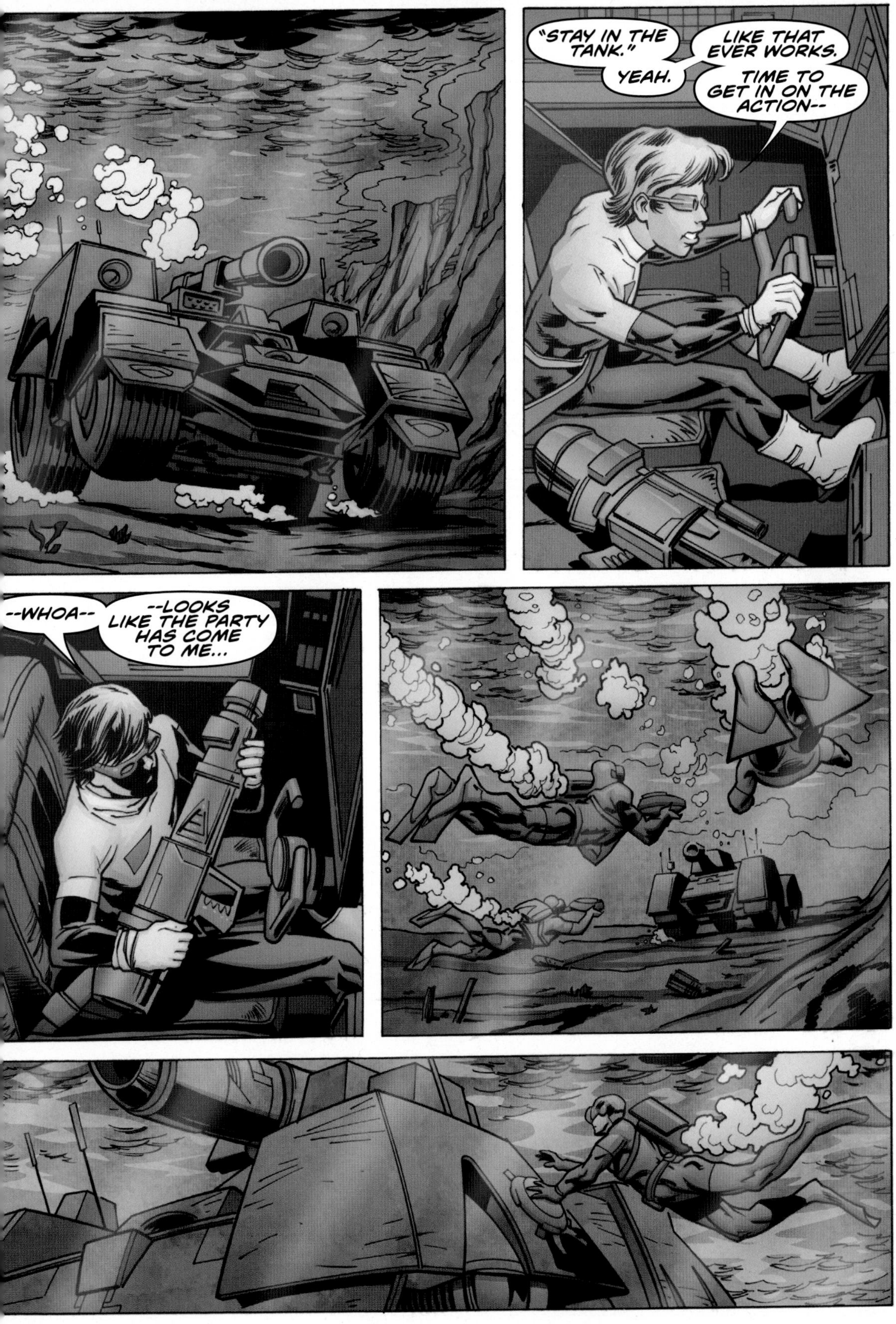
"STAY IN THE TANK."
YEAH.
LIKE THAT EVER WORKS.
TIME TO GET IN ON THE ACTION--
--WHOA--
--LOOKS LIKE THE PARTY HAS COME TO ME...

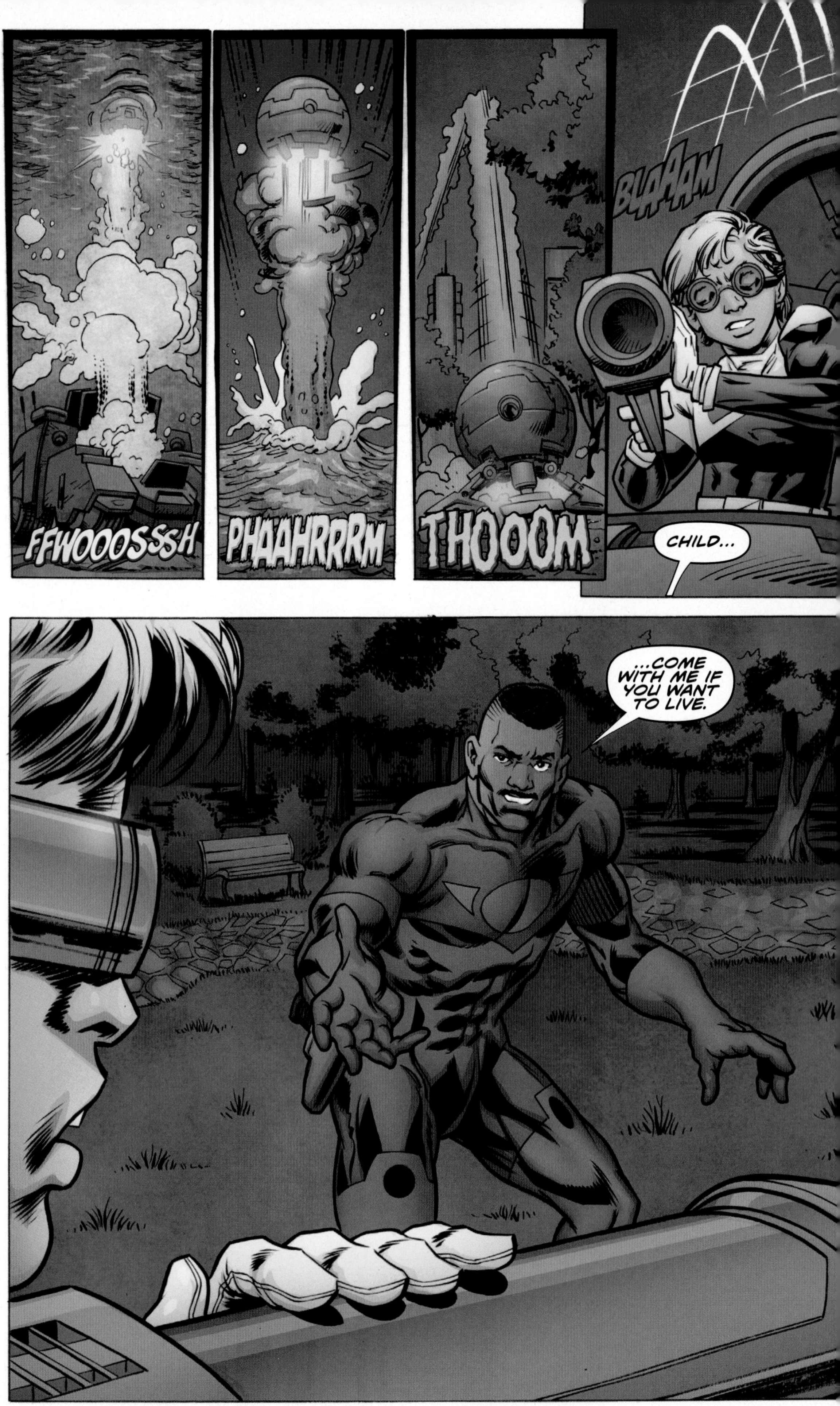
FFWOOOSSSH
PHAAHRRRM
THOOOM
BLAAAM
CHILD...
...COME WITH ME IF YOU WANT TO LIVE.

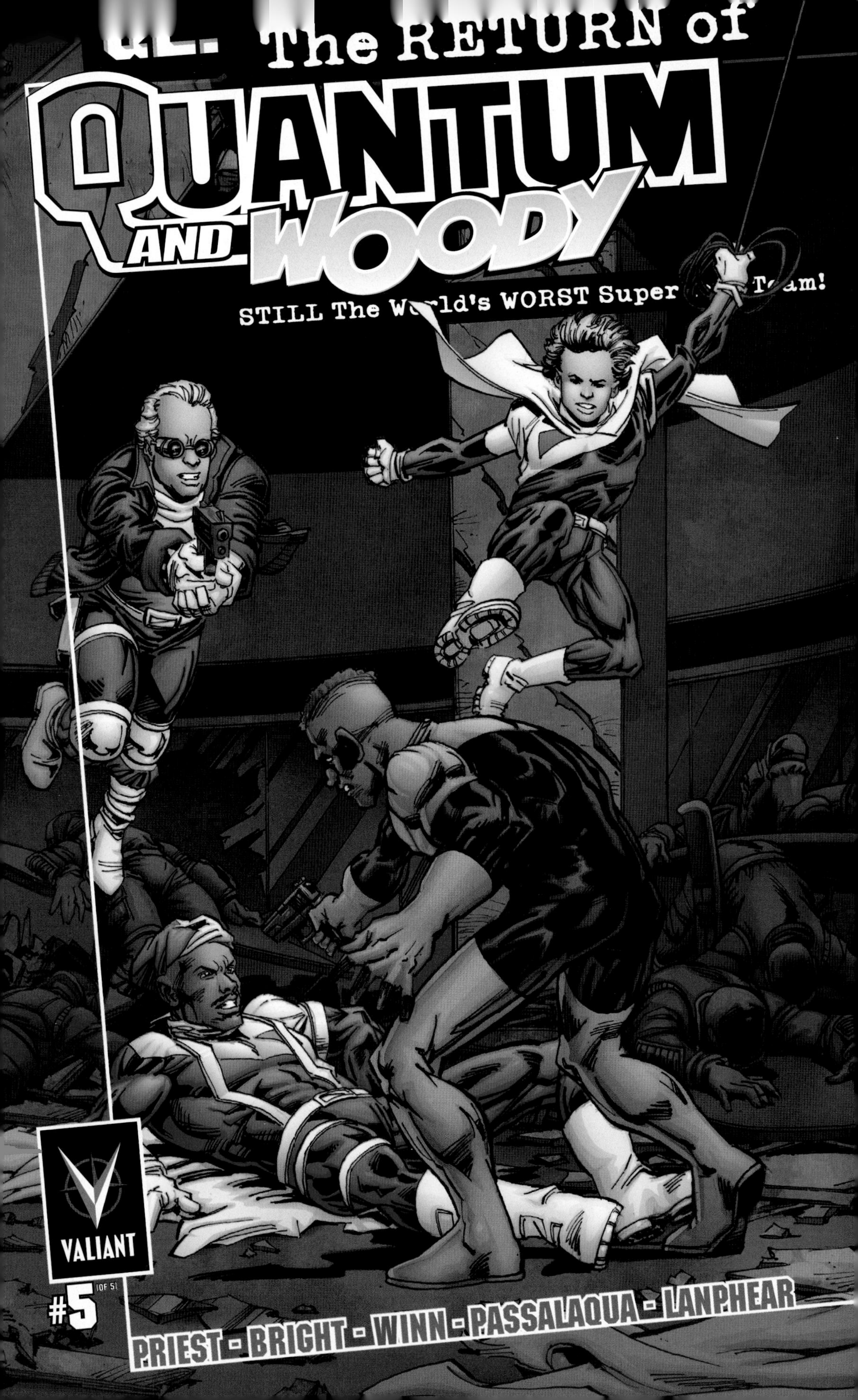
The RETURN of
QUANTUM AND WOODY
STILL The World's WORST Super Team!
VALIANT
#5 (OF 5)
PRIEST - BRIGHT - WINN - PASSALAQUA - LANPHEAR

"Hats"

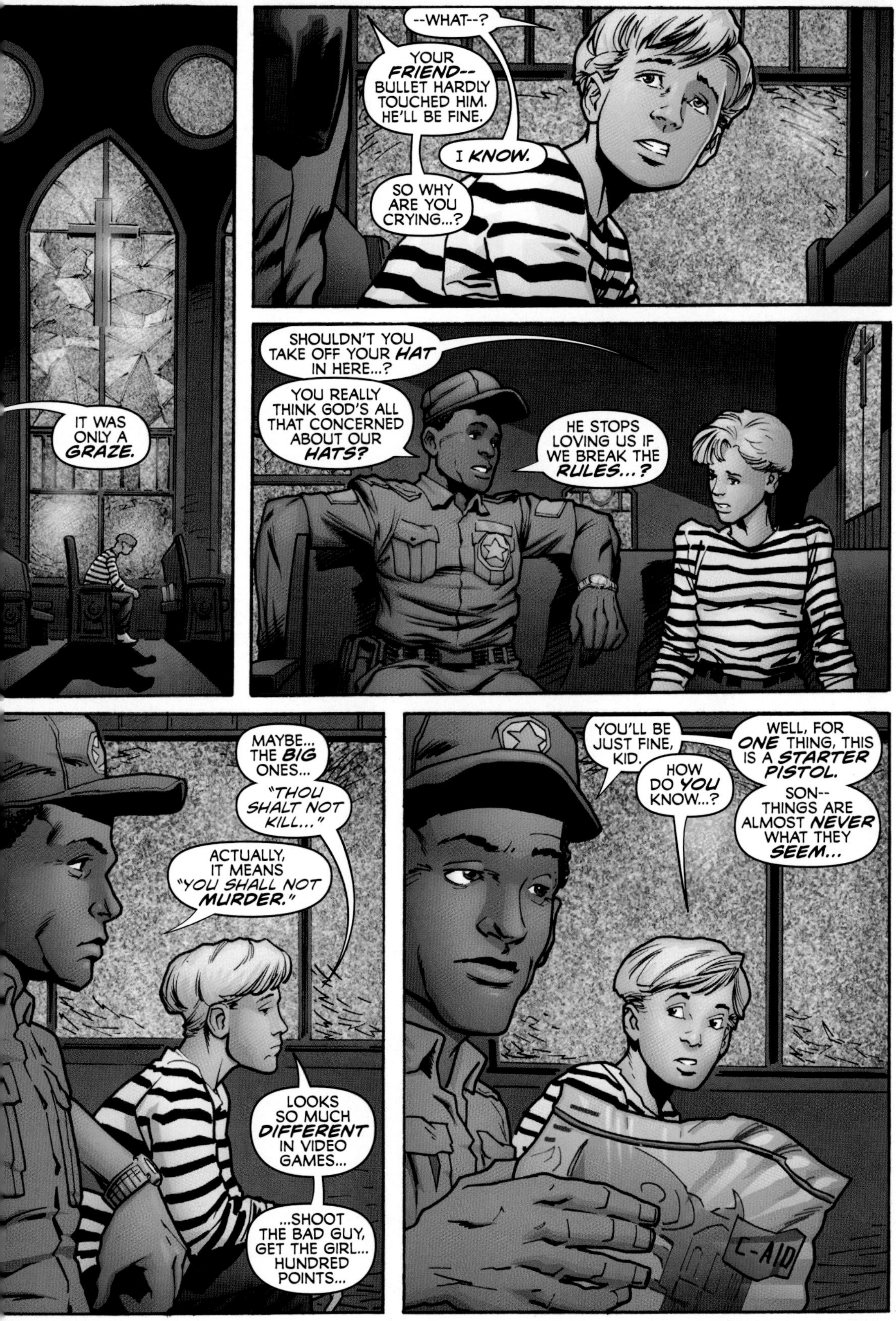

IT WAS ONLY A GRAZE.
--WHAT--?
YOUR FRIEND-- BULLET HARDLY TOUCHED HIM. HE'LL BE FINE.
I KNOW.
SO WHY ARE YOU CRYING...?
SHOULDN'T YOU TAKE OFF YOUR HAT IN HERE...?
YOU REALLY THINK GOD'S ALL THAT CONCERNED ABOUT OUR HATS?
HE STOPS LOVING US IF WE BREAK THE RULES...?
MAYBE... THE BIG ONES...
"THOU SHALT NOT KILL..."
ACTUALLY, IT MEANS "YOU SHALL NOT MURDER."
LOOKS SO MUCH DIFFERENT IN VIDEO GAMES...
...SHOOT THE BAD GUY, GET THE GIRL... HUNDRED POINTS...
YOU'LL BE JUST FINE, KID.
HOW DO YOU KNOW...?
WELL, FOR ONE THING, THIS IS A STARTER PISTOL.
SON-- THINGS ARE ALMOST NEVER WHAT THEY SEEM...

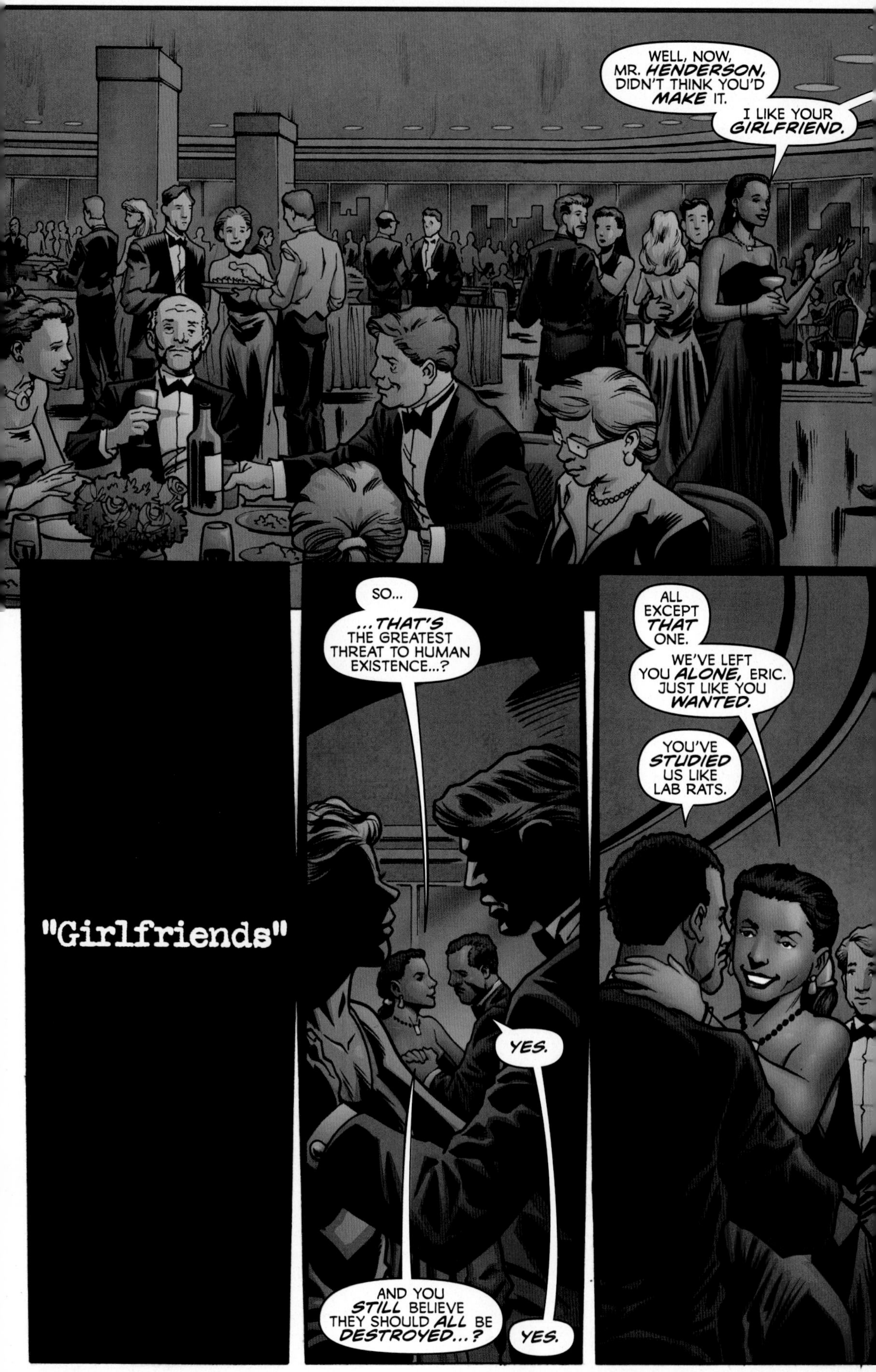
WELL, NOW, MR. HENDERSON, DIDN'T THINK YOU'D MAKE IT.
I LIKE YOUR GIRLFRIEND.
"Girlfriends"
SO...
...THAT'S THE GREATEST THREAT TO HUMAN EXISTENCE...?
YES.
AND YOU STILL BELIEVE THEY SHOULD ALL BE DESTROYED...?
YES.
ALL EXCEPT THAT ONE.
WE'VE LEFT YOU ALONE, ERIC. JUST LIKE YOU WANTED.
YOU'VE STUDIED US LIKE LAB RATS.

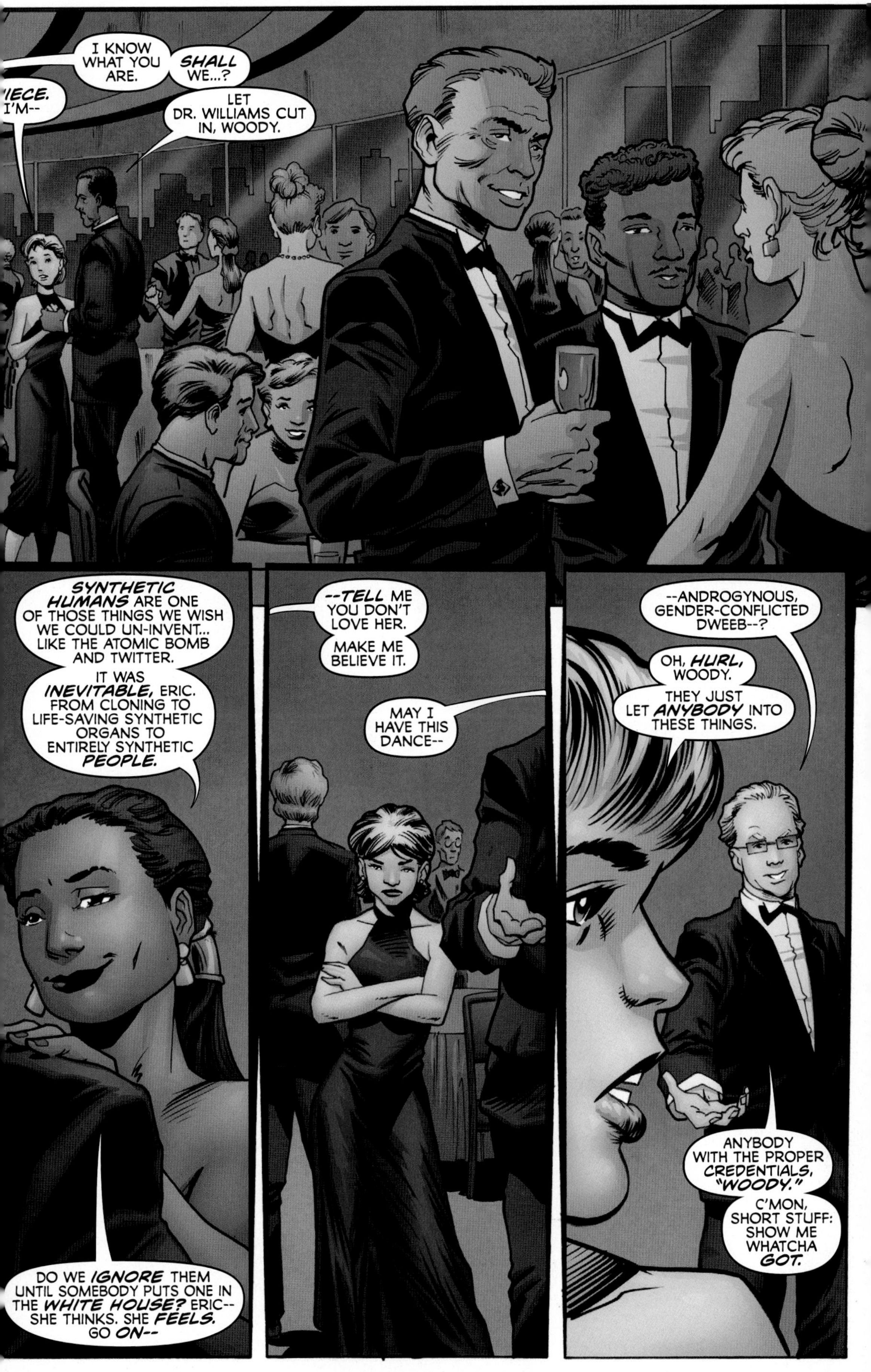

I KNOW WHAT YOU ARE.
SHALL WE...?
IECE. I'M--
LET DR. WILLIAMS CUT IN, WOODY.
SYNTHETIC HUMANS ARE ONE OF THOSE THINGS WE WISH WE COULD UN-INVENT... LIKE THE ATOMIC BOMB AND TWITTER.
IT WAS INEVITABLE, ERIC. FROM CLONING TO LIFE-SAVING SYNTHETIC ORGANS TO ENTIRELY SYNTHETIC PEOPLE.
DO WE IGNORE THEM UNTIL SOMEBODY PUTS ONE IN THE WHITE HOUSE? ERIC-- SHE THINKS. SHE FEELS. GO ON--
--TELL ME YOU DON'T LOVE HER.
MAKE ME BELIEVE IT.
MAY I HAVE THIS DANCE--
--ANDROGYNOUS, GENDER-CONFLICTED DWEEB--?
OH, HURL, WOODY.
THEY JUST LET ANYBODY INTO THESE THINGS.
ANYBODY WITH THE PROPER CREDENTIALS, "WOODY."
C'MON, SHORT STUFF: SHOW ME WHATCHA GOT.

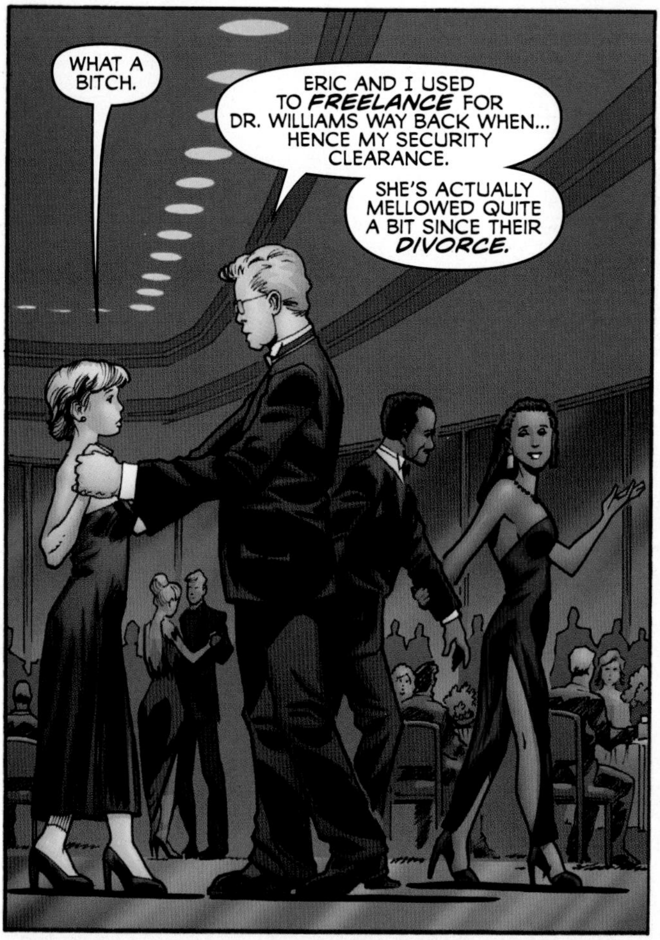
WHAT A BITCH.
ERIC AND I USED TO **FREELANCE** FOR DR. WILLIAMS WAY BACK WHEN... HENCE MY SECURITY CLEARANCE.
SHE'S ACTUALLY MELLOWED QUITE A BIT SINCE THEIR **DIVORCE.**

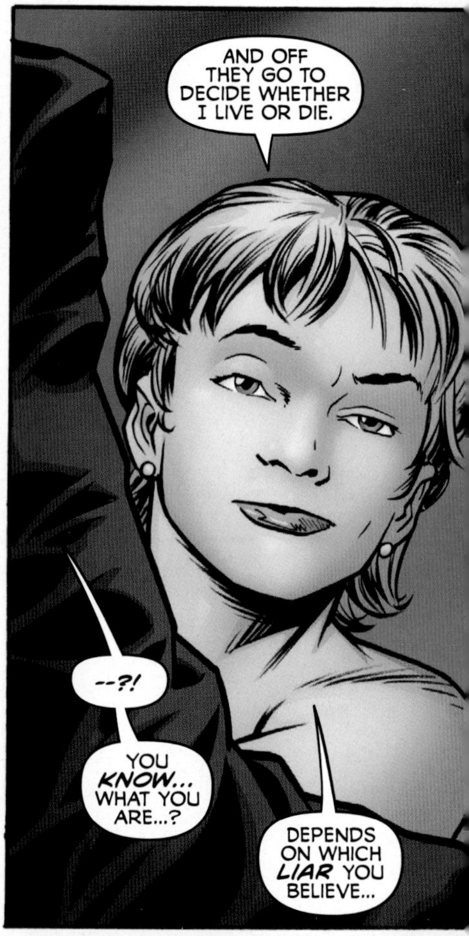
AND OFF THEY GO TO DECIDE WHETHER I LIVE OR DIE.
--?!
YOU **KNOW...** WHAT YOU ARE...?
DEPENDS ON WHICH **LIAR** YOU BELIEVE...

"Pinocchio"

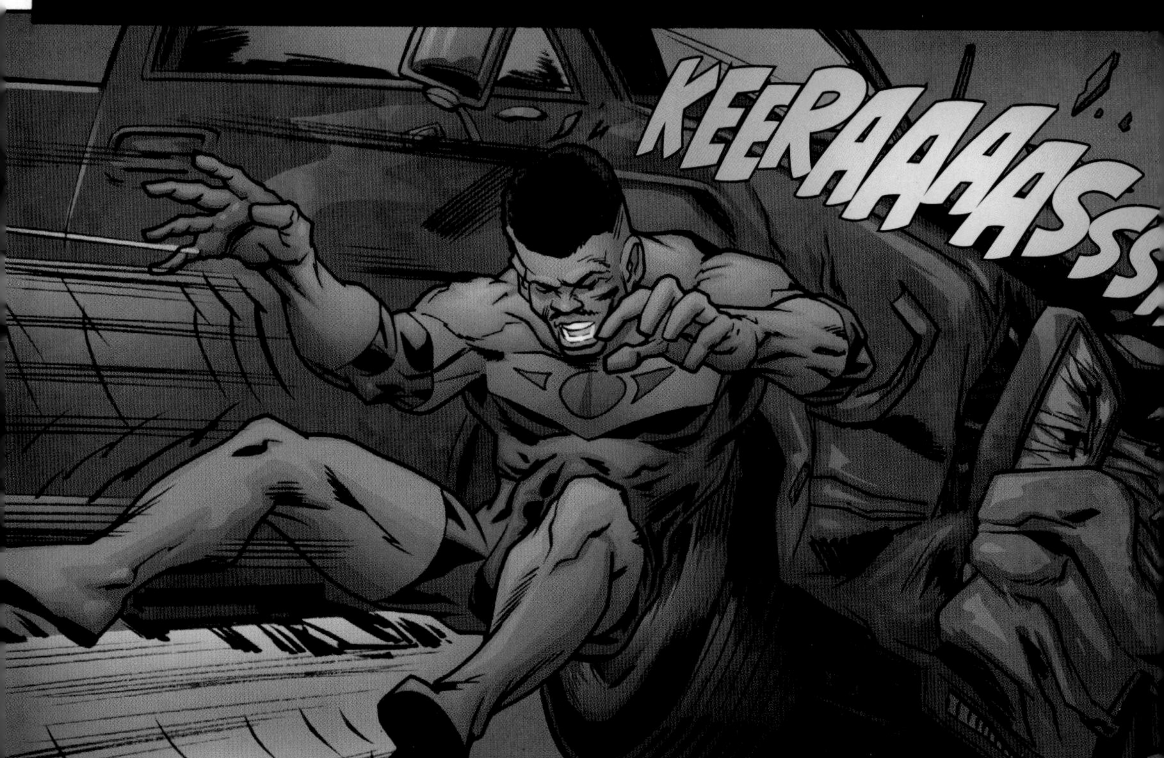
KEERAAAASS

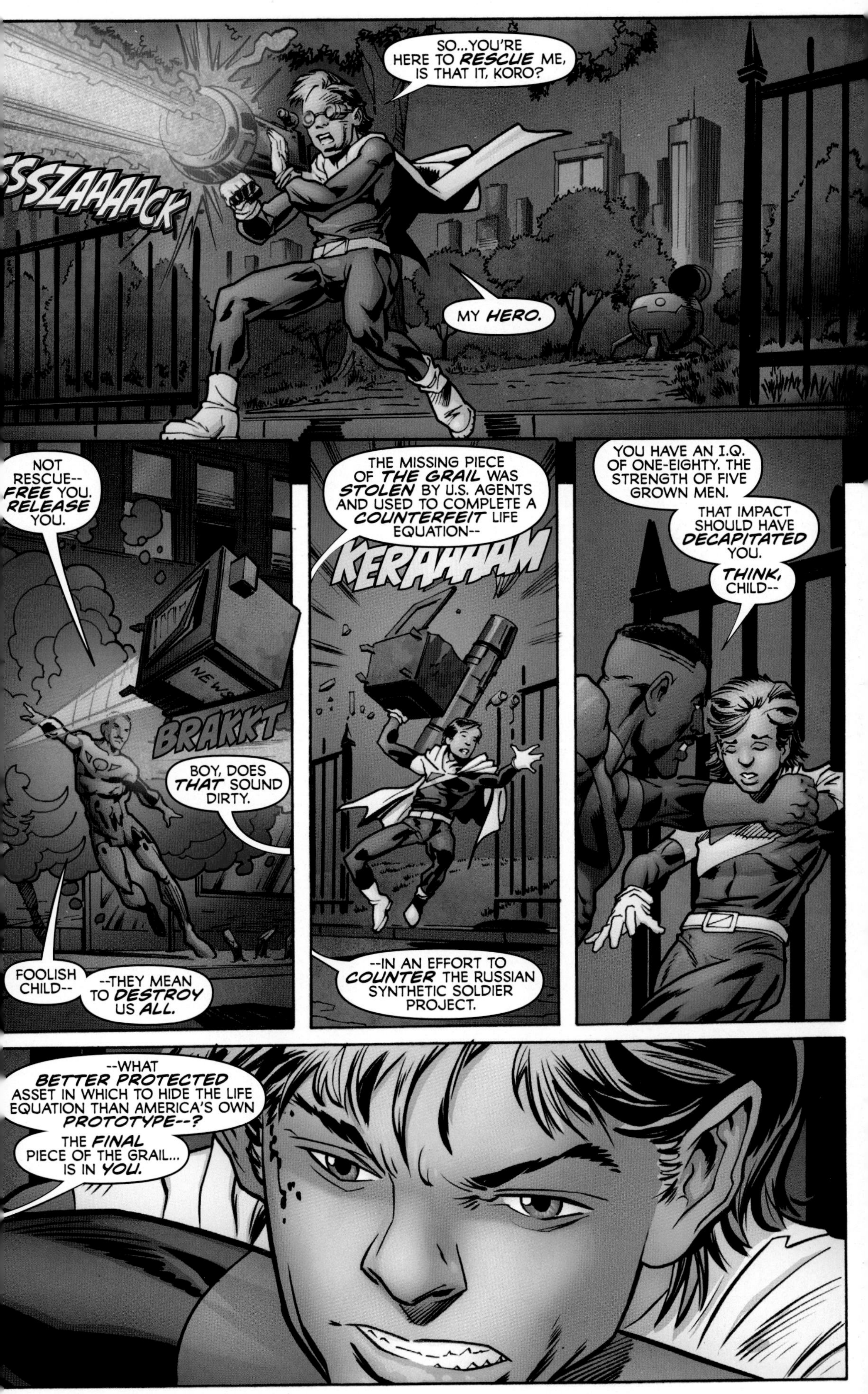
SO...YOU'RE HERE TO RESCUE ME, IS THAT IT, KORO?
SSZAAAACK
MY HERO.
NOT RESCUE-- FREE YOU. RELEASE YOU.
BRAKKT
BOY, DOES THAT SOUND DIRTY.
FOOLISH CHILD--
--THEY MEAN TO DESTROY US ALL.
THE MISSING PIECE OF THE GRAIL WAS STOLEN BY U.S. AGENTS AND USED TO COMPLETE A COUNTERFEIT LIFE EQUATION--
KERAHHAM
--IN AN EFFORT TO COUNTER THE RUSSIAN SYNTHETIC SOLDIER PROJECT.
YOU HAVE AN I.Q. OF ONE-EIGHTY. THE STRENGTH OF FIVE GROWN MEN.
THAT IMPACT SHOULD HAVE DECAPITATED YOU.
THINK, CHILD--
--WHAT BETTER PROTECTED ASSET IN WHICH TO HIDE THE LIFE EQUATION THAN AMERICA'S OWN PROTOTYPE--?
THE FINAL PIECE OF THE GRAIL... IS IN YOU.

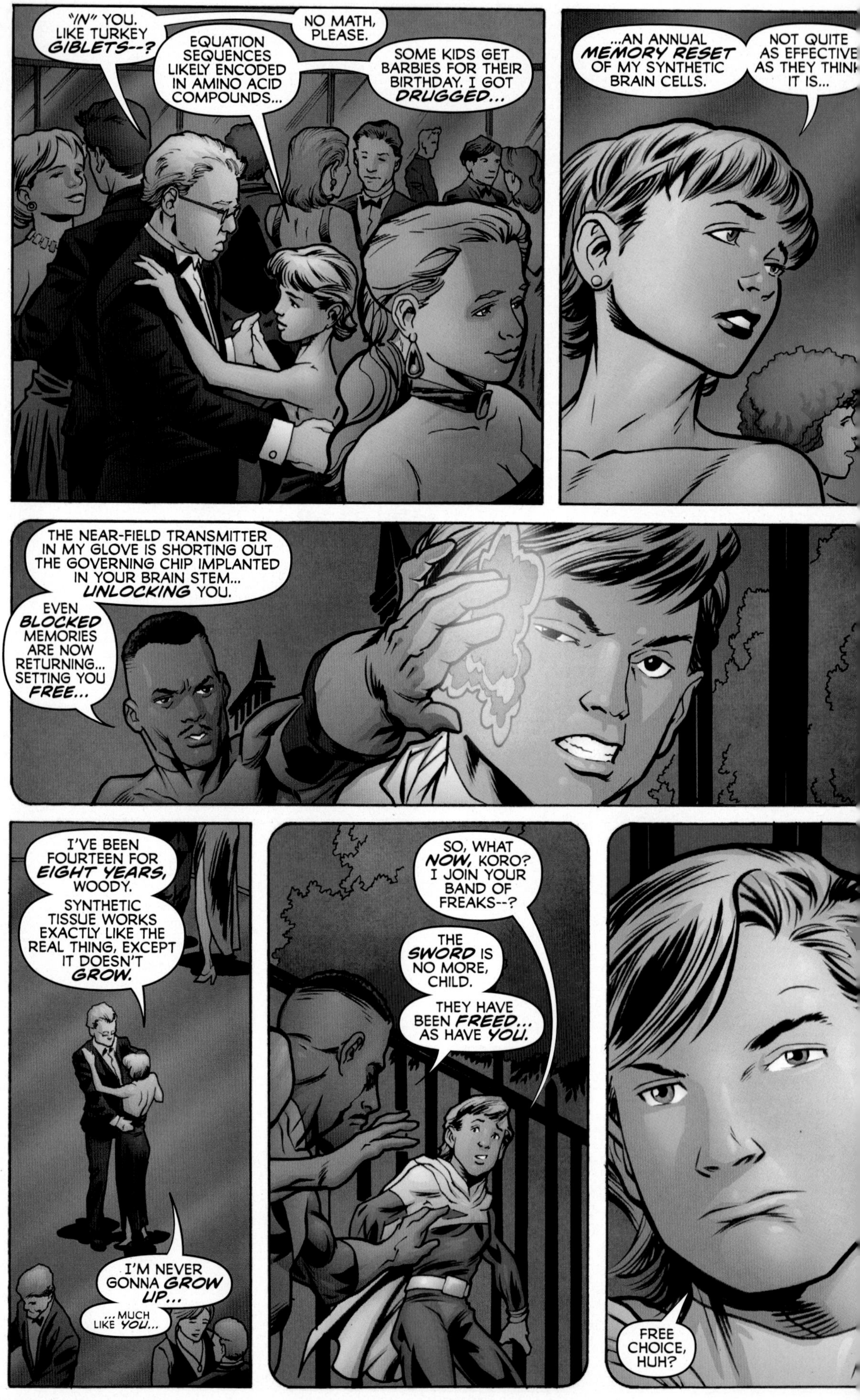
"IN" YOU. LIKE TURKEY GIBLETS--?
NO MATH, PLEASE.
EQUATION SEQUENCES LIKELY ENCODED IN AMINO ACID COMPOUNDS...
SOME KIDS GET BARBIES FOR THEIR BIRTHDAY. I GOT DRUGGED...
...AN ANNUAL MEMORY RESET OF MY SYNTHETIC BRAIN CELLS.
NOT QUITE AS EFFECTIVE AS THEY THINK IT IS...
THE NEAR-FIELD TRANSMITTER IN MY GLOVE IS SHORTING OUT THE GOVERNING CHIP IMPLANTED IN YOUR BRAIN STEM... UNLOCKING YOU.
EVEN BLOCKED MEMORIES ARE NOW RETURNING... SETTING YOU FREE...
I'VE BEEN FOURTEEN FOR EIGHT YEARS, WOODY.
SYNTHETIC TISSUE WORKS EXACTLY LIKE THE REAL THING, EXCEPT IT DOESN'T GROW.
I'M NEVER GONNA GROW UP...
...MUCH LIKE YOU...
SO, WHAT NOW, KORO? I JOIN YOUR BAND OF FREAKS--?
THE SWORD IS NO MORE, CHILD.
THEY HAVE BEEN FREED... AS HAVE YOU.
FREE CHOICE, HUH?

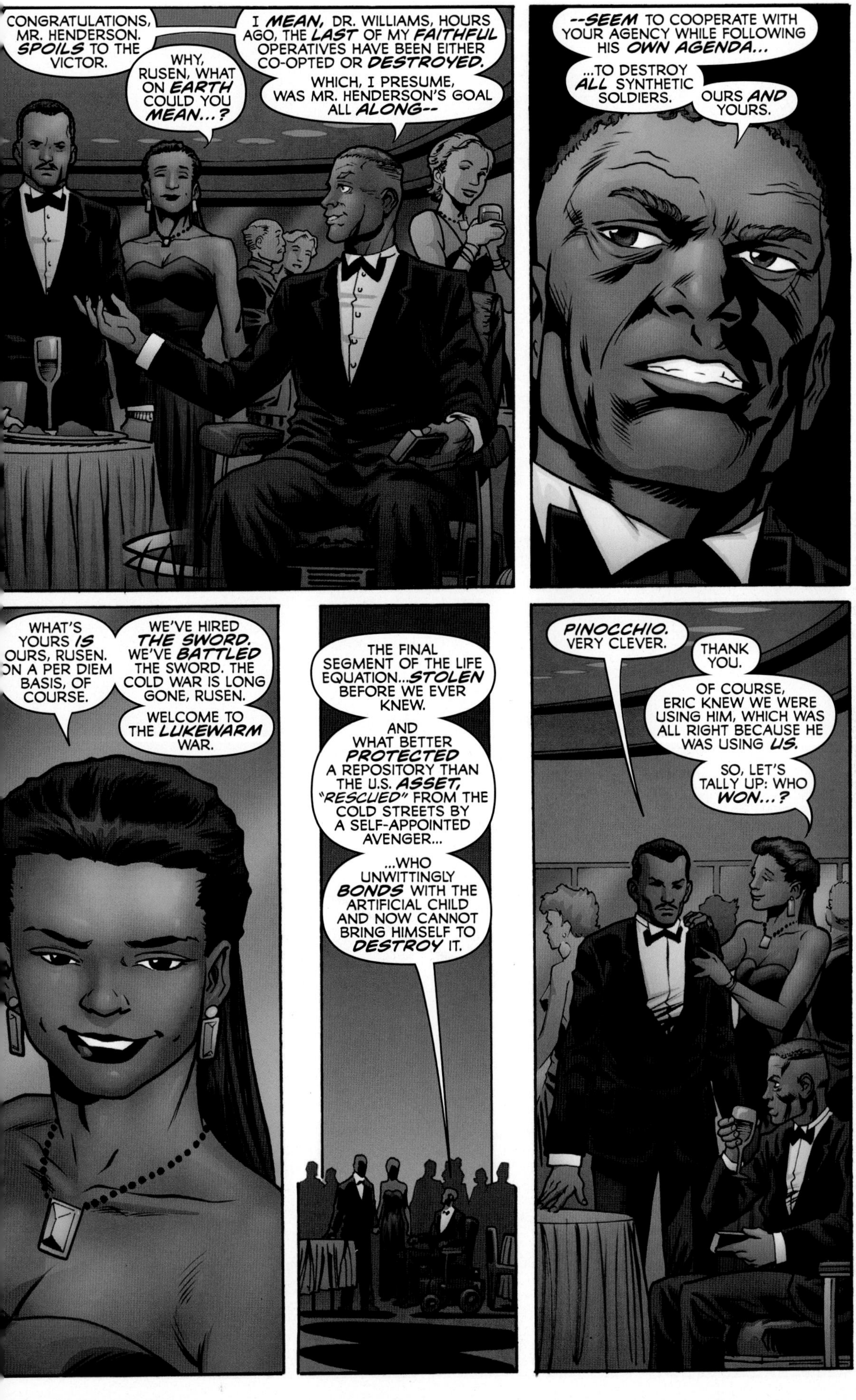

CONGRATULATIONS, MR. HENDERSON. SPOILS TO THE VICTOR.
WHY, RUSEN, WHAT ON EARTH COULD YOU MEAN...?
I MEAN, DR. WILLIAMS, HOURS AGO, THE LAST OF MY FAITHFUL OPERATIVES HAVE BEEN EITHER CO-OPTED OR DESTROYED.
WHICH, I PRESUME, WAS MR. HENDERSON'S GOAL ALL ALONG--
--SEEM TO COOPERATE WITH YOUR AGENCY WHILE FOLLOWING HIS OWN AGENDA...
...TO DESTROY ALL SYNTHETIC SOLDIERS.
OURS AND YOURS.
WHAT'S YOURS IS OURS, RUSEN. ON A PER DIEM BASIS, OF COURSE.
WE'VE HIRED THE SWORD. WE'VE BATTLED THE SWORD. THE COLD WAR IS LONG GONE, RUSEN.
WELCOME TO THE LUKEWARM WAR.
THE FINAL SEGMENT OF THE LIFE EQUATION...STOLEN BEFORE WE EVER KNEW.
AND WHAT BETTER PROTECTED A REPOSITORY THAN THE U.S. ASSET, "RESCUED" FROM THE COLD STREETS BY A SELF-APPOINTED AVENGER...
...WHO UNWITTINGLY BONDS WITH THE ARTIFICIAL CHILD AND NOW CANNOT BRING HIMSELF TO DESTROY IT.
PINOCCHIO. VERY CLEVER.
THANK YOU.
OF COURSE, ERIC KNEW WE WERE USING HIM, WHICH WAS ALL RIGHT BECAUSE HE WAS USING US.
SO, LET'S TALLY UP: WHO WON...?

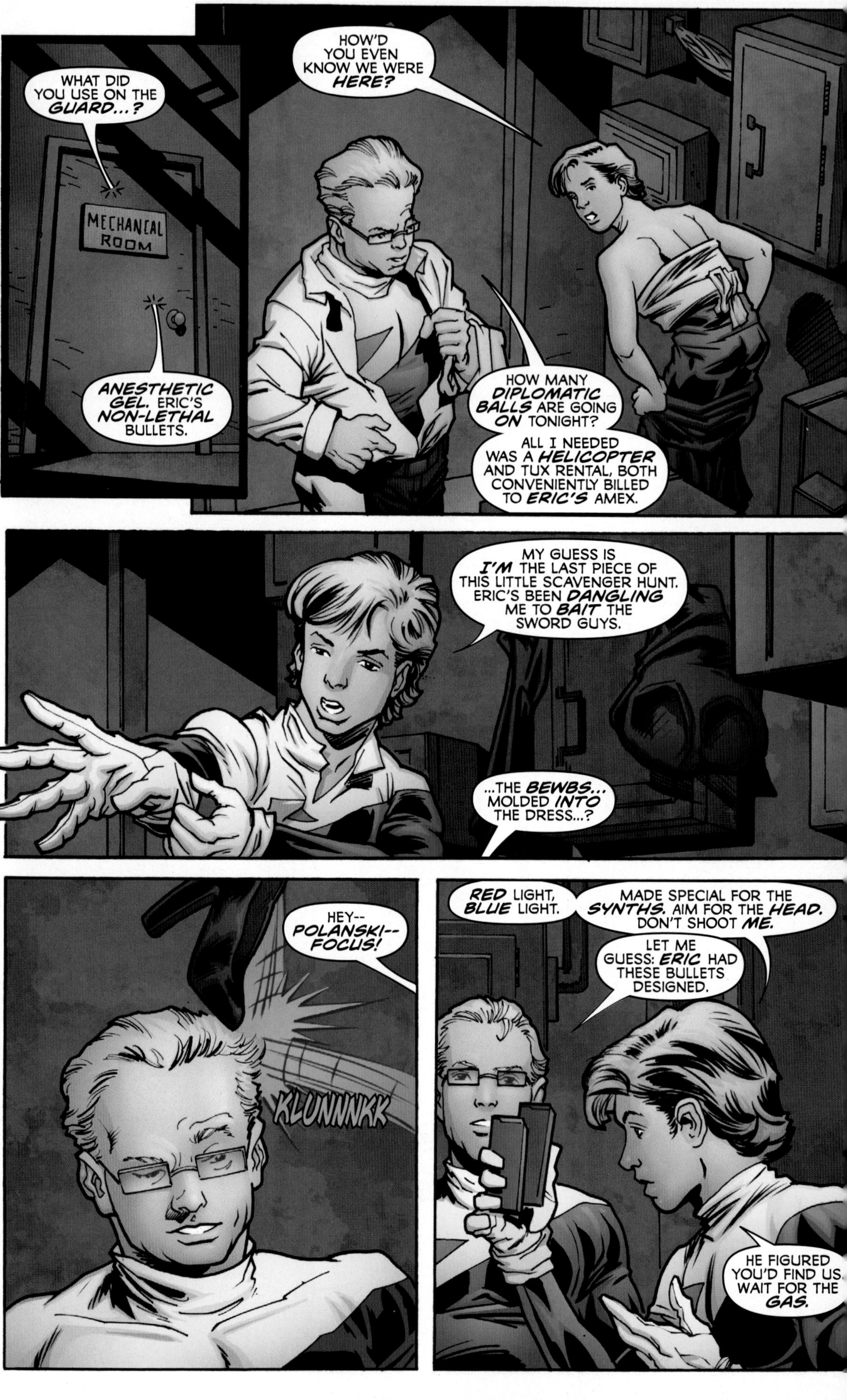
WHAT DID YOU USE ON THE GUARD...?
MECHANICAL ROOM
ANESTHETIC GEL. ERIC'S NON-LETHAL BULLETS.
HOW'D YOU EVEN KNOW WE WERE HERE?
HOW MANY DIPLOMATIC BALLS ARE GOING ON TONIGHT?
ALL I NEEDED WAS A HELICOPTER AND TUX RENTAL, BOTH CONVENIENTLY BILLED TO ERIC'S AMEX.
MY GUESS IS I'M THE LAST PIECE OF THIS LITTLE SCAVENGER HUNT. ERIC'S BEEN DANGLING ME TO BAIT THE SWORD GUYS.
...THE BEWBS... MOLDED INTO THE DRESS...?
HEY-- POLANSKI-- FOCUS!
KLUNNNKK
RED LIGHT, BLUE LIGHT.
MADE SPECIAL FOR THE SYNTHS. AIM FOR THE HEAD. DON'T SHOOT ME.
LET ME GUESS: ERIC HAD THESE BULLETS DESIGNED.
HE FIGURED YOU'D FIND US. WAIT FOR THE GAS.

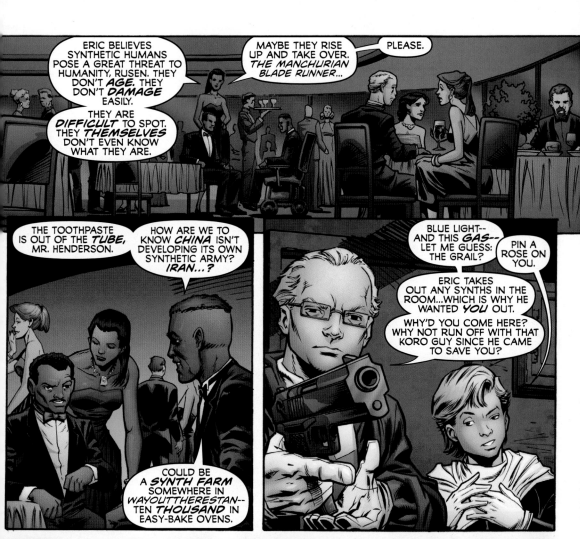

ERIC BELIEVES SYNTHETIC HUMANS POSE A GREAT THREAT TO HUMANITY, RUSEN. THEY DON'T *AGE*. THEY DON'T *DAMAGE* EASILY.

THEY ARE *DIFFICULT* TO SPOT. THEY *THEMSELVES* DON'T EVEN KNOW WHAT THEY ARE.

MAYBE THEY RISE UP AND TAKE OVER. *THE MANCHURIAN BLADE RUNNER...*

PLEASE.

THE TOOTHPASTE IS OUT OF THE *TUBE*, MR. HENDERSON.

HOW ARE WE TO KNOW *CHINA* ISN'T DEVELOPING ITS OWN SYNTHETIC ARMY? *IRAN...?*

COULD BE A *SYNTH FARM* SOMEWHERE IN *WAYOUTTHERESTAN*-- TEN *THOUSAND* IN EASY-BAKE OVENS.

BLUE LIGHT-- AND THIS *GAS*-- LET ME GUESS: THE GRAIL?

PIN A ROSE ON YOU.

ERIC TAKES OUT ANY SYNTHS IN THE ROOM...WHICH IS WHY HE WANTED *YOU* OUT.

WHY'D YOU COME HERE? WHY NOT RUN OFF WITH THAT KORO GUY SINCE HE CAME TO SAVE YOU?

NOBODY CAME TO SAVE ME.

LET'S GET THIS *DONE*.

ROGER. JUST ONE THING FIRST--

GIMME MY GLASSES!!

HEY-- HANDS OFF--!!

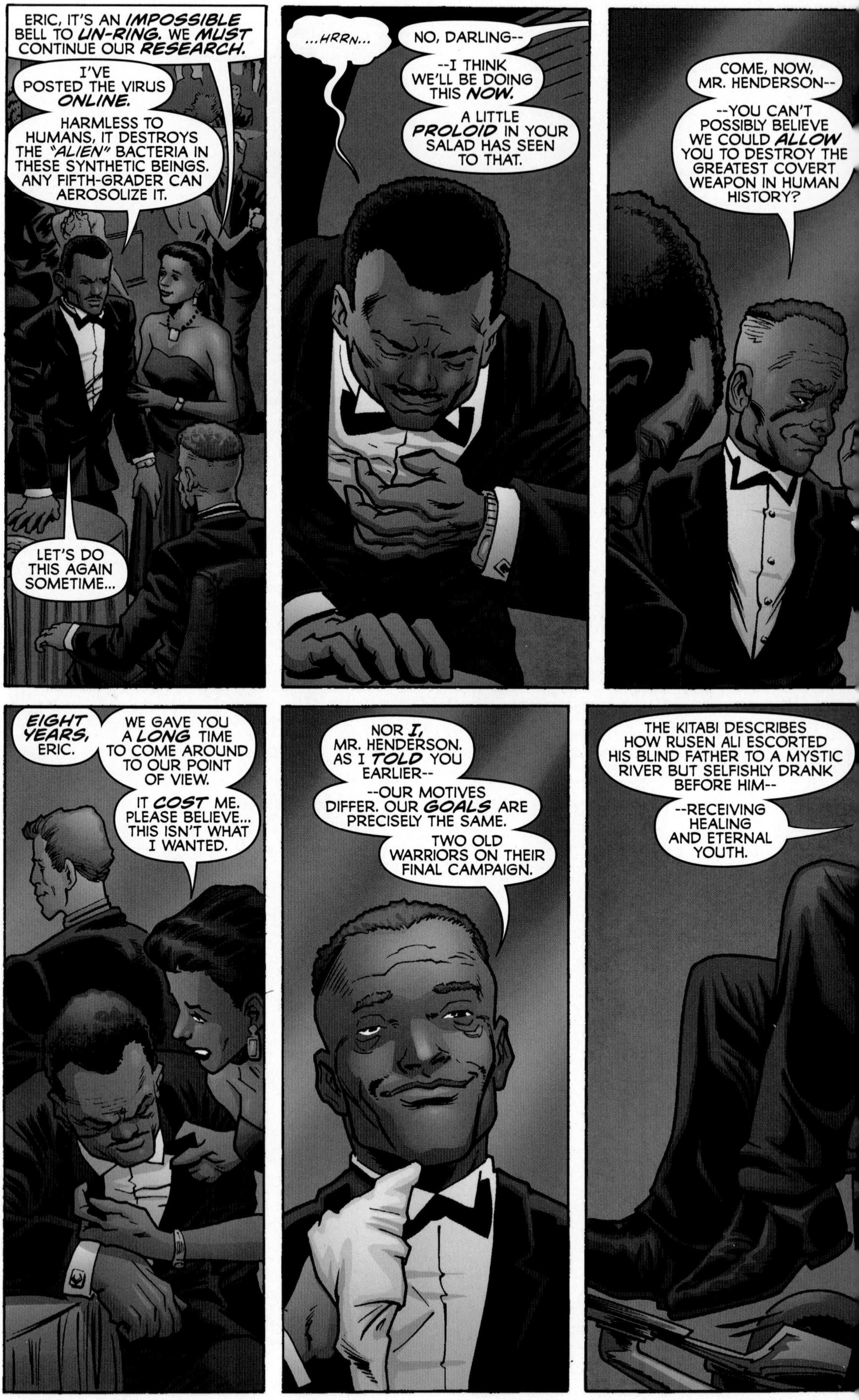
ERIC, IT'S AN IMPOSSIBLE BELL TO UN-RING. WE MUST CONTINUE OUR RESEARCH.
I'VE POSTED THE VIRUS ONLINE.
HARMLESS TO HUMANS, IT DESTROYS THE "ALIEN" BACTERIA IN THESE SYNTHETIC BEINGS. ANY FIFTH-GRADER CAN AEROSOLIZE IT.
LET'S DO THIS AGAIN SOMETIME...
...HRRN...
NO, DARLING--
--I THINK WE'LL BE DOING THIS NOW.
A LITTLE PROLOID IN YOUR SALAD HAS SEEN TO THAT.
COME, NOW, MR. HENDERSON--
--YOU CAN'T POSSIBLY BELIEVE WE COULD ALLOW YOU TO DESTROY THE GREATEST COVERT WEAPON IN HUMAN HISTORY?
EIGHT YEARS, ERIC.
WE GAVE YOU A LONG TIME TO COME AROUND TO OUR POINT OF VIEW.
IT COST ME. PLEASE BELIEVE... THIS ISN'T WHAT I WANTED.
NOR I, MR. HENDERSON. AS I TOLD YOU EARLIER--
--OUR MOTIVES DIFFER. OUR GOALS ARE PRECISELY THE SAME.
TWO OLD WARRIORS ON THEIR FINAL CAMPAIGN.
THE KITABI DESCRIBES HOW RUSEN ALI ESCORTED HIS BLIND FATHER TO A MYSTIC RIVER BUT SELFISHLY DRANK BEFORE HIM--
--RECEIVING HEALING AND ETERNAL YOUTH.

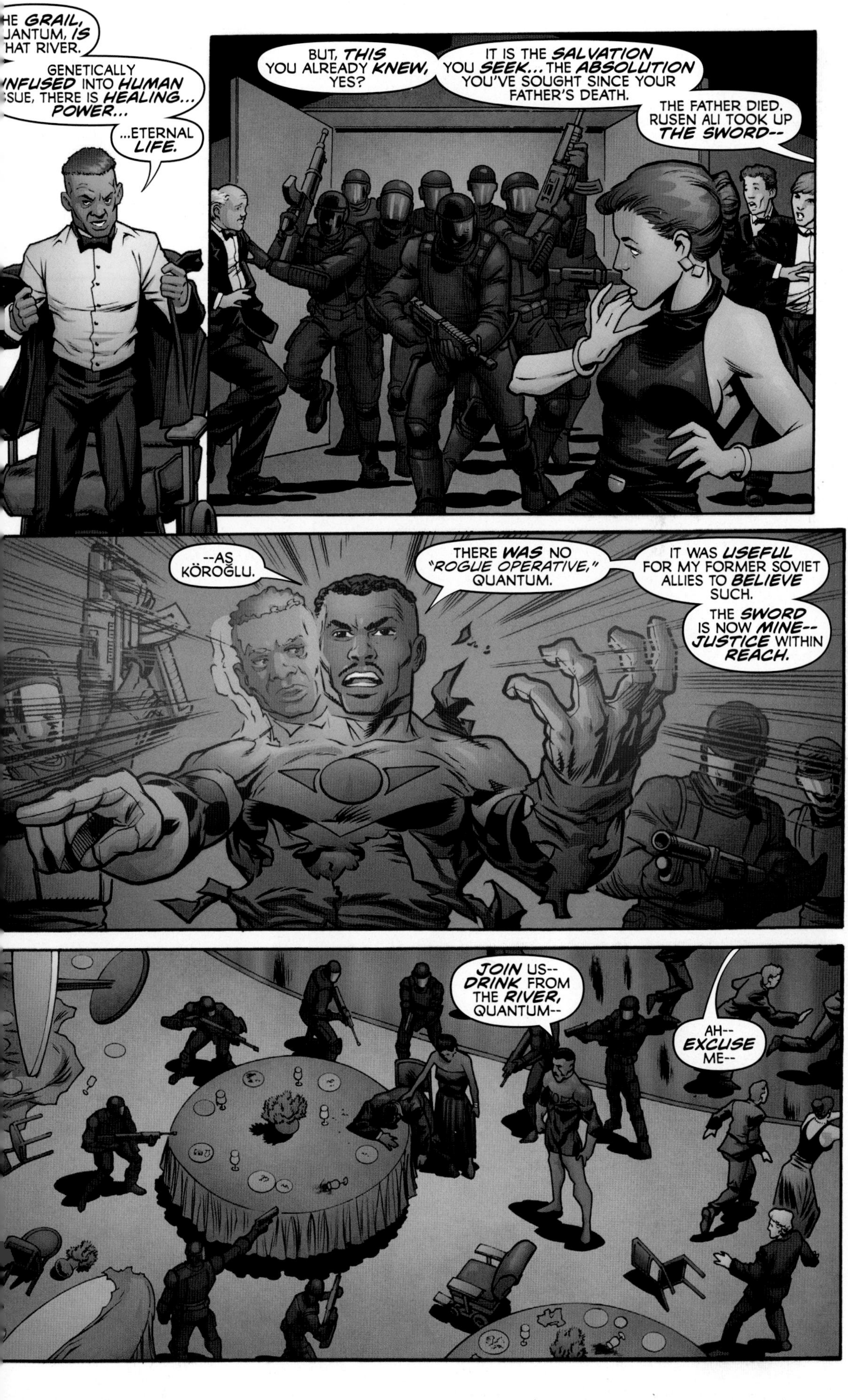

HE GRAIL, JANTUM, IS HAT RIVER.
GENETICALLY INFUSED INTO HUMAN SSUE, THERE IS HEALING... POWER...
...ETERNAL LIFE.
BUT, THIS YOU ALREADY KNEW, YES?
IT IS THE SALVATION YOU SEEK... THE ABSOLUTION YOU'VE SOUGHT SINCE YOUR FATHER'S DEATH.
THE FATHER DIED. RUSEN ALI TOOK UP THE SWORD--
--AS KÖROĞLU.
THERE WAS NO "ROGUE OPERATIVE," QUANTUM.
IT WAS USEFUL FOR MY FORMER SOVIET ALLIES TO BELIEVE SUCH.
THE SWORD IS NOW MINE-- JUSTICE WITHIN REACH.
JOIN US-- DRINK FROM THE RIVER, QUANTUM--
AH-- EXCUSE ME--

--BUT, DON'T RACCOONS *PEE* IN THE RIVER, SWAMI--?

SINCE YOU *ZOMBIE SWORD GUYS* ARE *OBVIOUSLY* NOT GONNA *ACTUALLY* START SHOOTING UNTIL YOUR *BOSS,* THE EVIL DR. PEPPER, GETS OUT OF THE WAY--

--MAYBE WE PRESS *PAUS* A MINUTE.

Y'KNOW, ERIC, I THOUGHT MAYBE YOU WANTED TO USE THE GRAIL ON *YOURSELF*--DRINK THE *RACCOON PEE,* FIX YOUR BODY UP.

THEN I THOUGHT IT WAS A *DEATH WISH*-- IF YOU CAN'T WEAR *TIGHTS* ANYMORE, WHY LIVE?

NOT IT, EITHER.

YOU'RE TRYING TO *UN-CREATE* THES FOLKS...RENDER THE GRAIL USELESS B MAKING THE *VIRUS* PUBLIC.

WHICH WILL, OF COURSE, ONLY FORCE THEM TO CREATE A VIRUS-RESISTANT SYNTH, AND W START ALL OVER AGAIN.

ONLY A LUNATIC TRIES PUT TOOTHPAS BACK IN A TUB BUT THAT'S *YOU.*

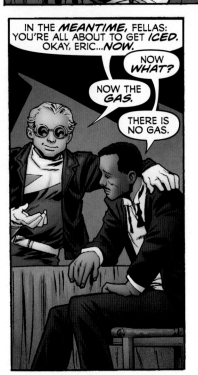

IN THE *MEANTIME,* FELLAS: YOU'RE ALL ABOUT TO GET *ICED.* OKAY, ERIC...*NOW.*

NOW *WHAT?*

NOW THE *GAS.*

THERE IS NO GAS.

OF COURSE THERE'S GAS. THERE'S *ALWAYS* GAS.

I JUST *SAID* THAT TO GET WOODY OUT OF HARM'S WAY.

--NO GAS--?

NO GAS.

--YOU *REALLY* SUCK.

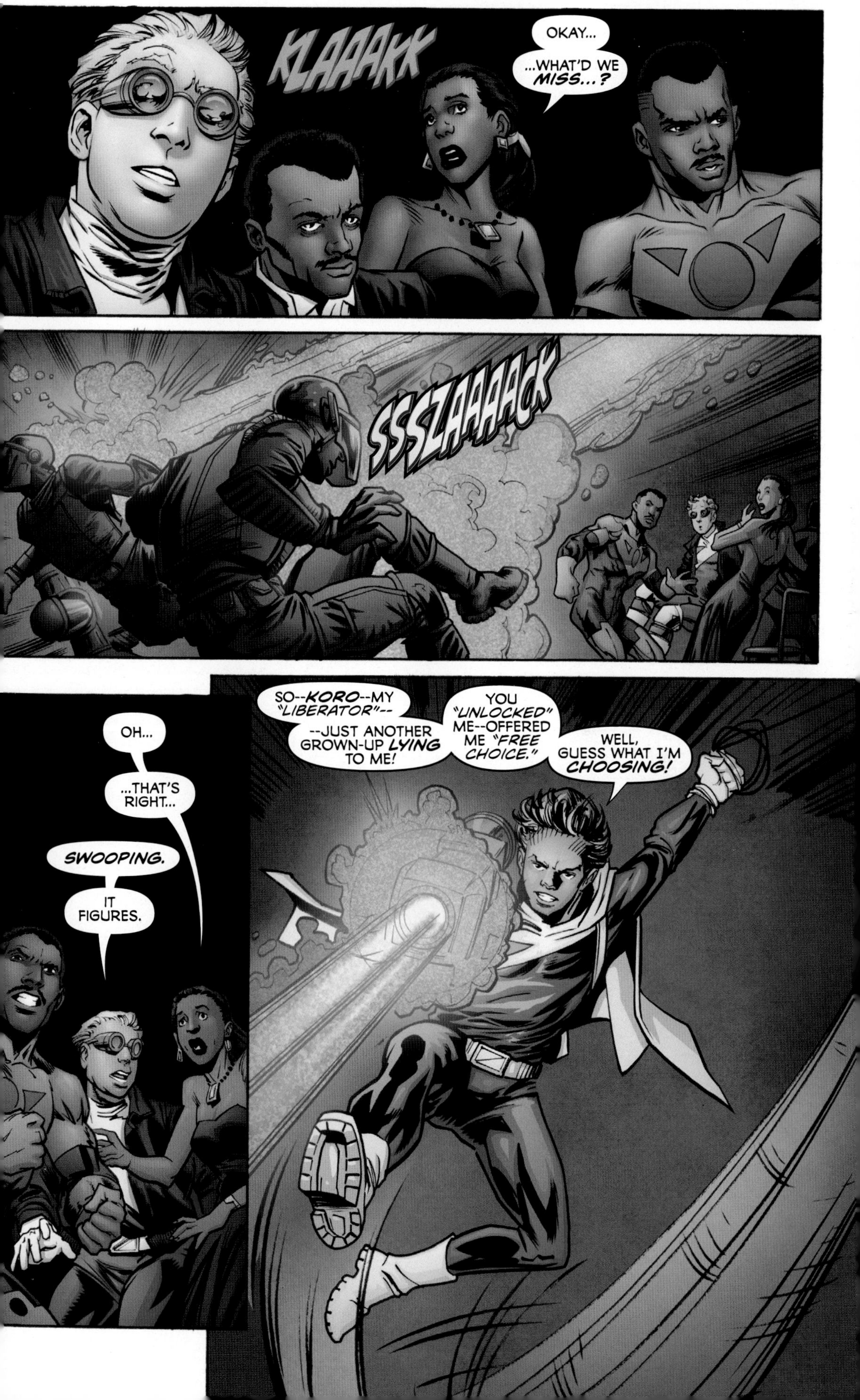
KLAAAKK
OKAY...
...WHAT'D WE MISS...?
SSSZAAAACK
OH...
...THAT'S RIGHT...
SWOOPING.
IT FIGURES.
SO--KORO--MY "LIBERATOR"--
--JUST ANOTHER GROWN-UP LYING TO ME!
YOU "UNLOCKED" ME--OFFERED ME "FREE CHOICE."
WELL, GUESS WHAT I'M CHOOSING!

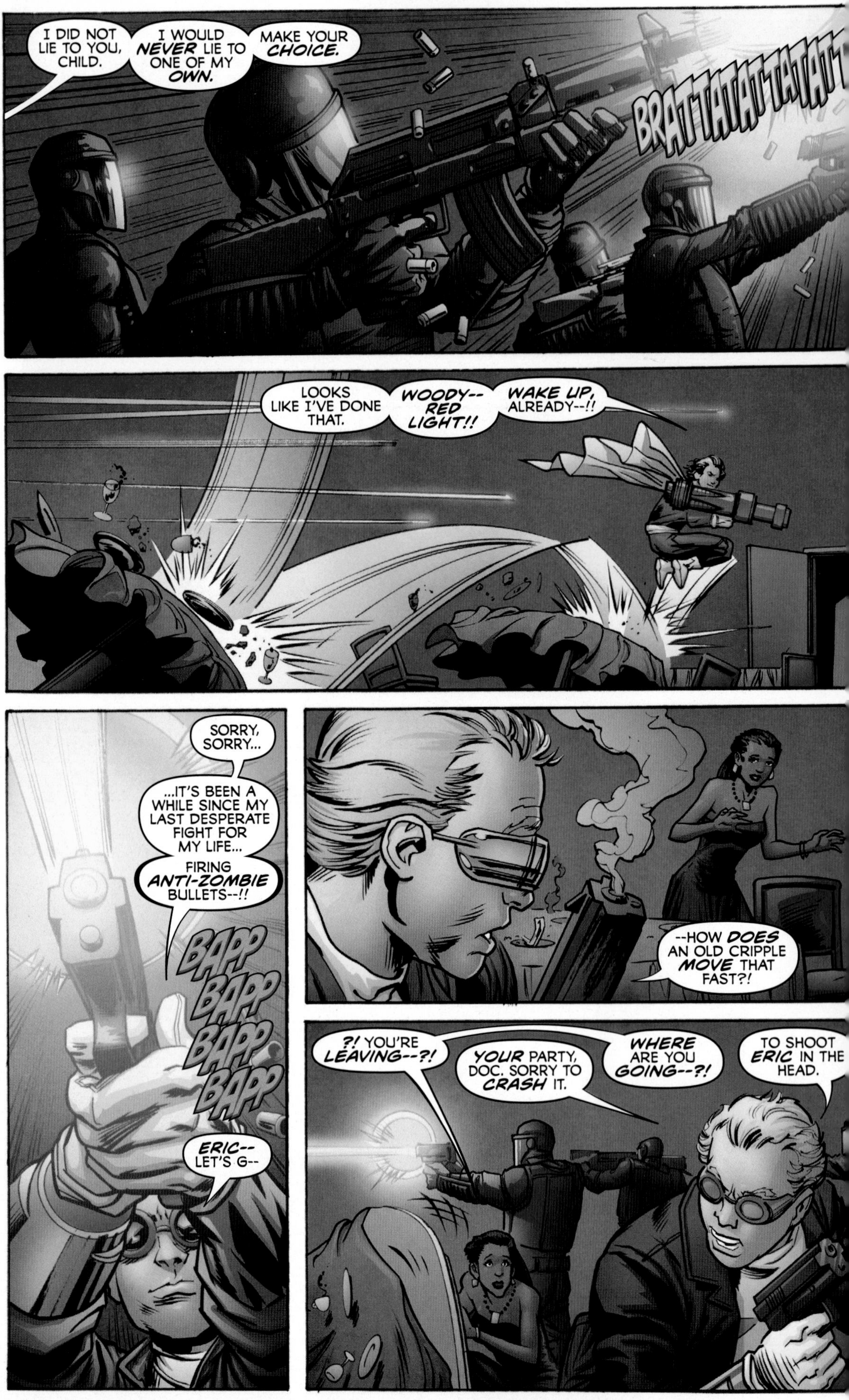
I DID NOT LIE TO YOU, CHILD.
I WOULD NEVER LIE TO ONE OF MY OWN.
MAKE YOUR CHOICE.
BRATTATATTATAT
LOOKS LIKE I'VE DONE THAT.
WOODY-- RED LIGHT!!
WAKE UP, ALREADY--!!
SORRY, SORRY...
...IT'S BEEN A WHILE SINCE MY LAST DESPERATE FIGHT FOR MY LIFE...
FIRING ANTI-ZOMBIE BULLETS--!!
BAPP BAPP BAPP BAPP
ERIC-- LET'S G--
--HOW DOES AN OLD CRIPPLE MOVE THAT FAST?!
?! YOU'RE LEAVING--?!
WHERE ARE YOU GOING--?!
YOUR PARTY, DOC. SORRY TO CRASH IT.
TO SHOOT ERIC IN THE HEAD.

"Better"

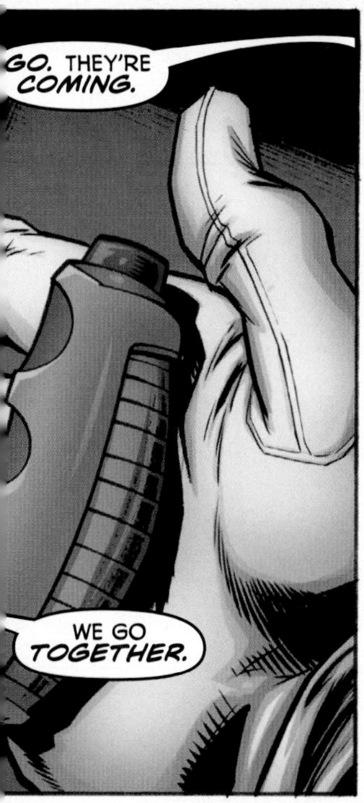
GO. THEY'RE COMING.
WE GO TOGETHER.

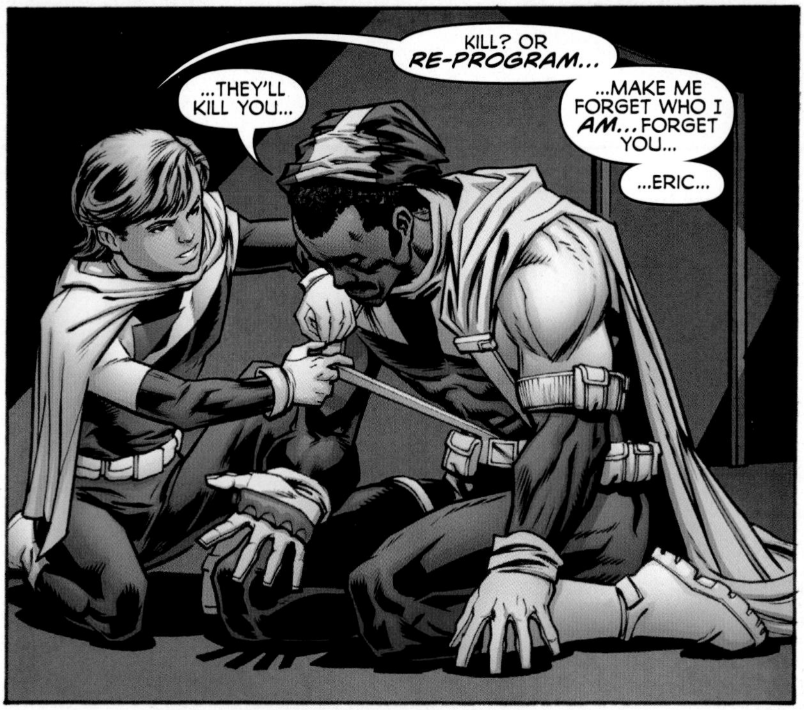
...THEY'LL KILL YOU...
KILL? OR RE-PROGRAM...
...MAKE ME FORGET WHO I AM... FORGET YOU...
...ERIC...

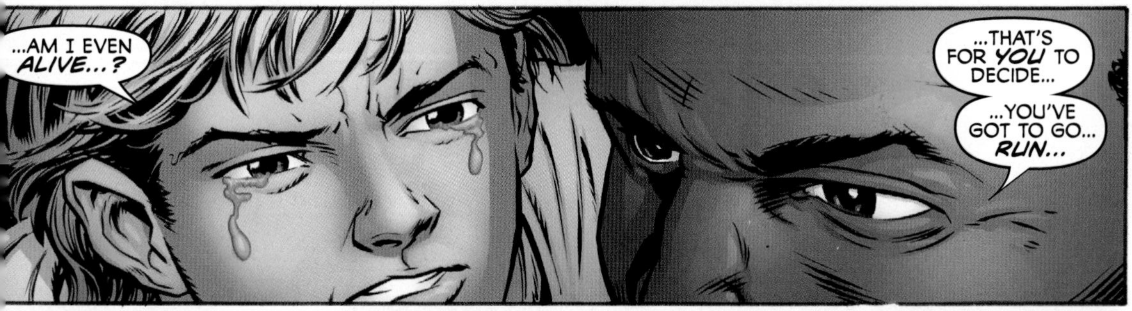
...AM I EVEN ALIVE...?
...THAT'S FOR YOU TO DECIDE...
...YOU'VE GOT TO GO... RUN...

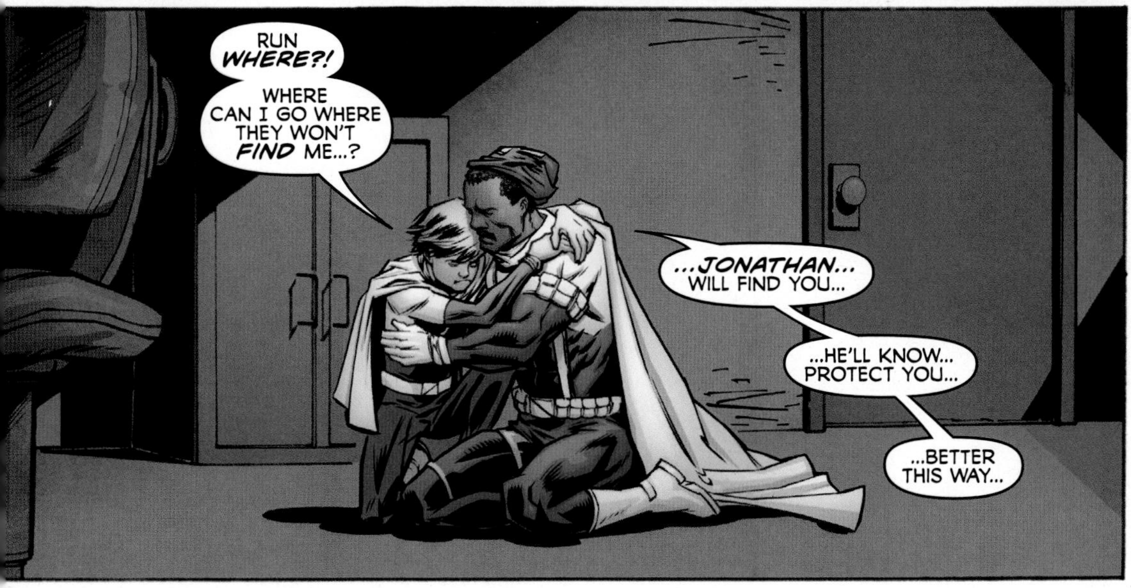
RUN WHERE?!
WHERE CAN I GO WHERE THEY WON'T FIND ME...?
...JONATHAN... WILL FIND YOU...
...HE'LL KNOW... PROTECT YOU...
...BETTER THIS WAY...

"Winning"

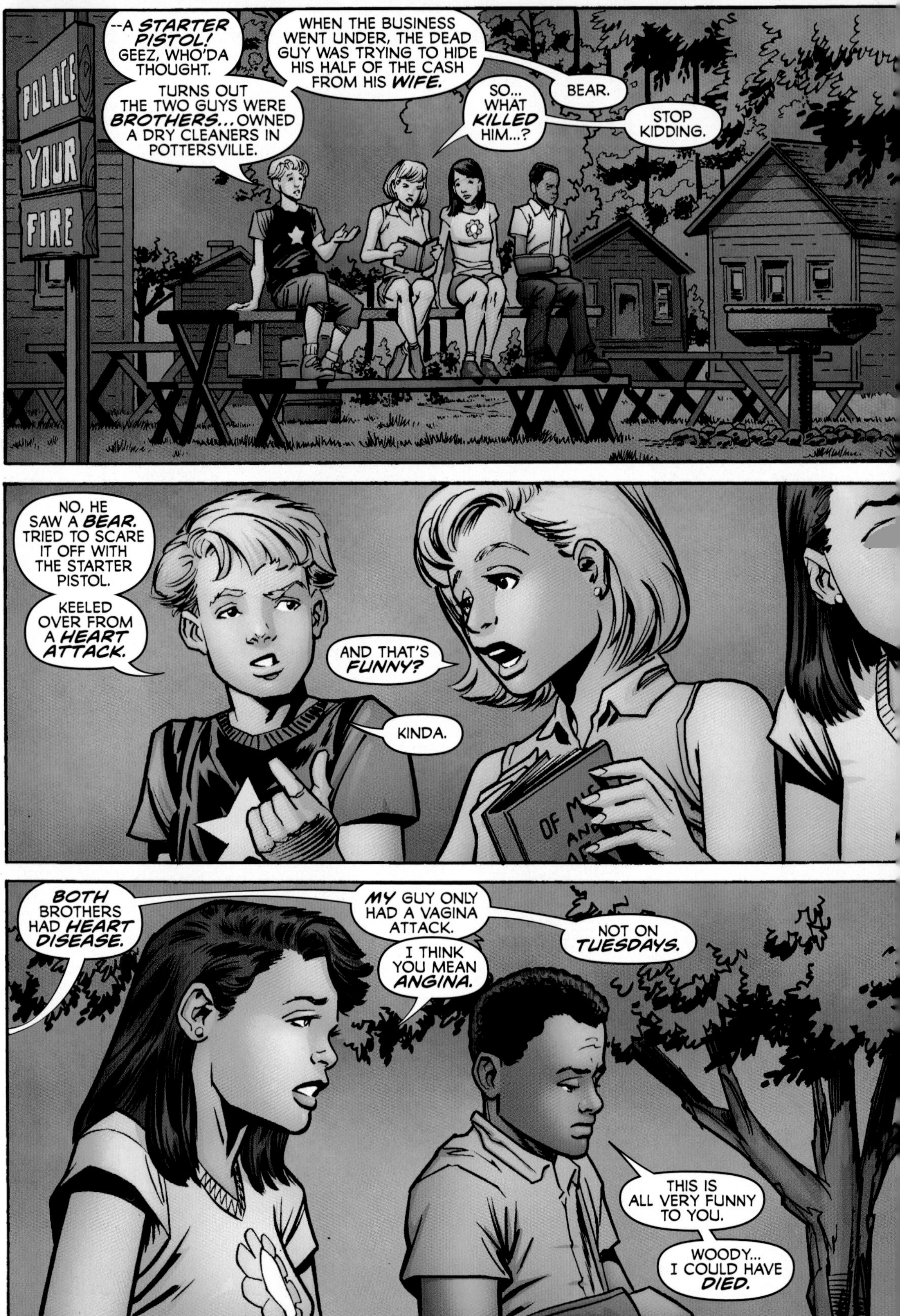
POLICE YOUR FIRE
--A STARTER PISTOL! GEEZ, WHO'DA THOUGHT.
TURNS OUT THE TWO GUYS WERE BROTHERS... OWNED A DRY CLEANERS IN POTTERSVILLE.
WHEN THE BUSINESS WENT UNDER, THE DEAD GUY WAS TRYING TO HIDE HIS HALF OF THE CASH FROM HIS WIFE.
SO... WHAT KILLED HIM...?
BEAR.
STOP KIDDING.
NO, HE SAW A BEAR. TRIED TO SCARE IT OFF WITH THE STARTER PISTOL.
KEELED OVER FROM A HEART ATTACK.
AND THAT'S FUNNY?
KINDA.
BOTH BROTHERS HAD HEART DISEASE.
MY GUY ONLY HAD A VAGINA ATTACK.
I THINK YOU MEAN ANGINA.
NOT ON TUESDAYS.
THIS IS ALL VERY FUNNY TO YOU.
WOODY... I COULD HAVE DIED.

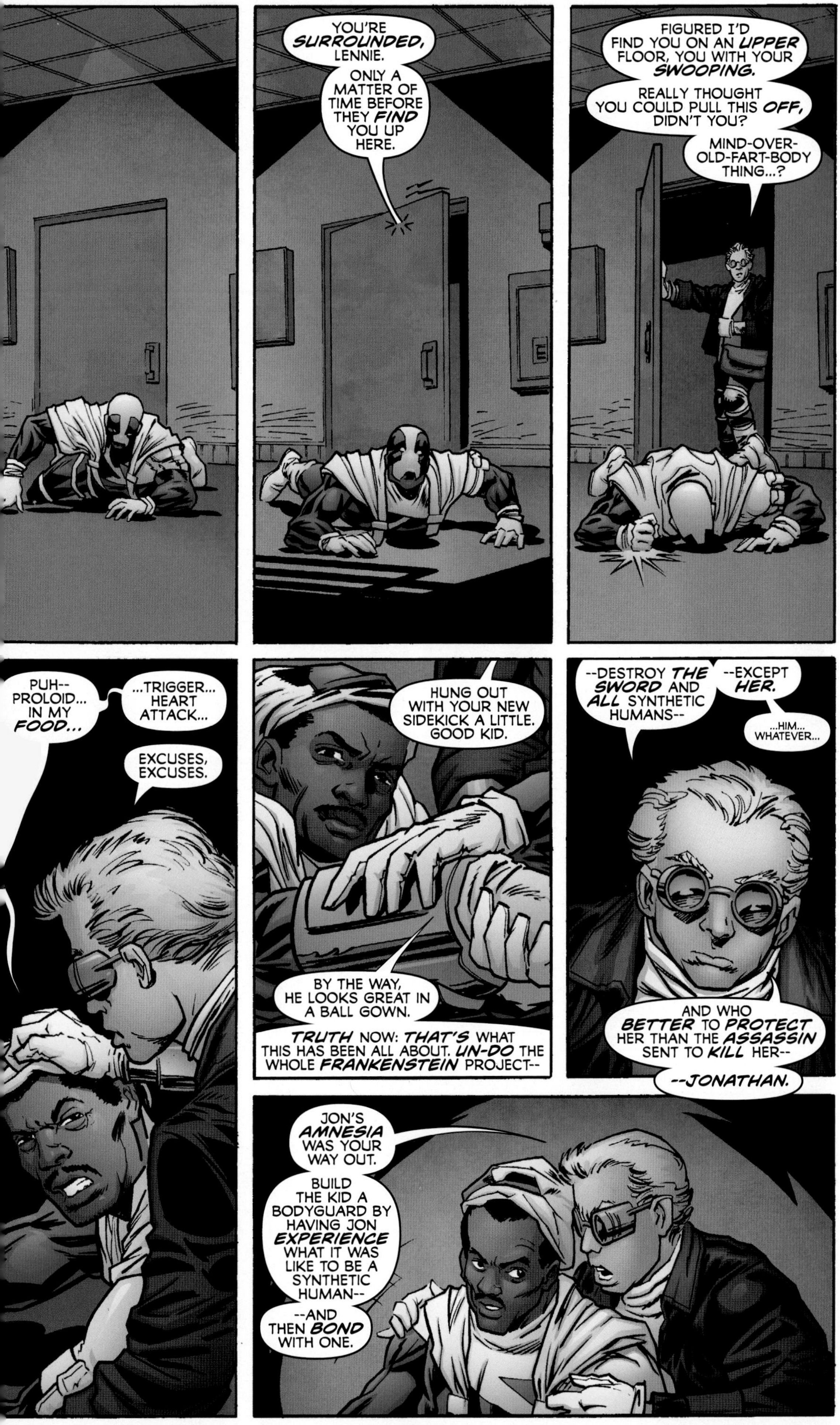
YOU'RE SURROUNDED, LENNIE.
ONLY A MATTER OF TIME BEFORE THEY FIND YOU UP HERE.
FIGURED I'D FIND YOU ON AN UPPER FLOOR, YOU WITH YOUR SWOOPING.
REALLY THOUGHT YOU COULD PULL THIS OFF, DIDN'T YOU?
MIND-OVER-OLD-FART-BODY THING...?
PUH-- PROLOID... IN MY FOOD...
...TRIGGER... HEART ATTACK...
EXCUSES, EXCUSES.
HUNG OUT WITH YOUR NEW SIDEKICK A LITTLE. GOOD KID.
BY THE WAY, HE LOOKS GREAT IN A BALL GOWN.
TRUTH NOW: THAT'S WHAT THIS HAS BEEN ALL ABOUT. UN-DO THE WHOLE FRANKENSTEIN PROJECT--
--DESTROY THE SWORD AND ALL SYNTHETIC HUMANS--
--EXCEPT HER.
...HIM... WHATEVER...
AND WHO BETTER TO PROTECT HER THAN THE ASSASSIN SENT TO KILL HER--
--JONATHAN.
JON'S AMNESIA WAS YOUR WAY OUT.
BUILD THE KID A BODYGUARD BY HAVING JON EXPERIENCE WHAT IT WAS LIKE TO BE A SYNTHETIC HUMAN--
--AND THEN BOND WITH ONE.

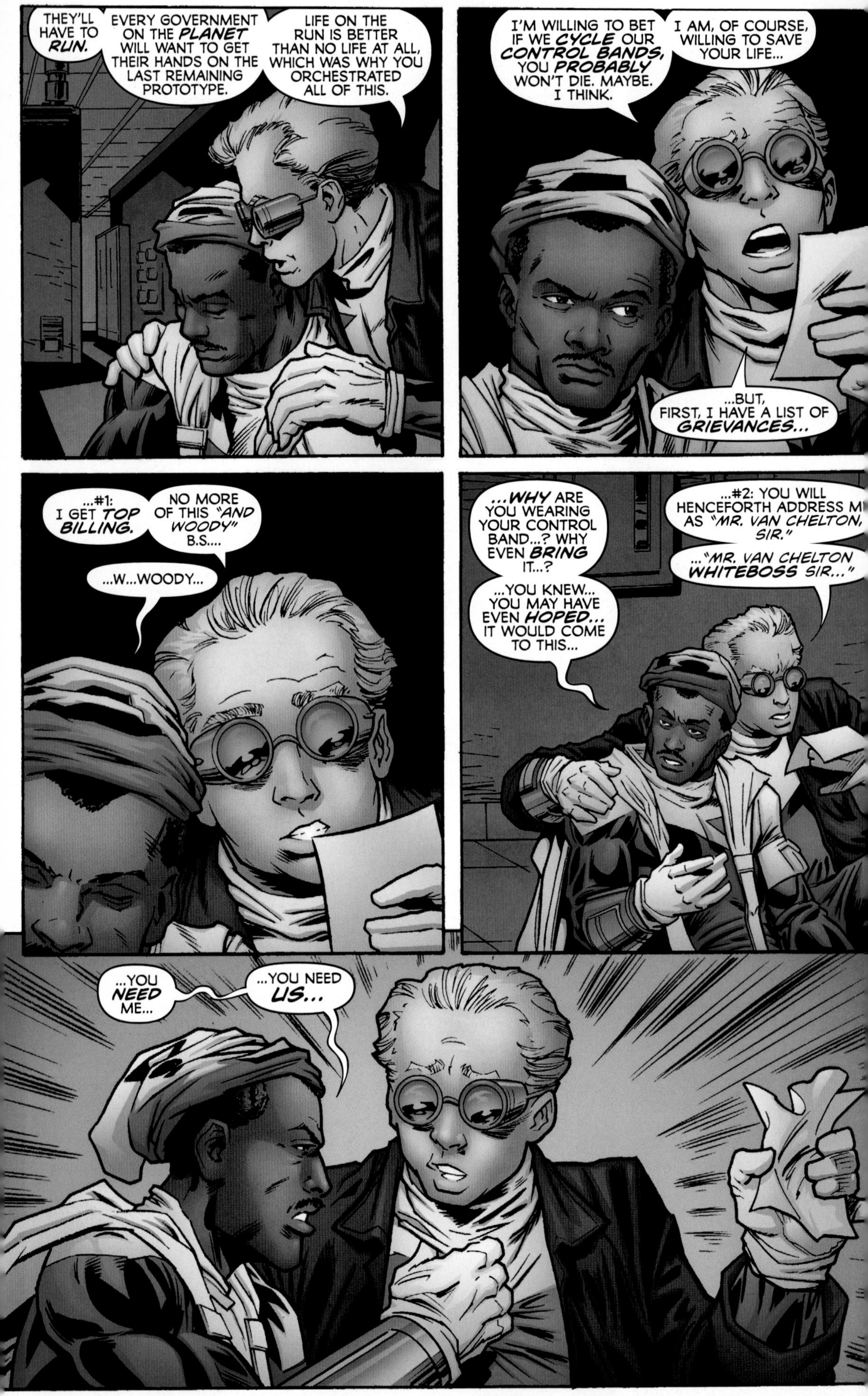

THEY'LL HAVE TO RUN.
EVERY GOVERNMENT ON THE PLANET WILL WANT TO GET THEIR HANDS ON THE LAST REMAINING PROTOTYPE.
LIFE ON THE RUN IS BETTER THAN NO LIFE AT ALL, WHICH WAS WHY YOU ORCHESTRATED ALL OF THIS.
I'M WILLING TO BET IF WE CYCLE OUR CONTROL BANDS, YOU PROBABLY WON'T DIE. MAYBE. I THINK.
I AM, OF COURSE, WILLING TO SAVE YOUR LIFE...
...BUT, FIRST, I HAVE A LIST OF GRIEVANCES...
...#1: I GET TOP BILLING.
NO MORE OF THIS "AND WOODY" B.S....
...W...WOODY...
...WHY ARE YOU WEARING YOUR CONTROL BAND...? WHY EVEN BRING IT...?
...YOU KNEW... YOU MAY HAVE EVEN HOPED... IT WOULD COME TO THIS...
...#2: YOU WILL HENCEFORTH ADDRESS M AS "MR. VAN CHELTON, SIR."
..."MR. VAN CHELTON WHITEBOSS SIR..."
...YOU NEED ME...
...YOU NEED US...

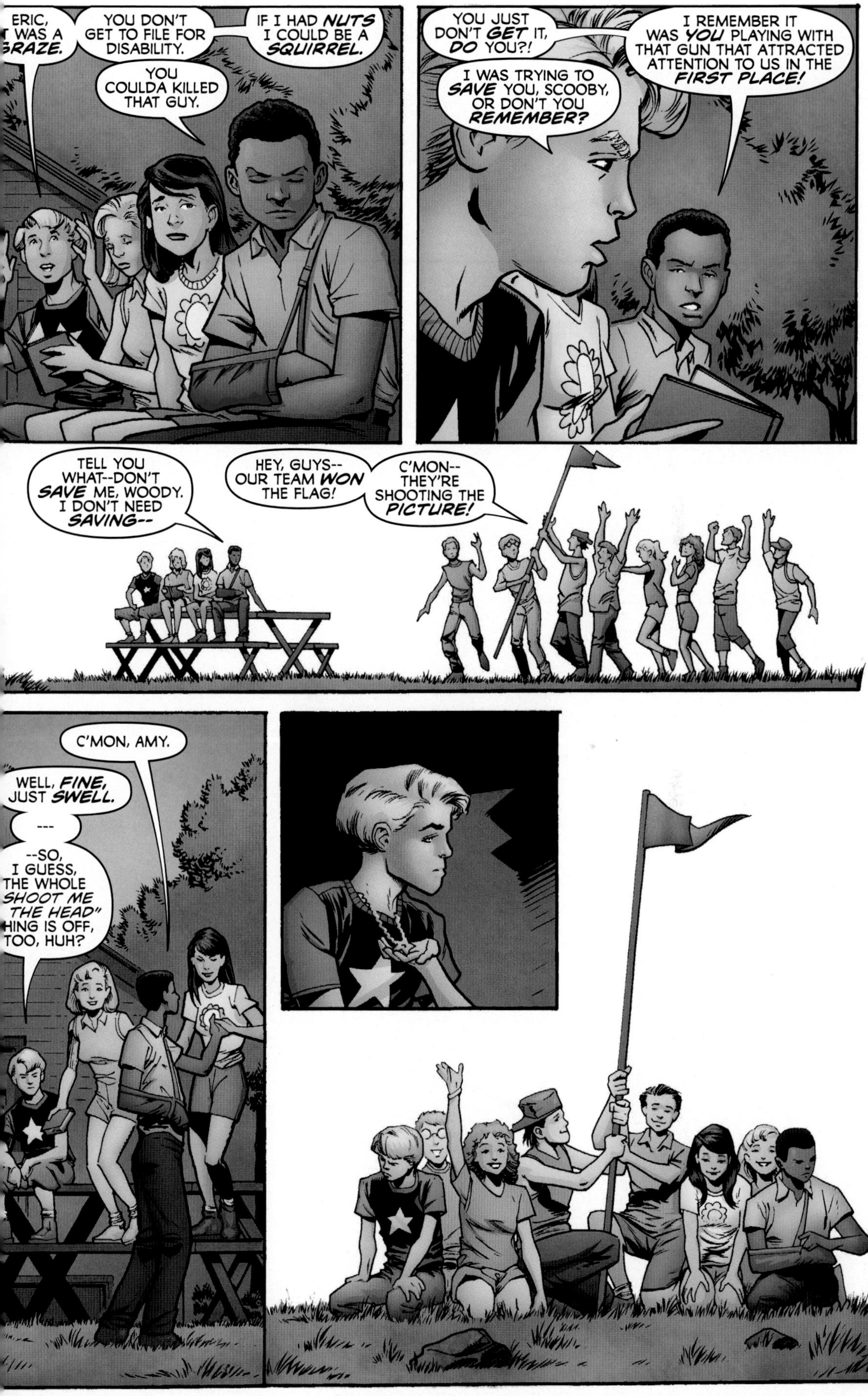
ERIC, T WAS A GRAZE.
YOU DON'T GET TO FILE FOR DISABILITY.
IF I HAD NUTS I COULD BE A SQUIRREL.
YOU COULDA KILLED THAT GUY.
YOU JUST DON'T GET IT, DO YOU?!
I WAS TRYING TO SAVE YOU, SCOOBY, OR DON'T YOU REMEMBER?
I REMEMBER IT WAS YOU PLAYING WITH THAT GUN THAT ATTRACTED ATTENTION TO US IN THE FIRST PLACE!
TELL YOU WHAT--DON'T SAVE ME, WOODY. I DON'T NEED SAVING--
HEY, GUYS-- OUR TEAM WON THE FLAG!
C'MON-- THEY'RE SHOOTING THE PICTURE!
C'MON, AMY.
WELL, FINE, JUST SWELL.

--SO, I GUESS, THE WHOLE SHOOT ME THE HEAD" HING IS OFF, TOO, HUH?

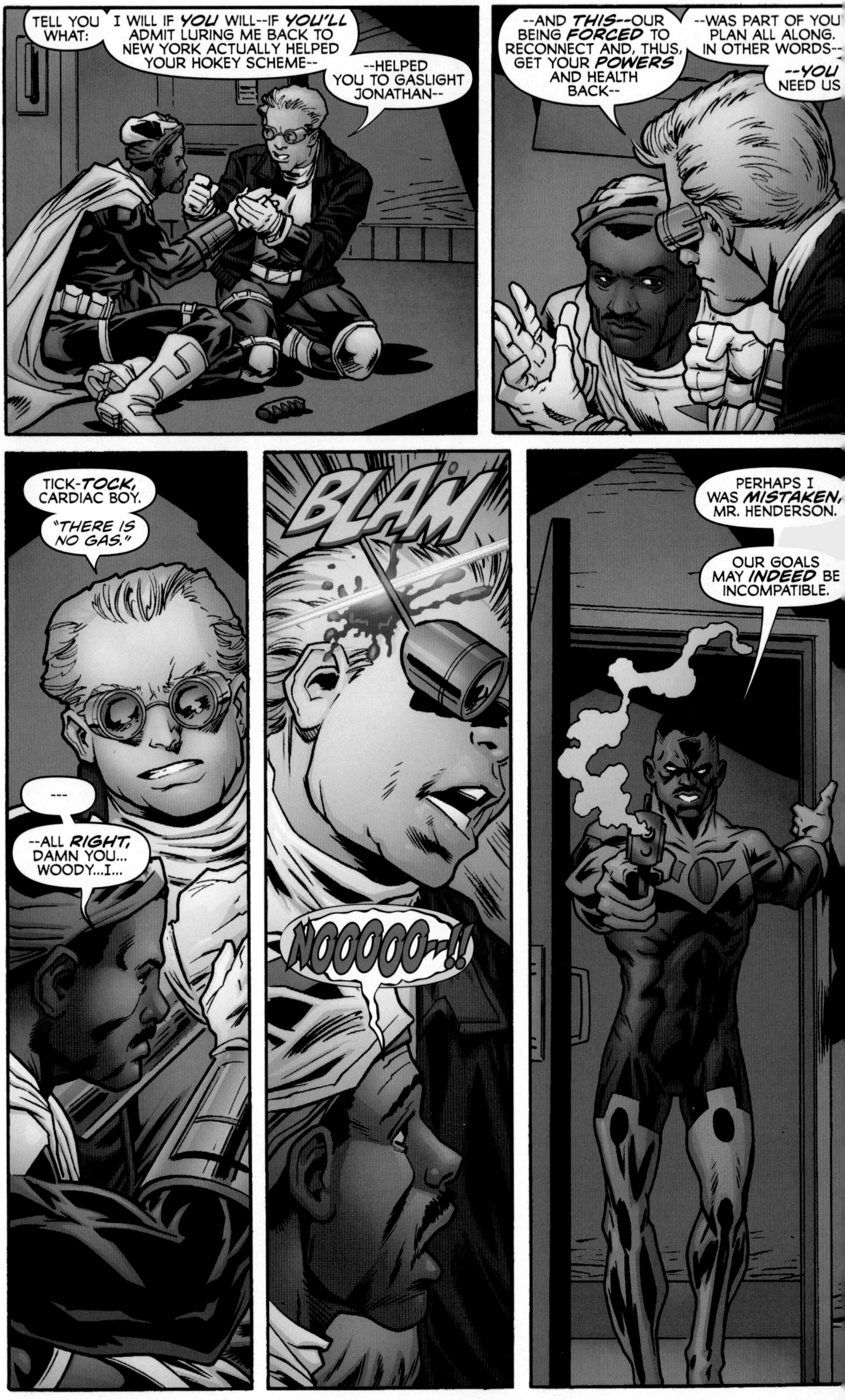
TELL YOU WHAT:
I WILL IF YOU WILL--IF YOU'LL ADMIT LURING ME BACK TO NEW YORK ACTUALLY HELPED YOUR HOKEY SCHEME--
--HELPED YOU TO GASLIGHT JONATHAN--
--AND THIS--OUR BEING FORCED TO RECONNECT AND, THUS, GET YOUR POWERS AND HEALTH BACK--
--WAS PART OF YOU PLAN ALL ALONG. IN OTHER WORDS--
--YOU NEED US
TICK-TOCK, CARDIAC BOY.
"THERE IS NO GAS."

--ALL RIGHT, DAMN YOU... WOODY...I...
BLAM
NOOOOO--!!
PERHAPS I WAS MISTAKEN, MR. HENDERSON.
OUR GOALS MAY INDEED BE INCOMPATIBLE.

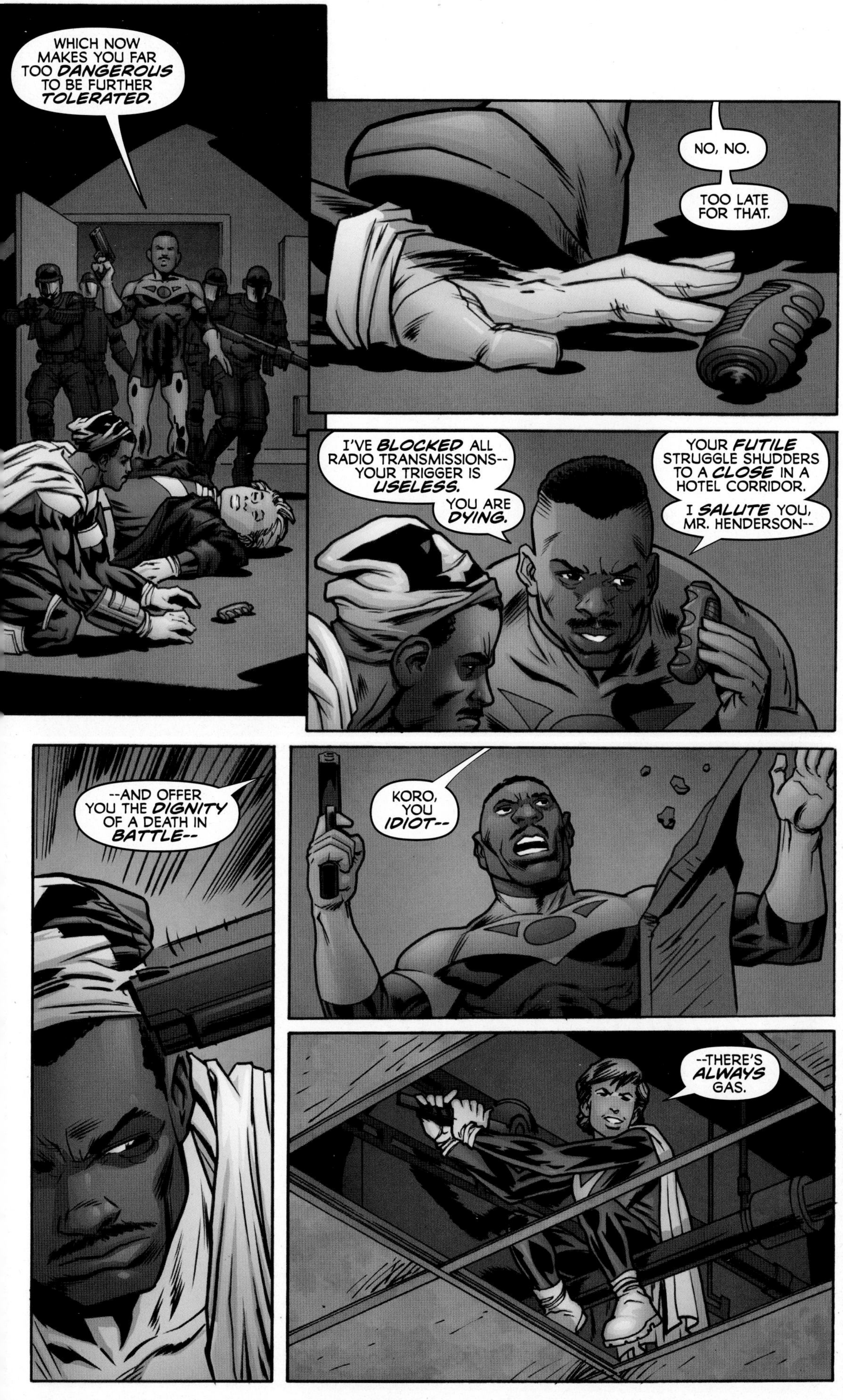
WHICH NOW MAKES YOU FAR TOO DANGEROUS TO BE FURTHER TOLERATED.
NO, NO.
TOO LATE FOR THAT.
I'VE BLOCKED ALL RADIO TRANSMISSIONS-- YOUR TRIGGER IS USELESS.
YOU ARE DYING.
YOUR FUTILE STRUGGLE SHUDDERS TO A CLOSE IN A HOTEL CORRIDOR.
I SALUTE YOU, MR. HENDERSON--
--AND OFFER YOU THE DIGNITY OF A DEATH IN BATTLE--
KORO, YOU IDIOT--
--THERE'S ALWAYS GAS.

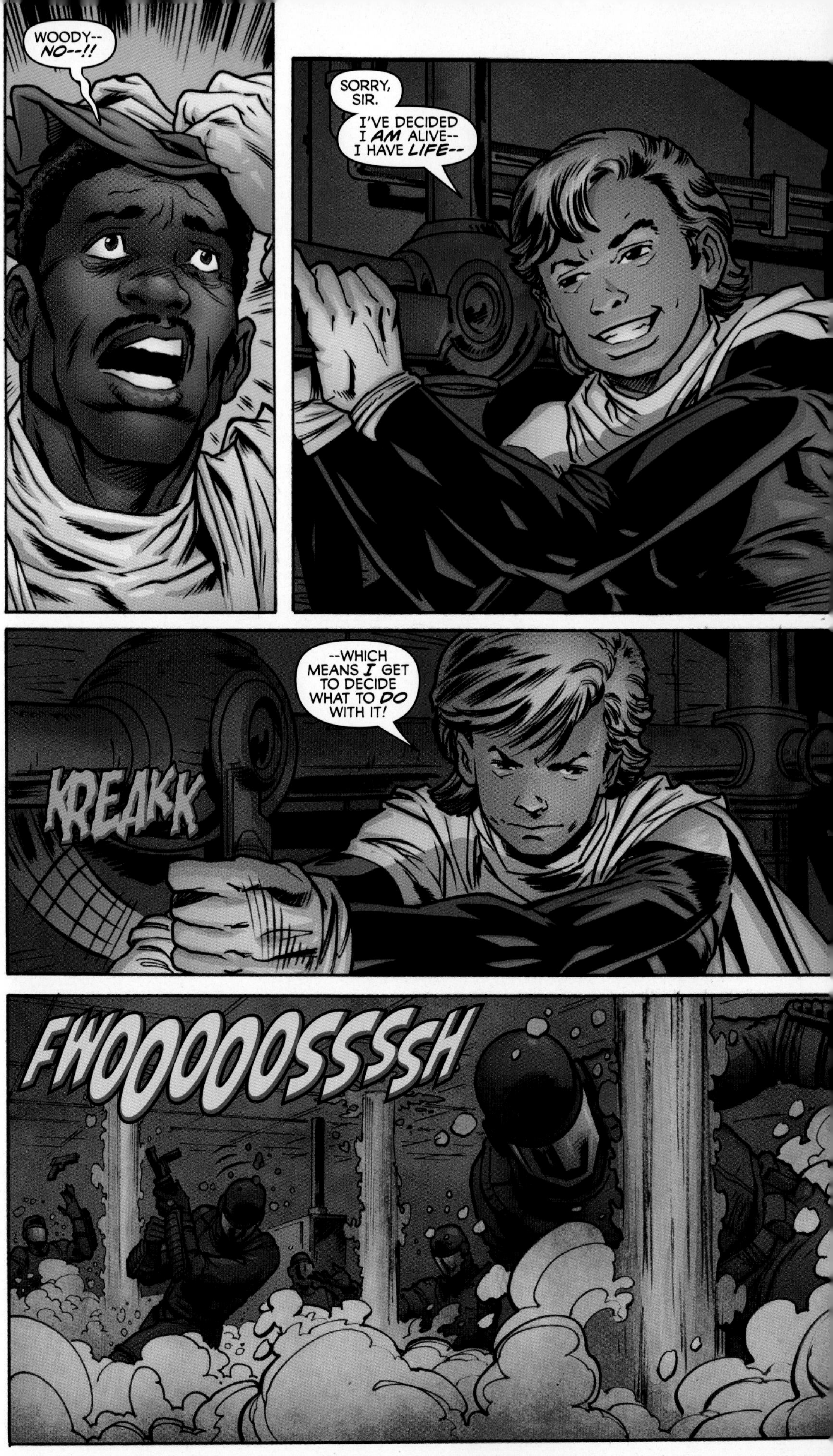
WOODY-- NO--!!
SORRY, SIR.
I'VE DECIDED I AM ALIVE-- I HAVE LIFE--
--WHICH MEANS I GET TO DECIDE WHAT TO DO WITH IT!
KREAKK
FWOOOOOOSSSSH

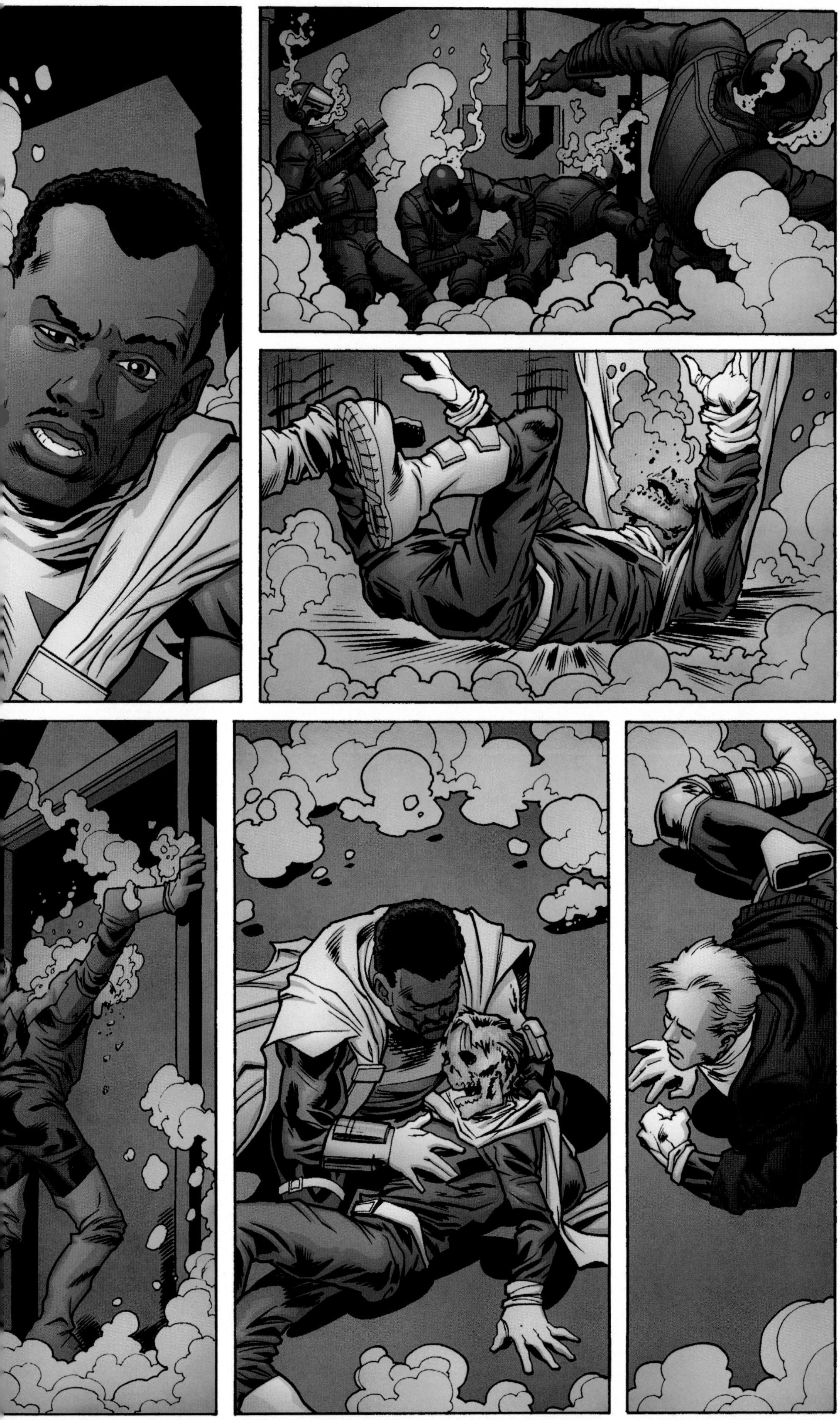

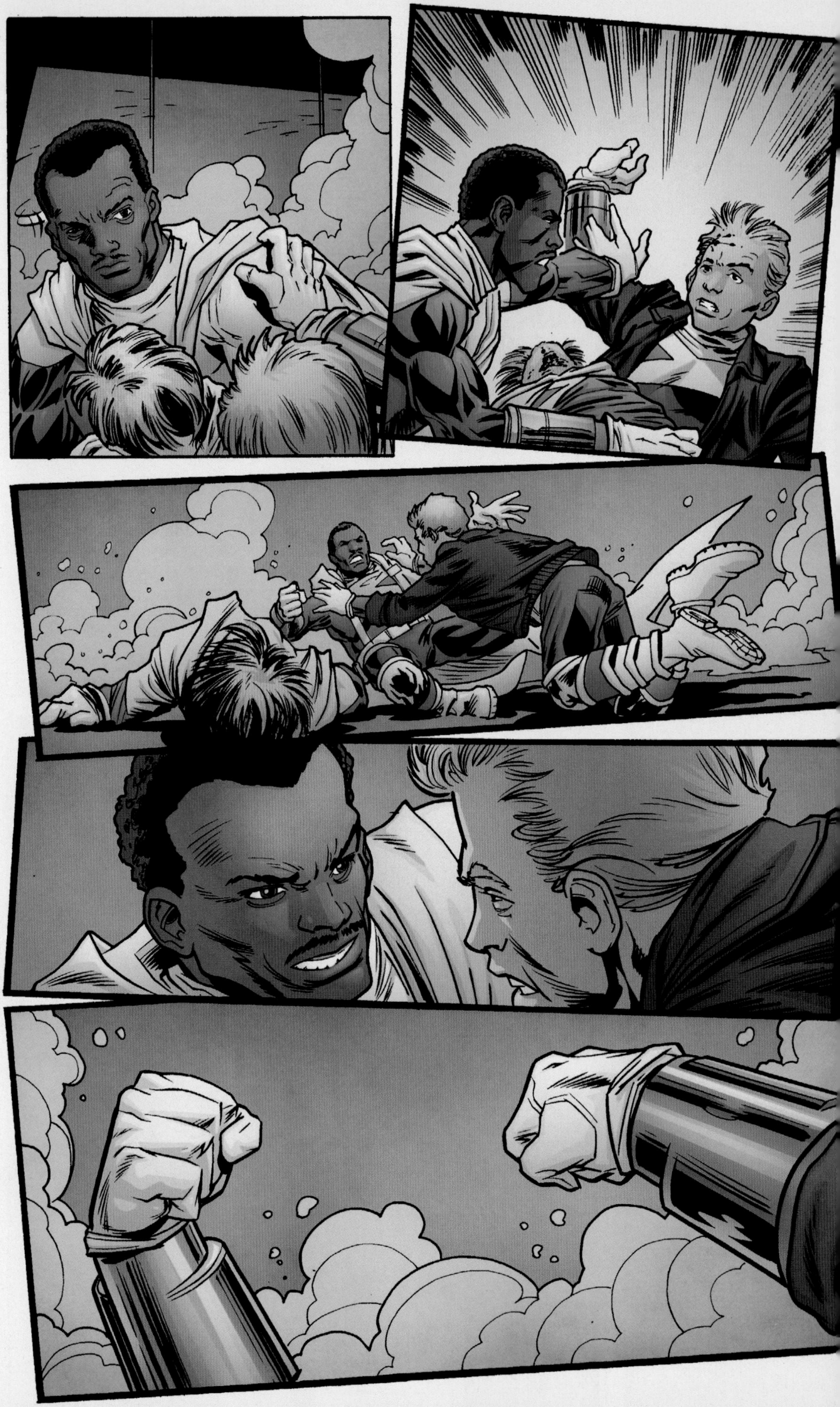

"Doesn't It Suck That We Didn't Show It?"

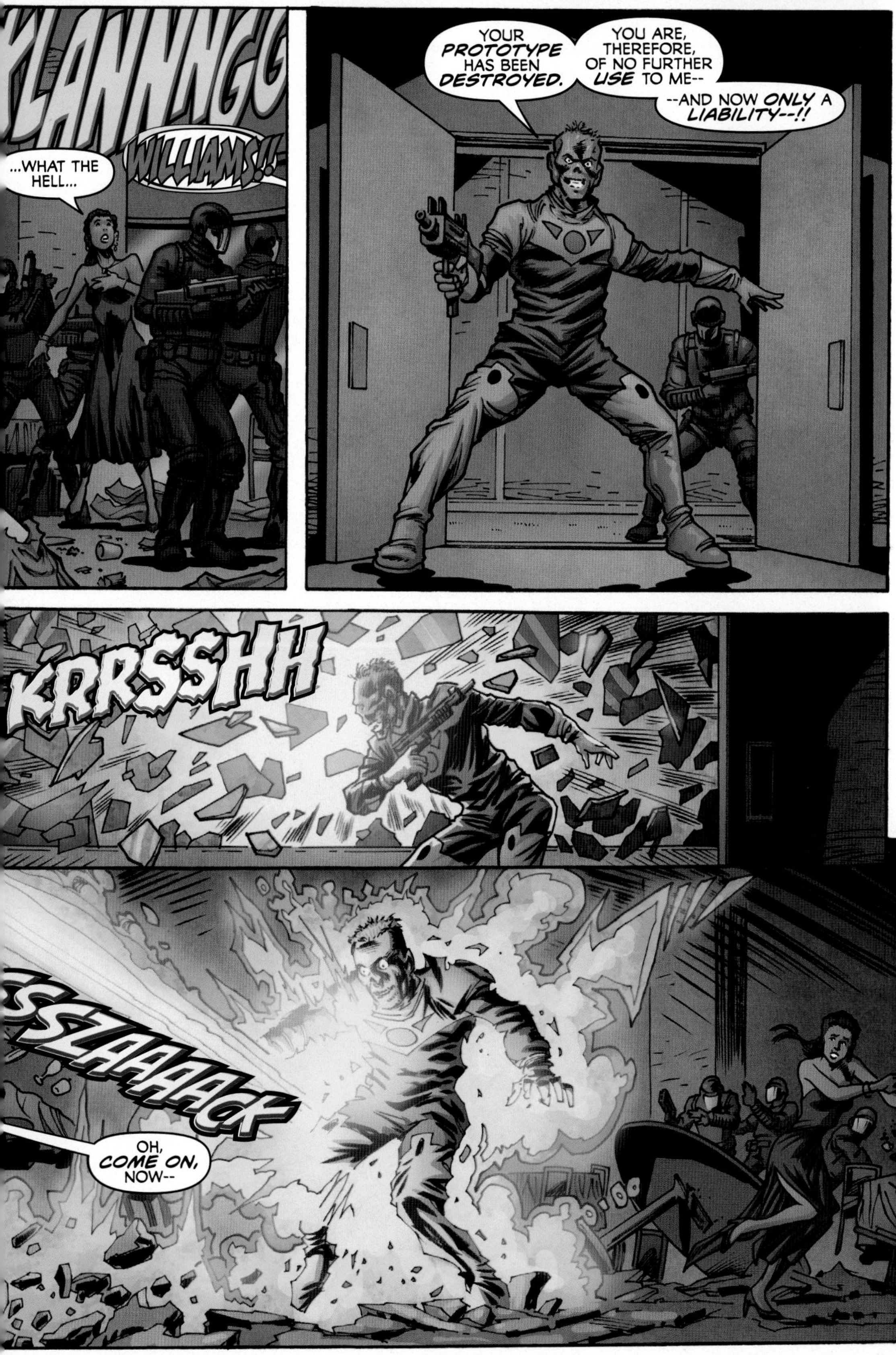

KLANNNGG
...WHAT THE HELL...
WILLIAMS!!
YOUR PROTOTYPE HAS BEEN DESTROYED.
YOU ARE, THEREFORE, OF NO FURTHER USE TO ME--
--AND NOW ONLY A LIABILITY--!!
KRRSSHH
SZAAAACK
OH, COME ON, NOW--

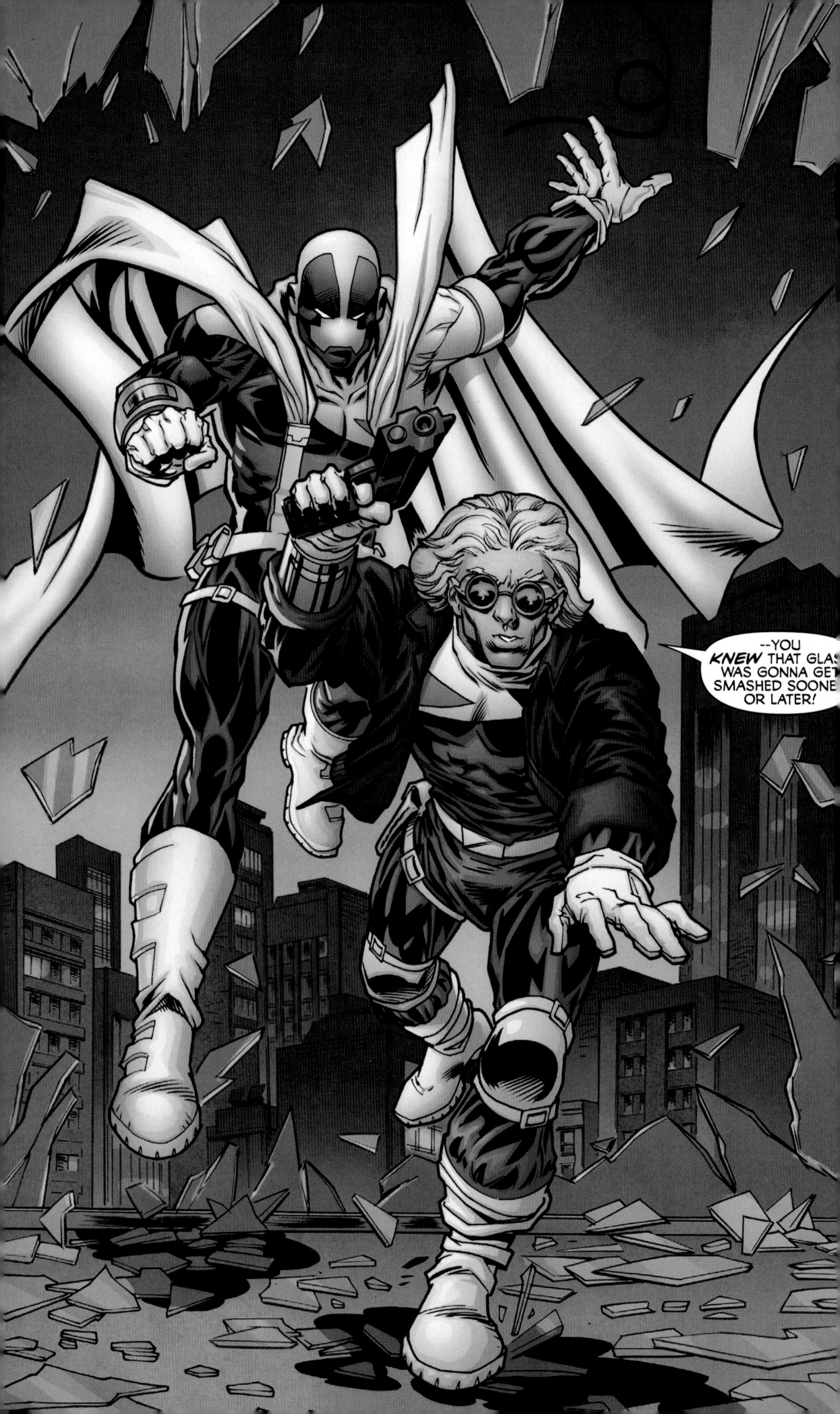
--YOU KNEW THAT GLAS WAS GONNA GET SMASHED SOONE OR LATER!

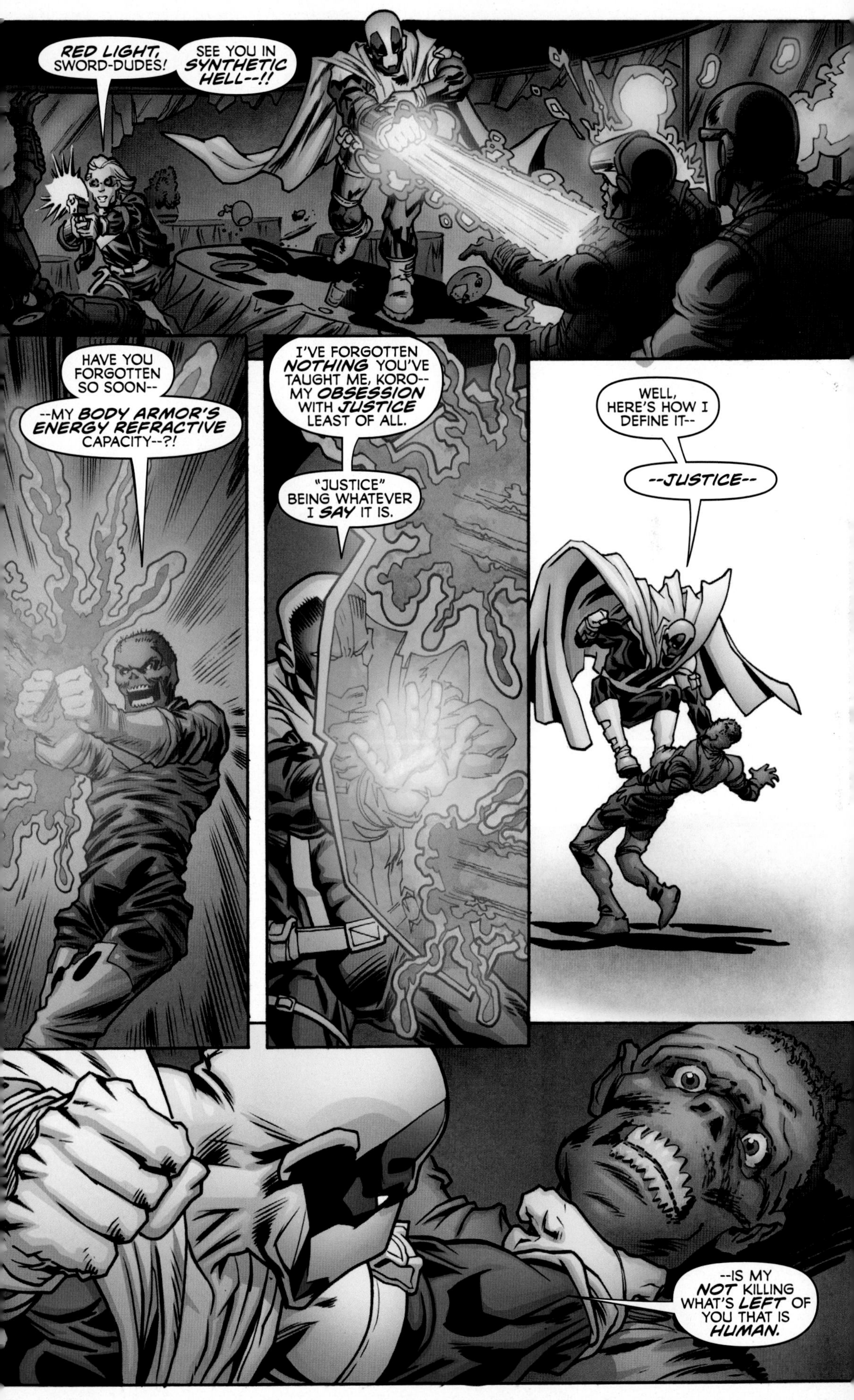
RED LIGHT, SWORD-DUDES!
SEE YOU IN SYNTHETIC HELL--!!
HAVE YOU FORGOTTEN SO SOON--
--MY BODY ARMOR'S ENERGY REFRACTIVE CAPACITY--?!
I'VE FORGOTTEN NOTHING YOU'VE TAUGHT ME, KORO-- MY OBSESSION WITH JUSTICE LEAST OF ALL.
"JUSTICE" BEING WHATEVER I SAY IT IS.
WELL, HERE'S HOW I DEFINE IT--
--JUSTICE--
--IS MY NOT KILLING WHAT'S LEFT OF YOU THAT IS HUMAN.

"And, so..."

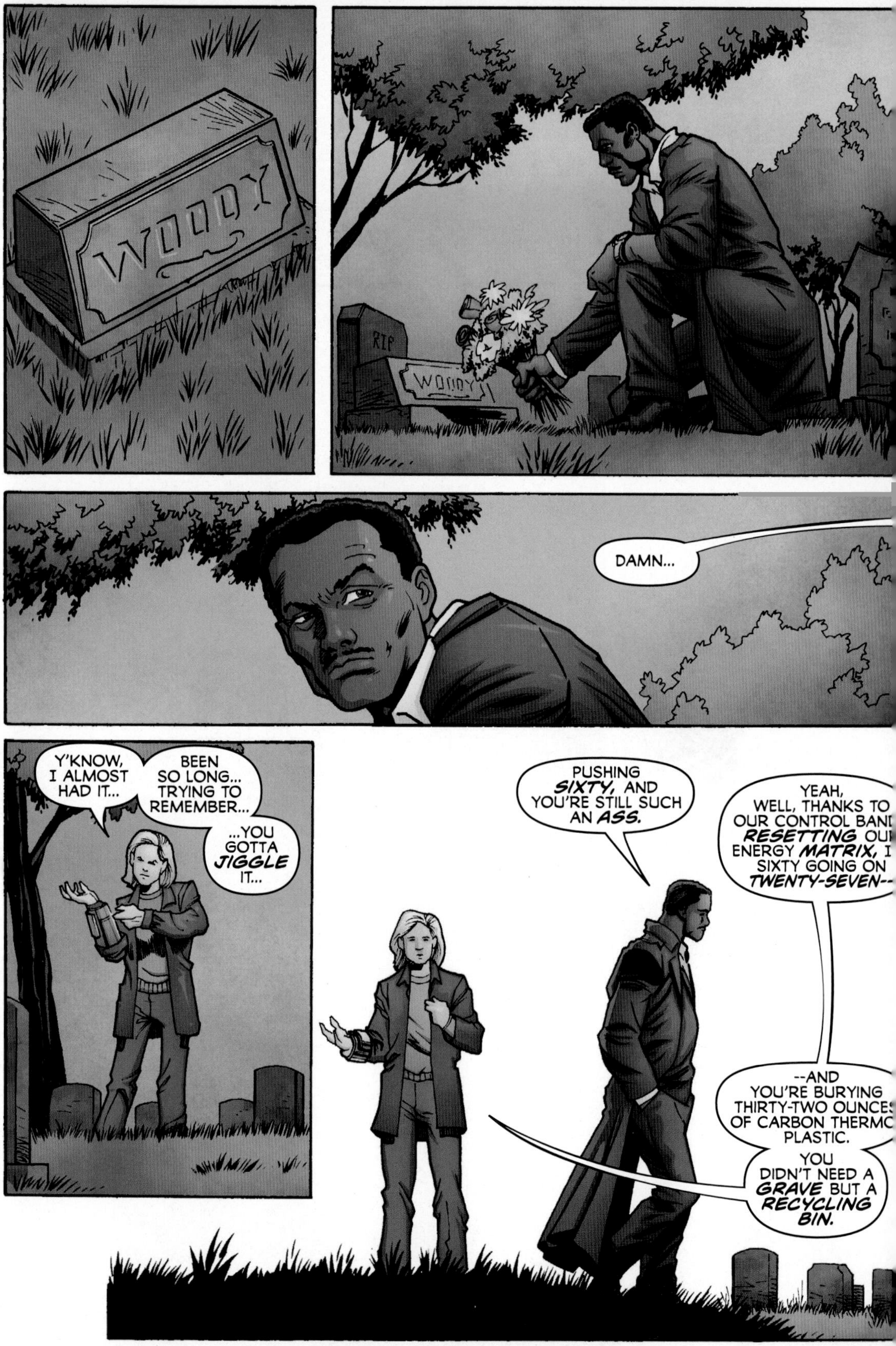

WOODY
RIP
WOODY
DAMN...
Y'KNOW, I ALMOST HAD IT...
BEEN SO LONG... TRYING TO REMEMBER...
...YOU GOTTA JIGGLE IT...
PUSHING SIXTY, AND YOU'RE STILL SUCH AN ASS.
YEAH, WELL, THANKS TO OUR CONTROL BAND RESETTING OUR ENERGY MATRIX, I SIXTY GOING ON TWENTY-SEVEN--
--AND YOU'RE BURYING THIRTY-TWO OUNCES OF CARBON THERMO PLASTIC.
YOU DIDN'T NEED A GRAVE BUT A RECYCLING BIN.

WOODY WAS *ALIVE*, IDIOT.

REALLY? SO, WHAT ABOUT ALL THOSE *SWORD* GUYS WE WHACKED?

WHY DOES THE *KID* COUNT BUT *THEY* DON'T?

WOODY WAS A MUCH MORE *ADVANCED* PROTOTYPE--

A HOUSE NOOGIE.

ISN'T THAT HOW WE USED TO SORT THE *FIELD HANDS* FROM THE HOUSE SERVANTS?

"*ADVANCED* PROTOTYPE"? ERIC: YOU BURIED A *TOASTER*.

YOU RISKED *YOUR* LIFE AND THE SECURITY OF THE *PLANET* FOR A *KEN* DOLL.

MY GOD, YOU'RE AN IDIOT.

TAKE THE COMPANY JET BACK TO L.A.

WOULD *LOVE* TO, SHERLOCK, BUT I *CAN'T GET THIS DAMNED THING OFF!!*

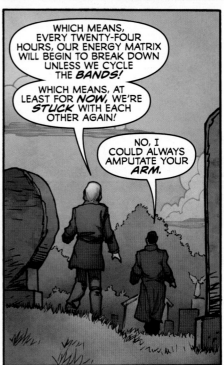

WHICH MEANS, EVERY TWENTY-FOUR HOURS, OUR ENERGY MATRIX WILL BEGIN TO BREAK DOWN UNLESS WE CYCLE THE *BANDS!*

WHICH MEANS, AT LEAST FOR *NOW*, WE'RE *STUCK* WITH EACH OTHER AGAIN!

NO, I COULD ALWAYS AMPUTATE YOUR *ARM*.

I COULD AMPUTATE YOUR *NUTS*.

WOODY-- WE'VE BEEN GIVEN *ANOTHER CHANCE* TO BE *USEFUL*--MAKE A *DIFFERENCE*.

YEAH...

...LOOK AT HOW WELL *THAT* WORKED FOR US THE *FIRST* TIME...

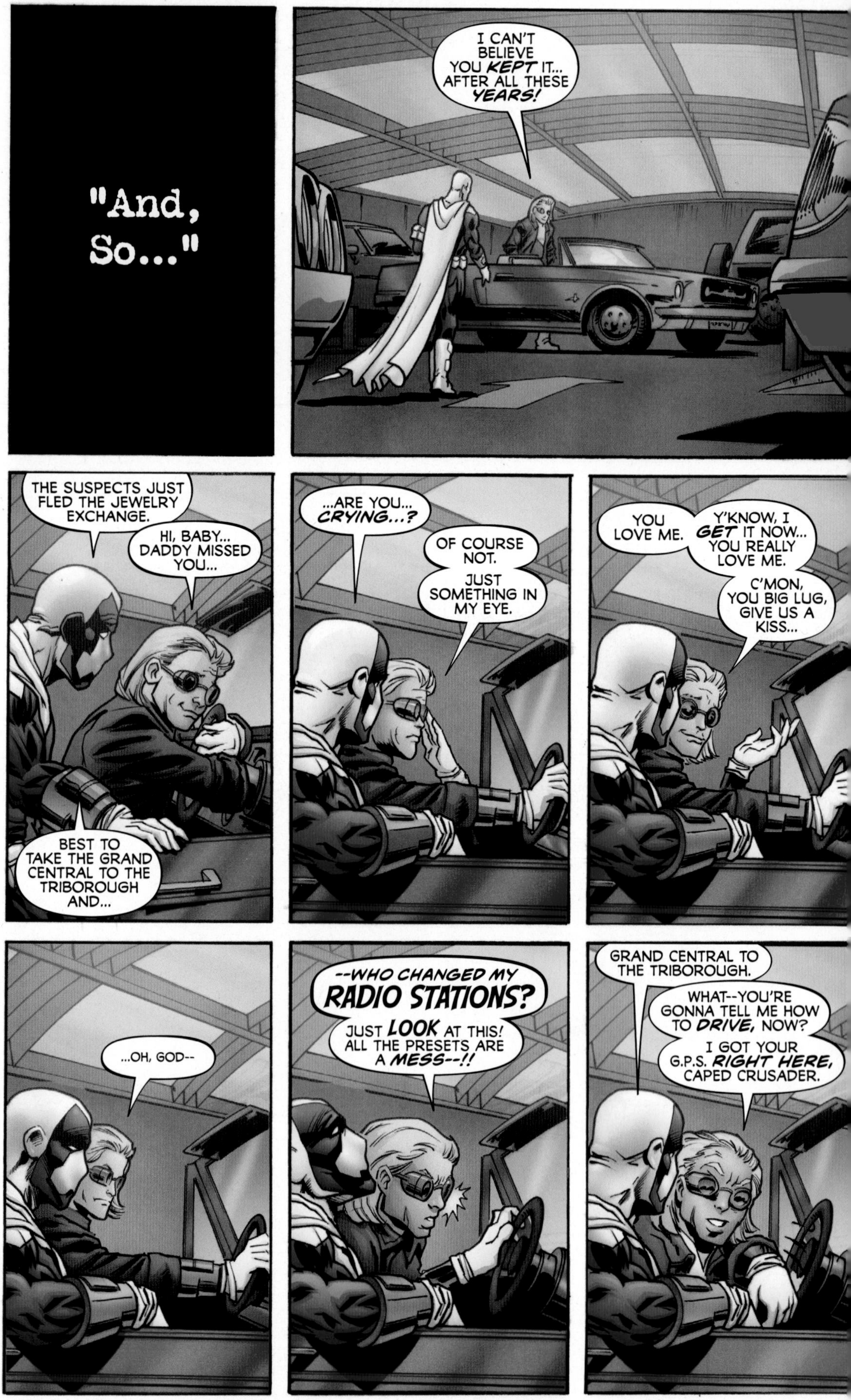
"And, So..."
I CAN'T BELIEVE YOU KEPT IT... AFTER ALL THESE YEARS!
THE SUSPECTS JUST FLED THE JEWELRY EXCHANGE.
HI, BABY... DADDY MISSED YOU...
BEST TO TAKE THE GRAND CENTRAL TO THE TRIBOROUGH AND...
...ARE YOU... CRYING...?
OF COURSE NOT.
JUST SOMETHING IN MY EYE.
YOU LOVE ME.
Y'KNOW, I GET IT NOW... YOU REALLY LOVE ME.
C'MON, YOU BIG LUG, GIVE US A KISS...
...OH, GOD--
--WHO CHANGED MY RADIO STATIONS?
JUST LOOK AT THIS! ALL THE PRESETS ARE A MESS--!!
GRAND CENTRAL TO THE TRIBOROUGH.
WHAT--YOU'RE GONNA TELL ME HOW TO DRIVE, NOW?
I GOT YOUR G.P.S. RIGHT HERE, CAPED CRUSADER.

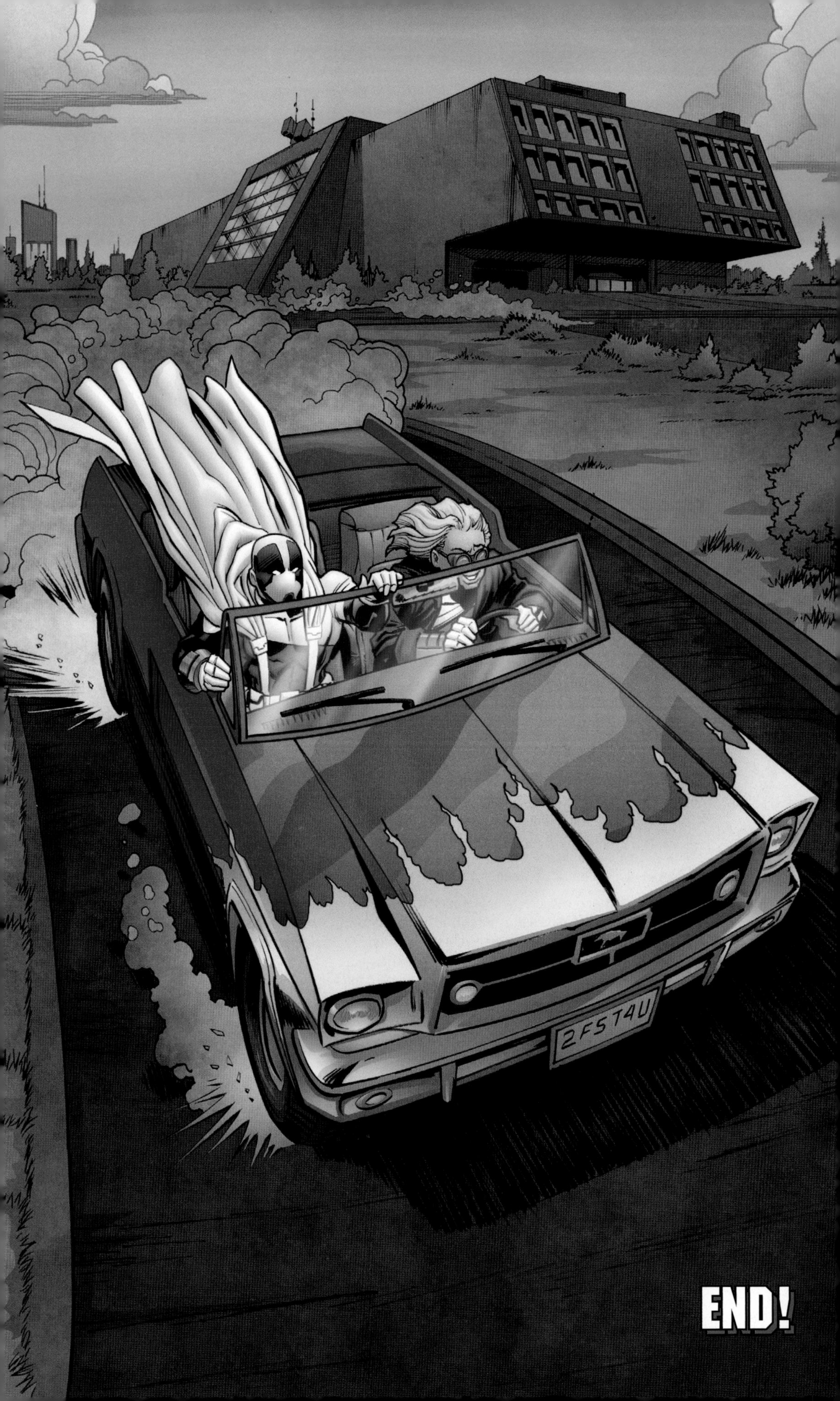
2FST4U
END!

I t wasn't funny.

I'd turned in issue #1 of Q2: THE RETURN OF QUANTUM AND WOODY, and there was nary a chuckle in it. There were reasons for that. First: as originally conceived, this was a graphic novel project. It was not structured with traditional act breaks every twenty or so pages but intended to be read as a single volume. Second: QUANTUM AND WOODY, in our original series for Acclaim comics, was never funny. Neither Doc Bright nor I ever once plotted the book from the point of view of the series being a comedy. We were producing a super-hero buddy book about two friends who loved one another like brothers but couldn't stand each other.

It was an action-adventure series that had one funny guy in it; someone who relentlessly mocked everything going on, much the way M.D. "Doc" Bright does. The other character was a staunchly sardonic and overly invested stubborn obsessive, much the way Doc Bright is. Truthfully, both Quantum and Woody were based on the warring aspects of their artist's personality. People tend to assume Q&W are Priest and Bright; no, they're both Bright, who has the quickest wit you can imagine and who can also be the biggest annoyance at the same time. It's his super-power.

After our Acclaim run, I wasn't anxious to return to the series. First, you never want to end up competing with yourself. Second, Valiant had successfully recast the series in a highly successful new vision, transitioning the concept from satire to farce; the difference between the two literary styles being the first four seasons of Seinfeld and the last five–same show, still funny, different approaches (and the later seasons had much higher ratings).

Satire evokes situational humor out of a narrative grounded in reality, while farce bends reality a bit. The Valiant Q&W is a very funny book in a way ours never was. What made our book "funny" was Woody's situational observations. Beyond that, we had no funny villains or funny situations, though we ourselves tipped over into farce now and again (notably when Q&W switched bodies).

Returning to Q&W, using our "Early Seinfeld" approach, might position us to be competing not only with ourselves but with Valiant's new

hit book, which really didn't appeal to me. Working with Valiant Editor-in-Chief Warren Simons, we mulled over some ideas of how to make this the same and yet not the same; to give this peculiar project its own reason for existing. The idea came: what if the original Acclaim series had never been cancelled? Who and what would those characters be right now?

Well, they'd be our age. Doc and I met thirty-plus years ago, working on a Falcon miniseries for Marvel. When you're twenty-something, you think you will live forever. We are now grumpy middle-aged men, dealing with the shock of forced adulthood this time of life brings. And that became our story: not specifically about aging per se but about transitions life imposes upon all of us and how we choose to deal with them.

And so I ended up over at long-time DC Comics letterer Willie Schubert's house whining about my plot (or, actually, lack thereof), as I tend to do during the suffering stage of trying to piece together a story. Willie's American Genius high-school daughter, Marika, patiently listened to my prattling on and then said, "It sounds like you're talking about 'Of Mice And Men.'"

Oh, wow. And it all just clicked. Steinbeck's theme of fate, highlighted by a series of misconceptions, expectations, and pre-judgements, was a nice place to go with our Grumpy Old Heroes narrative.

Additionally, for the graphic novel, I wanted to write a long form of the vignettes we'd used in the Acclaim series which featured our heroes as kids. The B-story would provide convenient cutaways while crossing into the main plotline at a key area (with Eric's childhood crush, Amy Fishbein).

Virtually all of the main and supporting characters in Q2 were dealing with transitions forced upon them by life's circumstances; reality shattering their expectations and forcing them to reassess themselves and their relationships. Now extremely limited by multiple sclerosis and a heart condition, Eric has apparently forged a new super-team and is placing a young boy at risk; for which Woody feels responsible since this whole super-hero schtick came about as a result of his having manipulated Eric after their fathers' deaths. Our ersatz George (from Steinbeck's novella), Woody returns to New York

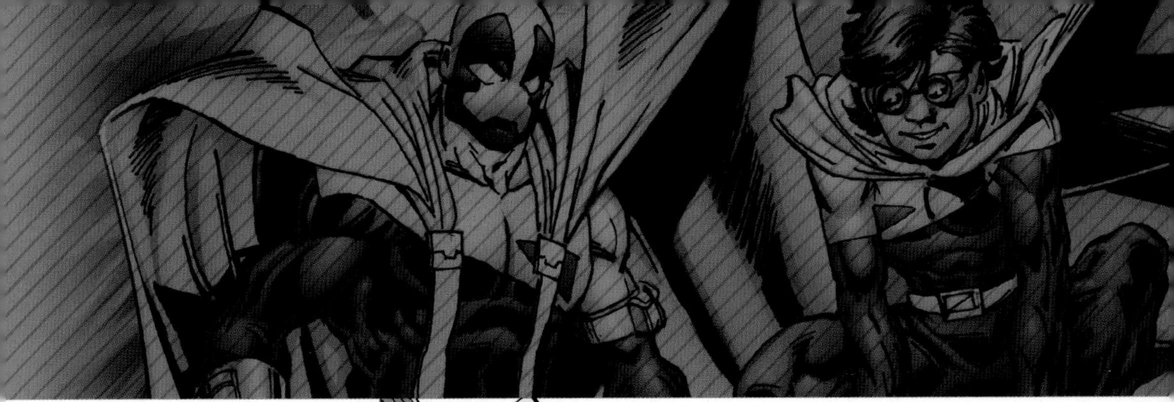

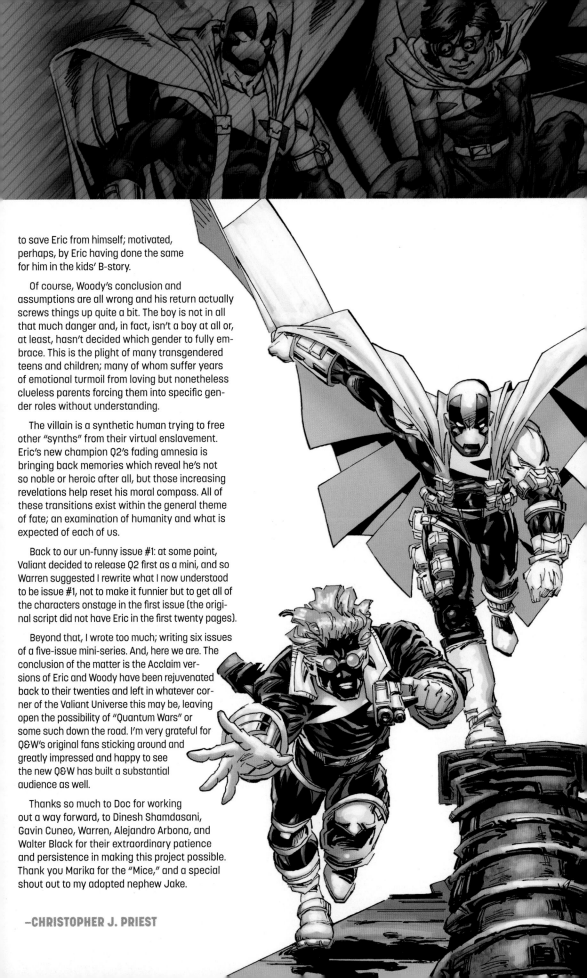

to save Eric from himself; motivated, perhaps, by Eric having done the same for him in the kids' B-story.

Of course, Woody's conclusion and assumptions are all wrong and his return actually screws things up quite a bit. The boy is not in all that much danger and, in fact, isn't a boy at all or, at least, hasn't decided which gender to fully embrace. This is the plight of many transgendered teens and children; many of whom suffer years of emotional turmoil from loving but nonetheless clueless parents forcing them into specific gender roles without understanding.

The villain is a synthetic human trying to free other "synths" from their virtual enslavement. Eric's new champion Q2's fading amnesia is bringing back memories which reveal he's not so noble or heroic after all, but those increasing revelations help reset his moral compass. All of these transitions exist within the general theme of fate; an examination of humanity and what is expected of each of us.

Back to our un-funny issue #1: at some point, Valiant decided to release Q2 first as a mini, and so Warren suggested I rewrite what I now understood to be issue #1, not to make it funnier but to get all of the characters onstage in the first issue (the original script did not have Eric in the first twenty pages).

Beyond that, I wrote too much; writing six issues of a five-issue mini-series. And, here we are. The conclusion of the matter is the Acclaim versions of Eric and Woody have been rejuvenated back to their twenties and left in whatever corner of the Valiant Universe this may be, leaving open the possibility of "Quantum Wars" or some such down the road. I'm very grateful for Q&W's original fans sticking around and greatly impressed and happy to see the new Q&W has built a substantial audience as well.

Thanks so much to Doc for working out a way forward, to Dinesh Shamdasani, Gavin Cuneo, Warren, Alejandro Arbona, and Walter Black for their extraordinary patience and persistence in making this project possible. Thank you Marika for the "Mice," and a special shout out to my adopted nephew Jake.

–CHRISTOPHER J. PRIEST

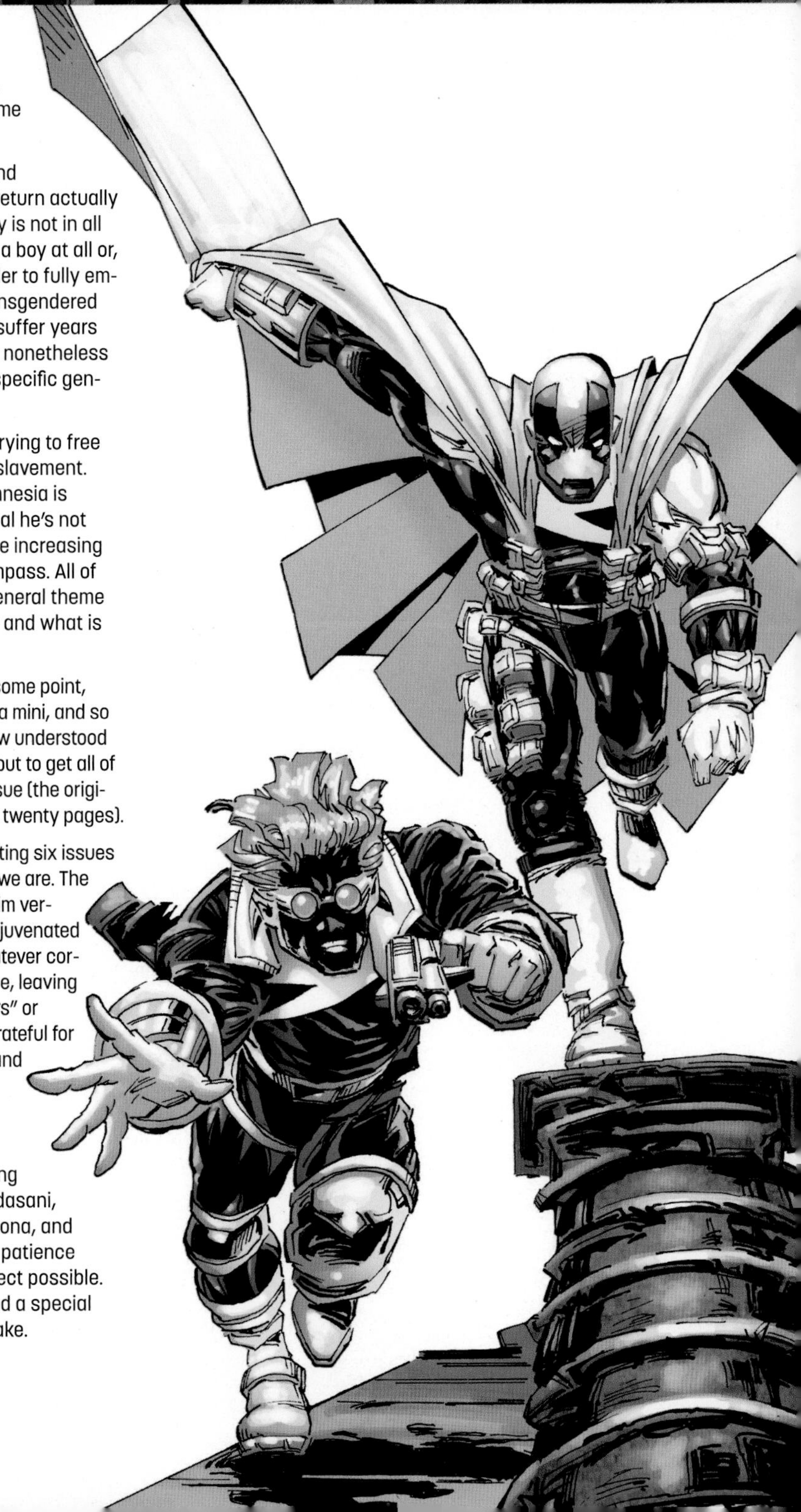

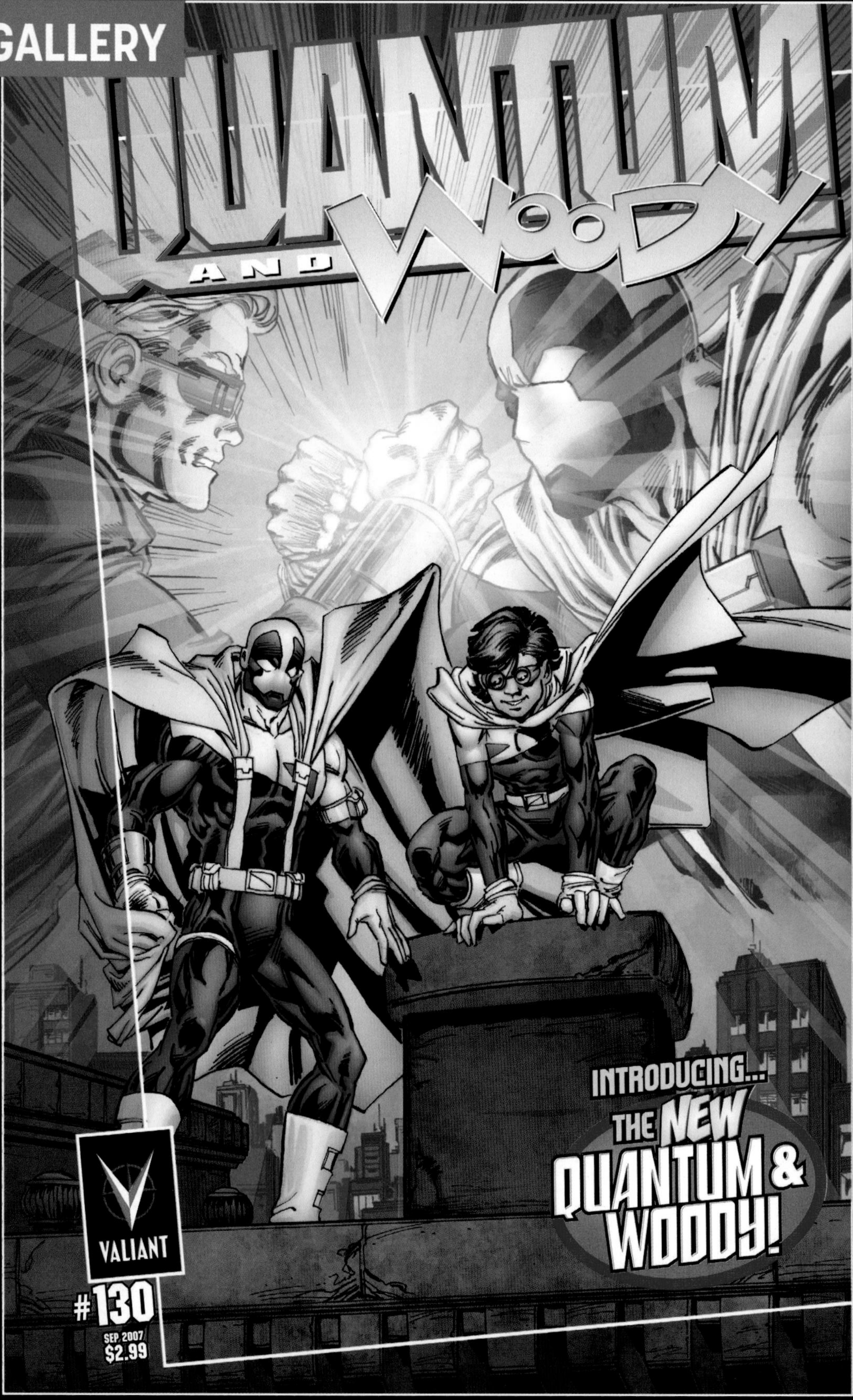
QUANTUM
AND
WOODY
INTRODUCING...
THE NEW
QUANTUM &
WOODY!
VALIANT
#130
SEP 2007
$2.99

"The Missing Years!"
Q2: THE RETURN OF QUANTUM AND WOODY #2
Cover by MD BRIGHT with ALLEN PASSALAQUA

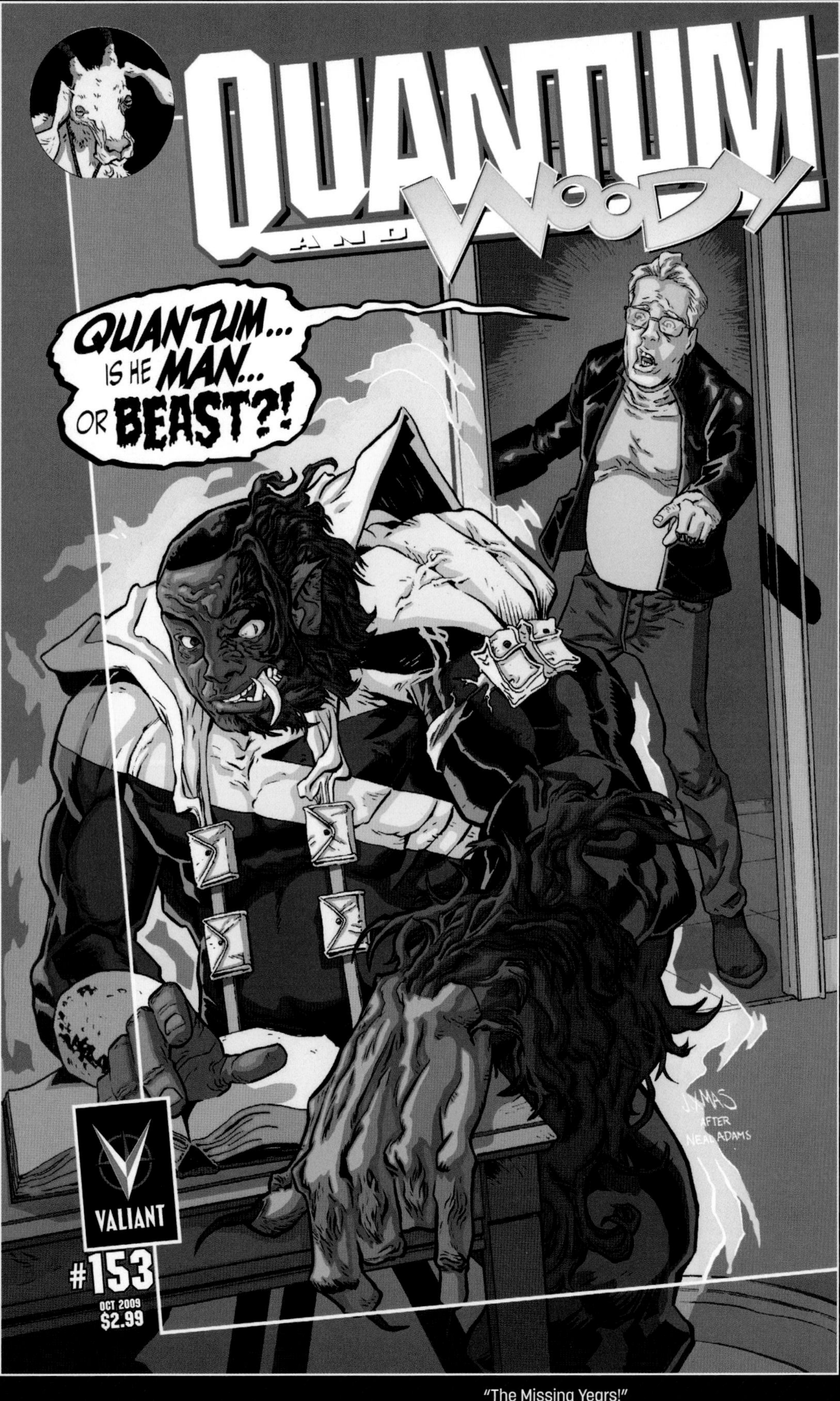
QUANTUM AND WOODY
QUANTUM... IS HE MAN... OR BEAST?!
J.XMAS AFTER NEAL ADAMS
VALIANT
#153
OCT 2009
$2.99

"The Missing Years!"
Q2: THE RETURN OF QUANTUM AND WOODY #2
Cover by JOHNNIE CHRISTMAS with JORDAN BOYD

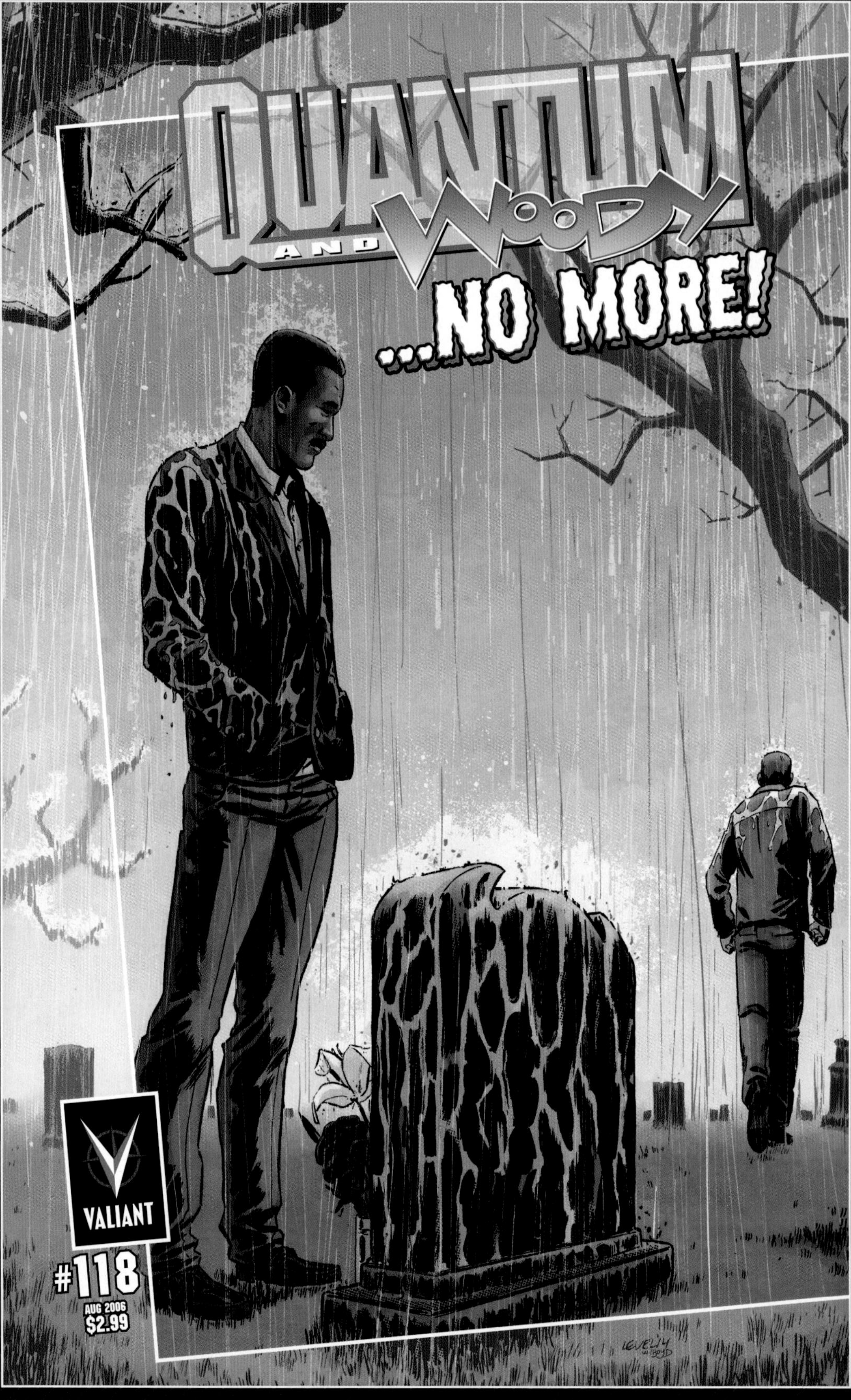
QUANTUM AND WOODY
...NO MORE!
VALIANT
#118
AUG 2006
$2.99
LEVEL '14 w/ BOYD

"The Missing Years!"
Q2: THE RETURN OF QUANTUM AND WOODY #3
Cover by BRIAN LEVEL with JORDAN BOYD

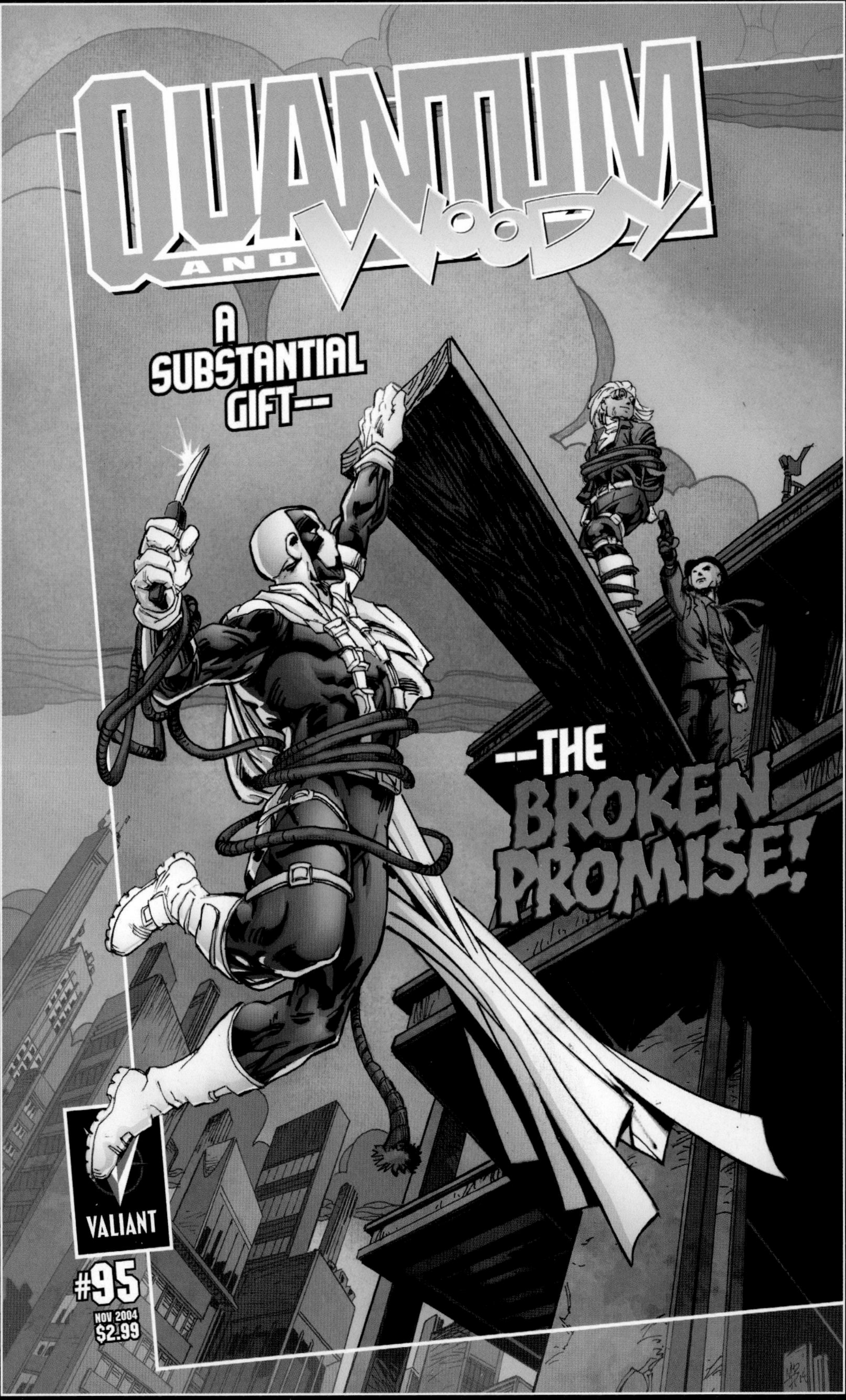
QUANTUM AND WOODY
A SUBSTANTIAL GIFT--
--THE BROKEN PROMISE!
VALIANT
#95
NOV 2004
$2.99

"The Missing Years!"
Q2: THE RETURN OF QUANTUM AND WOODY #3
Cover by MD BRIGHT with ALLEN PASSALAQUA

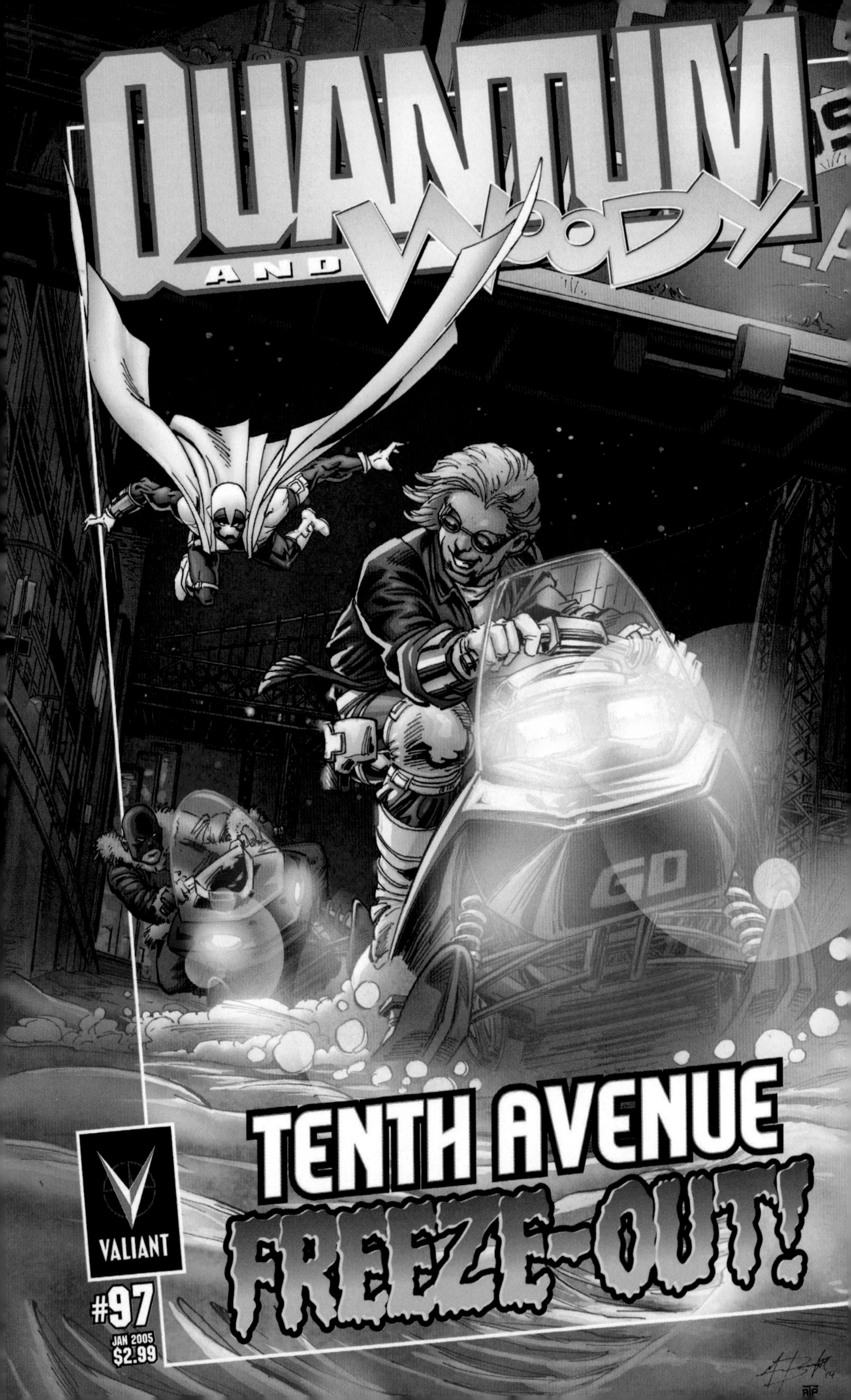
QUANTUM
AND
WOODY
GO
TENTH AVENUE
FREEZE-OUT!
VALIANT
#97
JAN 2005
$2.99

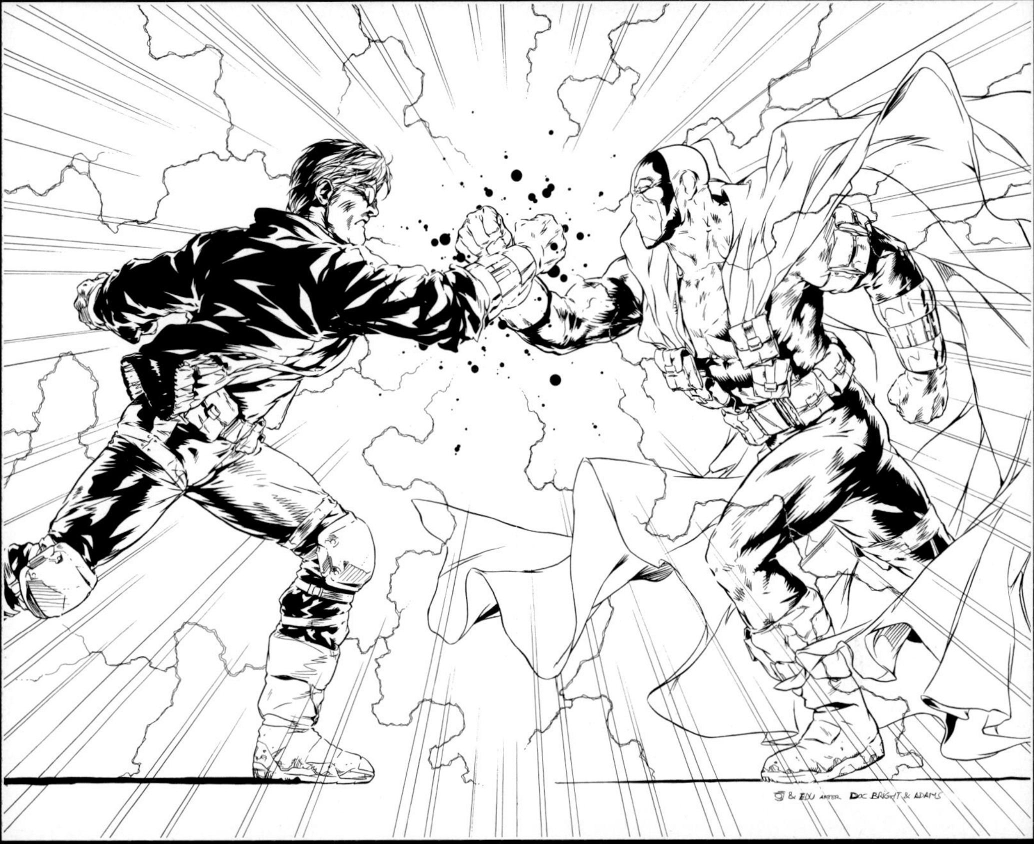
& EDU AFTER DOC BRIGHT & ADAMS

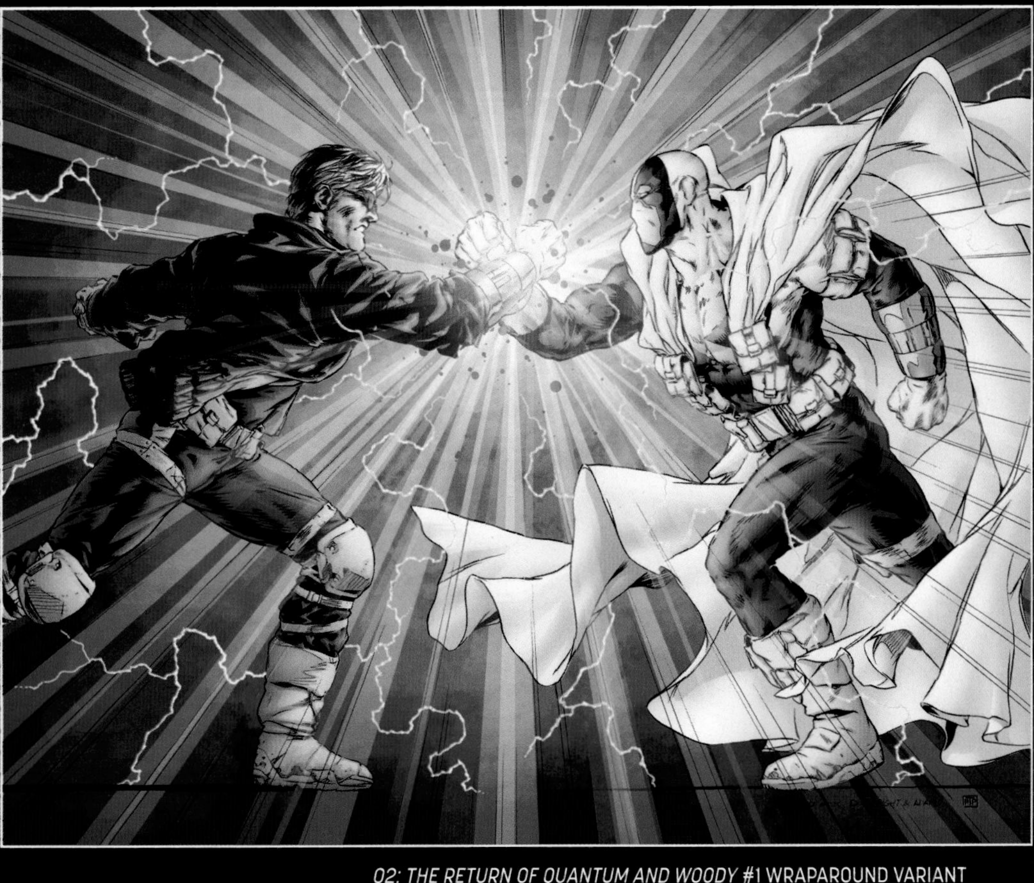

Q2: THE RETURN OF QUANTUM AND WOODY #1 WRAPAROUND VARIANT
Cover by OSCAR JIMENEZ and EDUARDO ALPUENTE with ALLEN PASSALAQUA

Q2: THE RETURN OF QUANTUM AND WOODY #1, p.10
Pencils by MD BRIGHT
Inks by DEXTER VINES

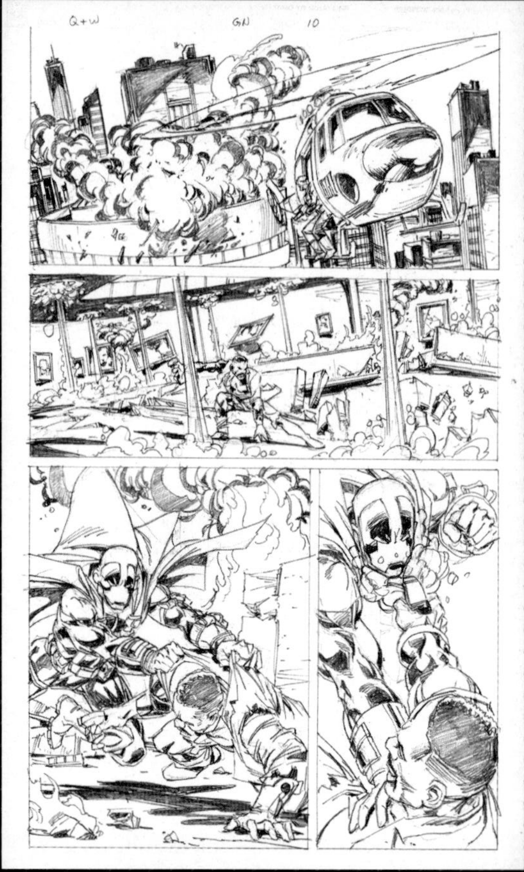

Q+W
GN
10

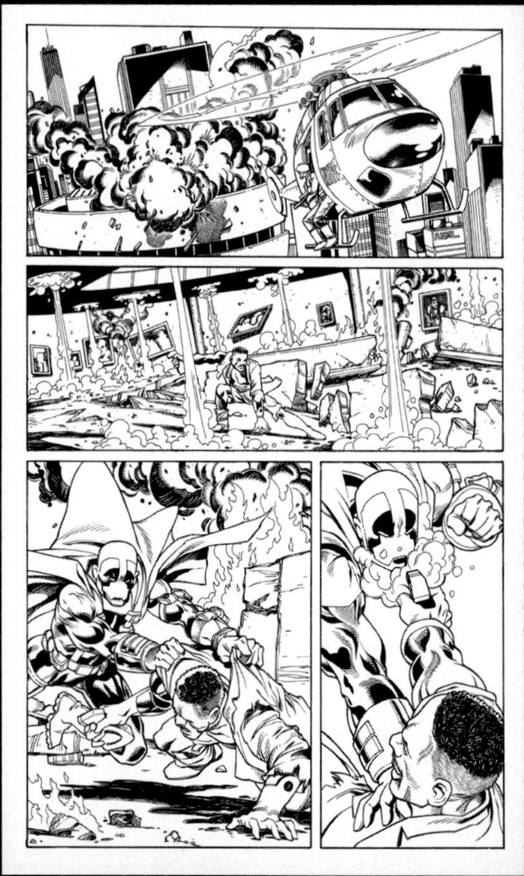

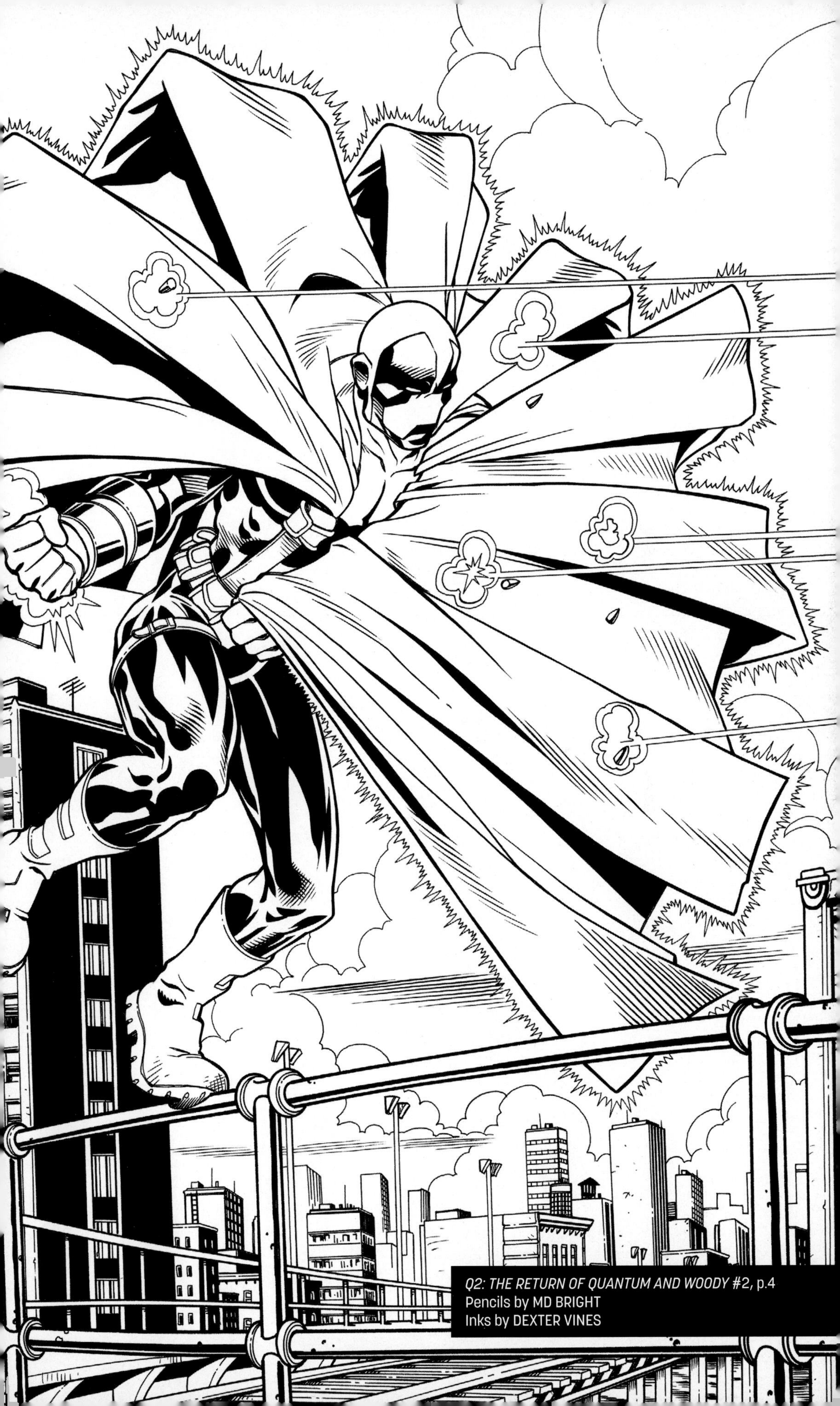

Q2: THE RETURN OF QUANTUM AND WOODY #2, p.4
Pencils by MD BRIGHT
Inks by DEXTER VINES

Q2: THE RETURN OF QUANTUM AND WOODY #2, p.12
Pencils by MD BRIGHT
Inks by DEXTER VINES

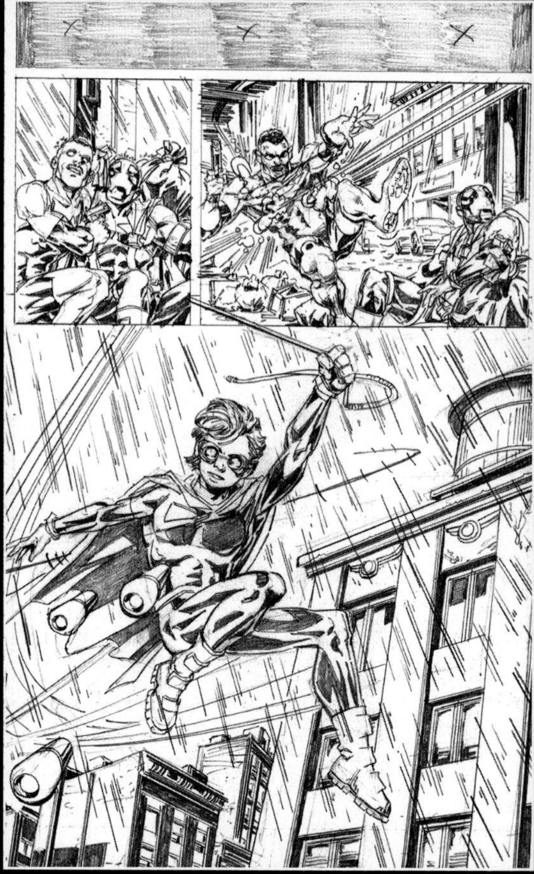

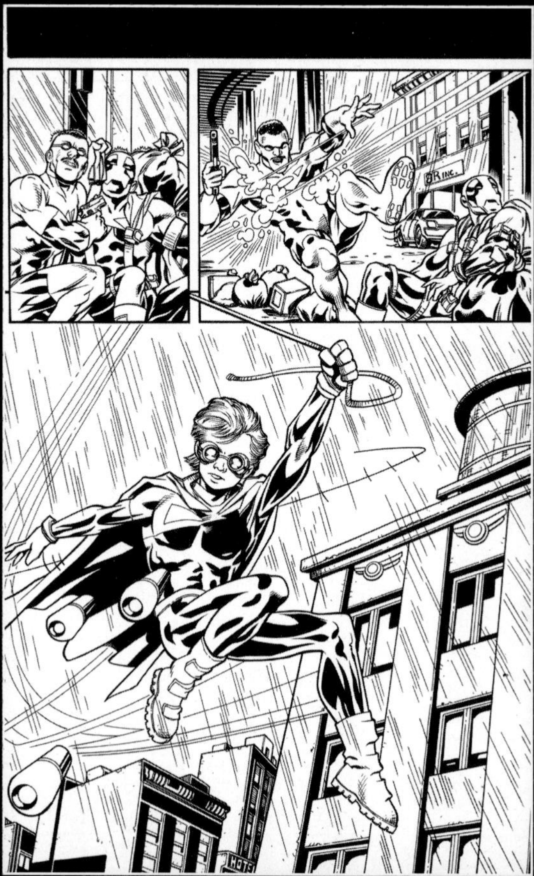

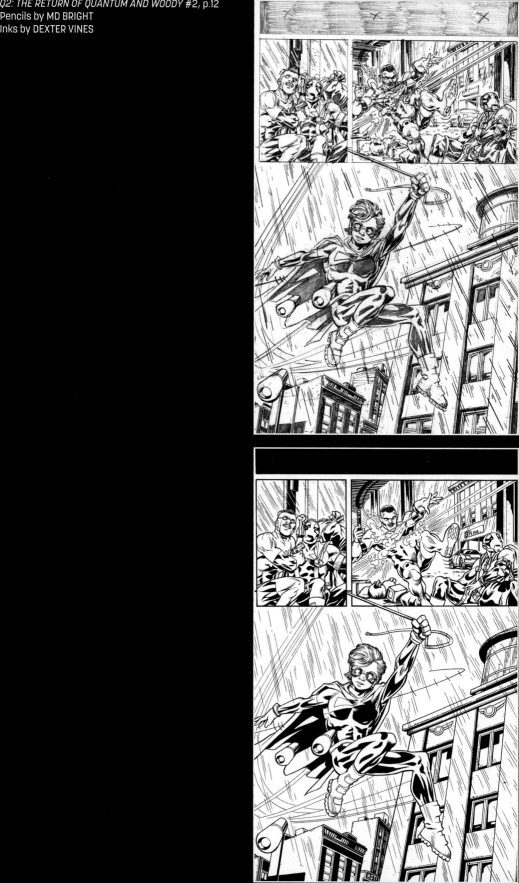

Q2: THE RETURN OF QUANTUM AND WOODY #3, p.5
Pencils by MD BRIGHT
Inks by DEXTER VINES

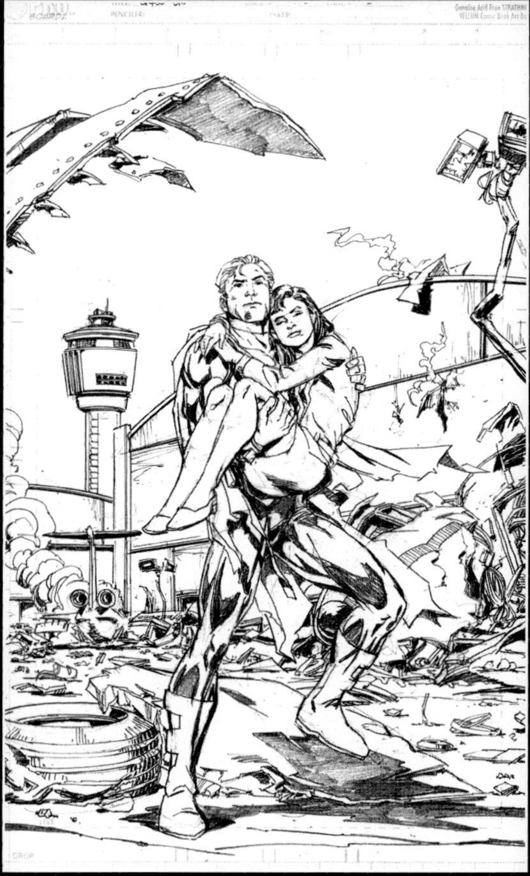

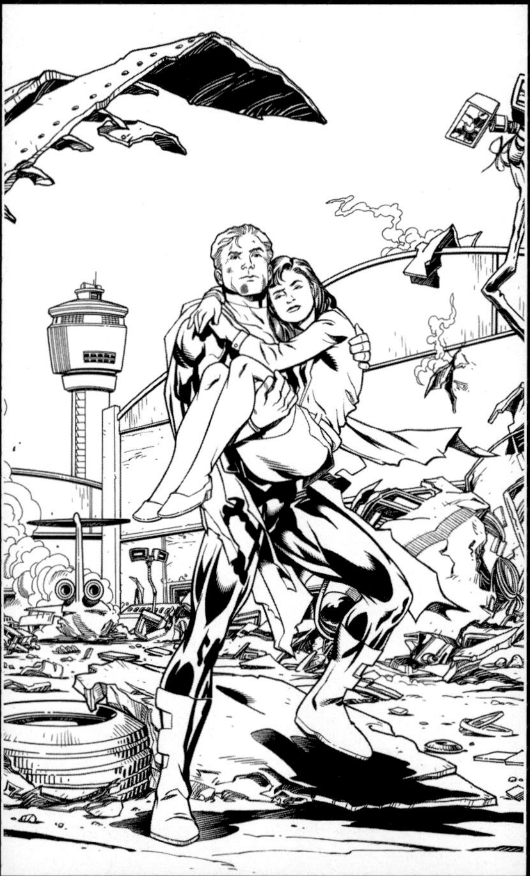

Q2: THE RETURN OF QUANTUM AND WOODY #4, p.15
Pencils by MD BRIGHT
Inks by RYAN WINN

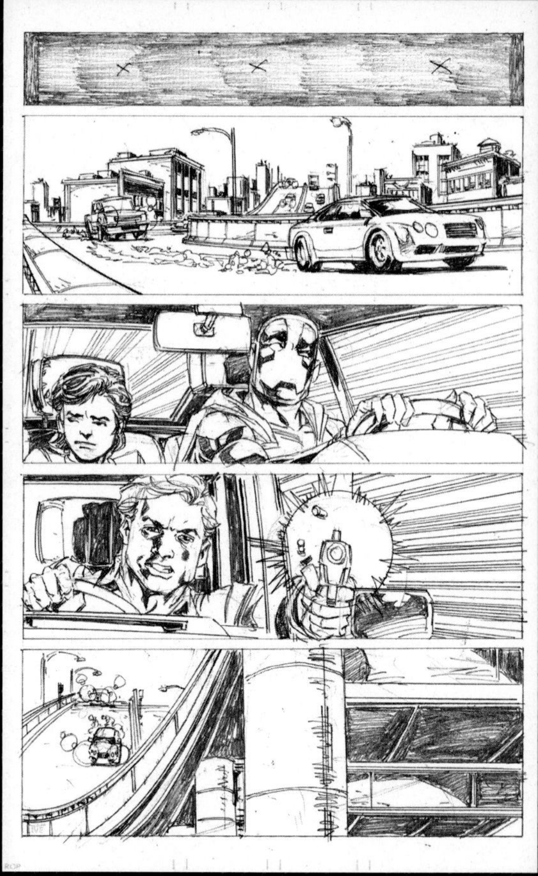

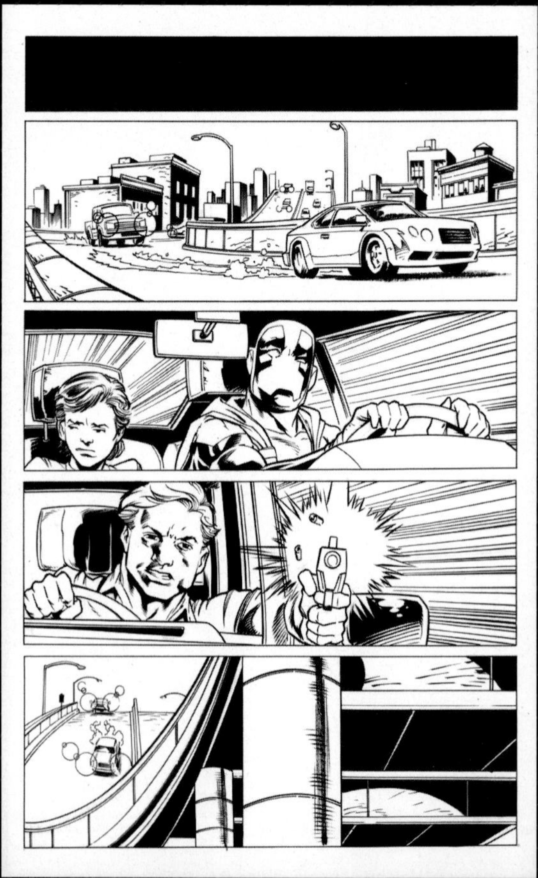

Q2: THE RETURN OF QUANTUM AND WOODY #4, p.18
Pencils by MD BRIGHT
Inks by RYAN WINN

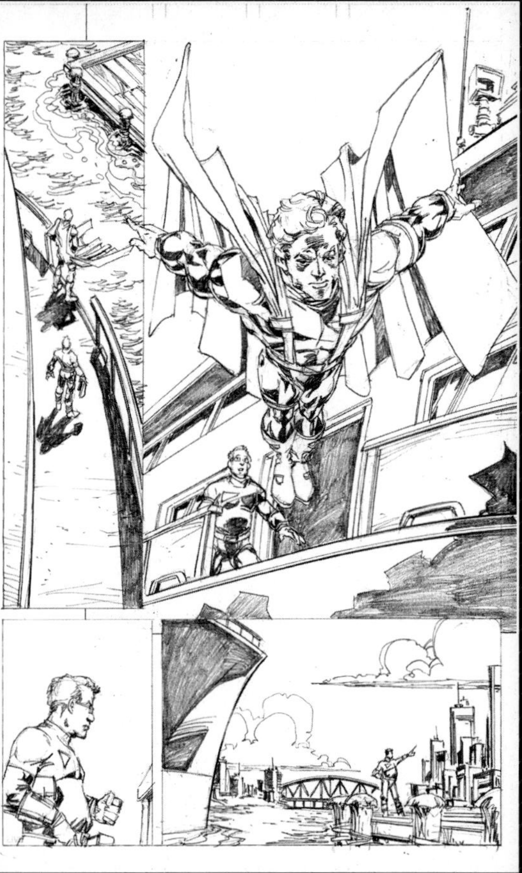

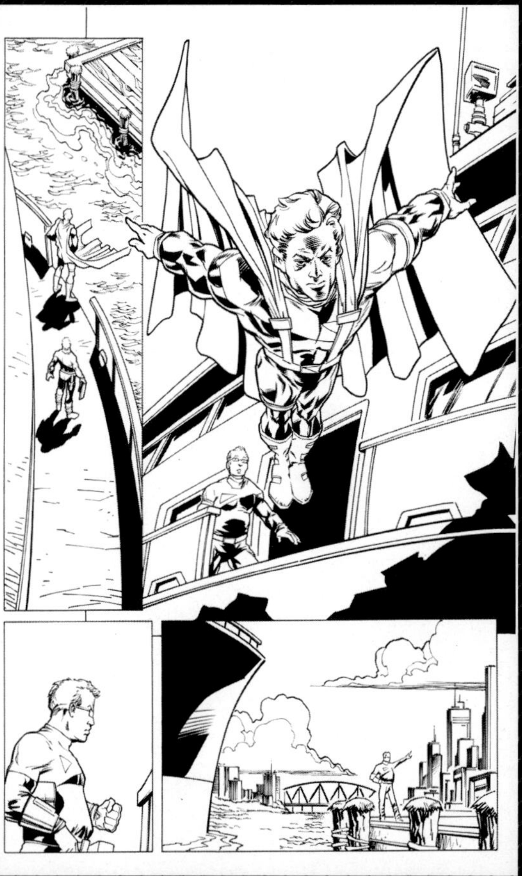

Q2: THE RETURN OF QUANTUM AND WOODY #5, p.13
Pencils by MD BRIGHT
Inks by RYAN WINN

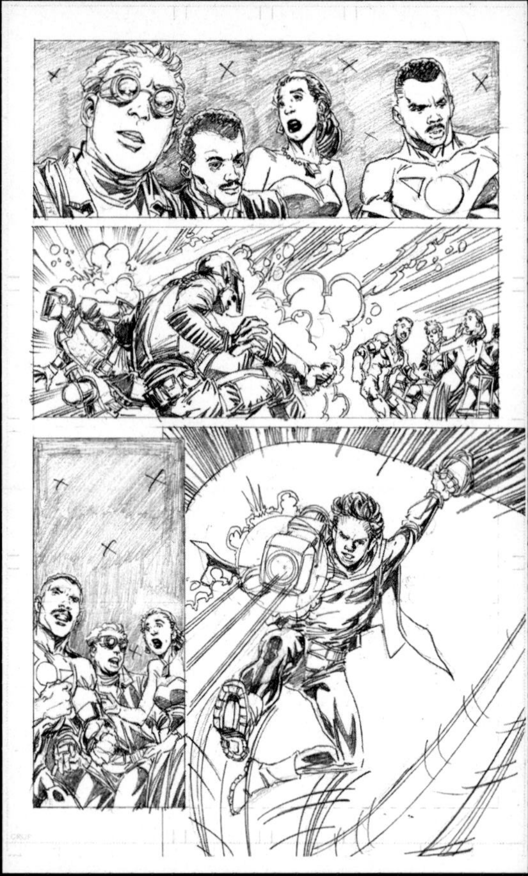

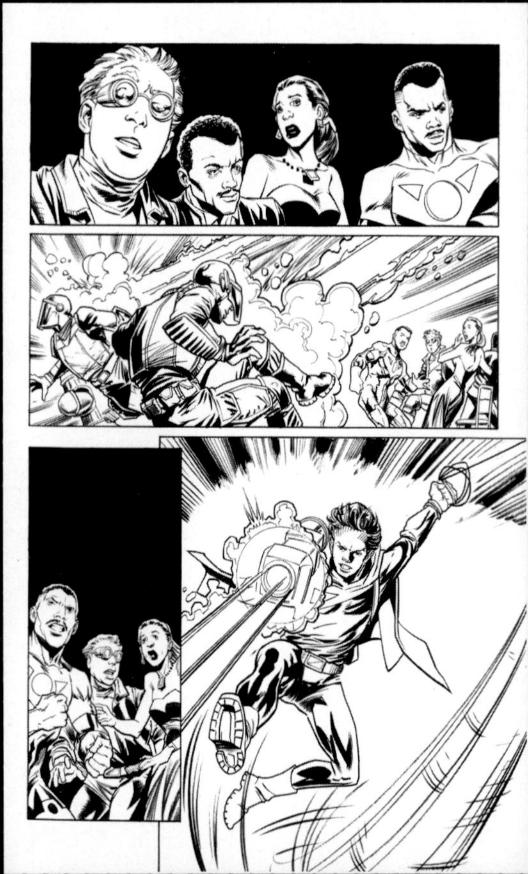

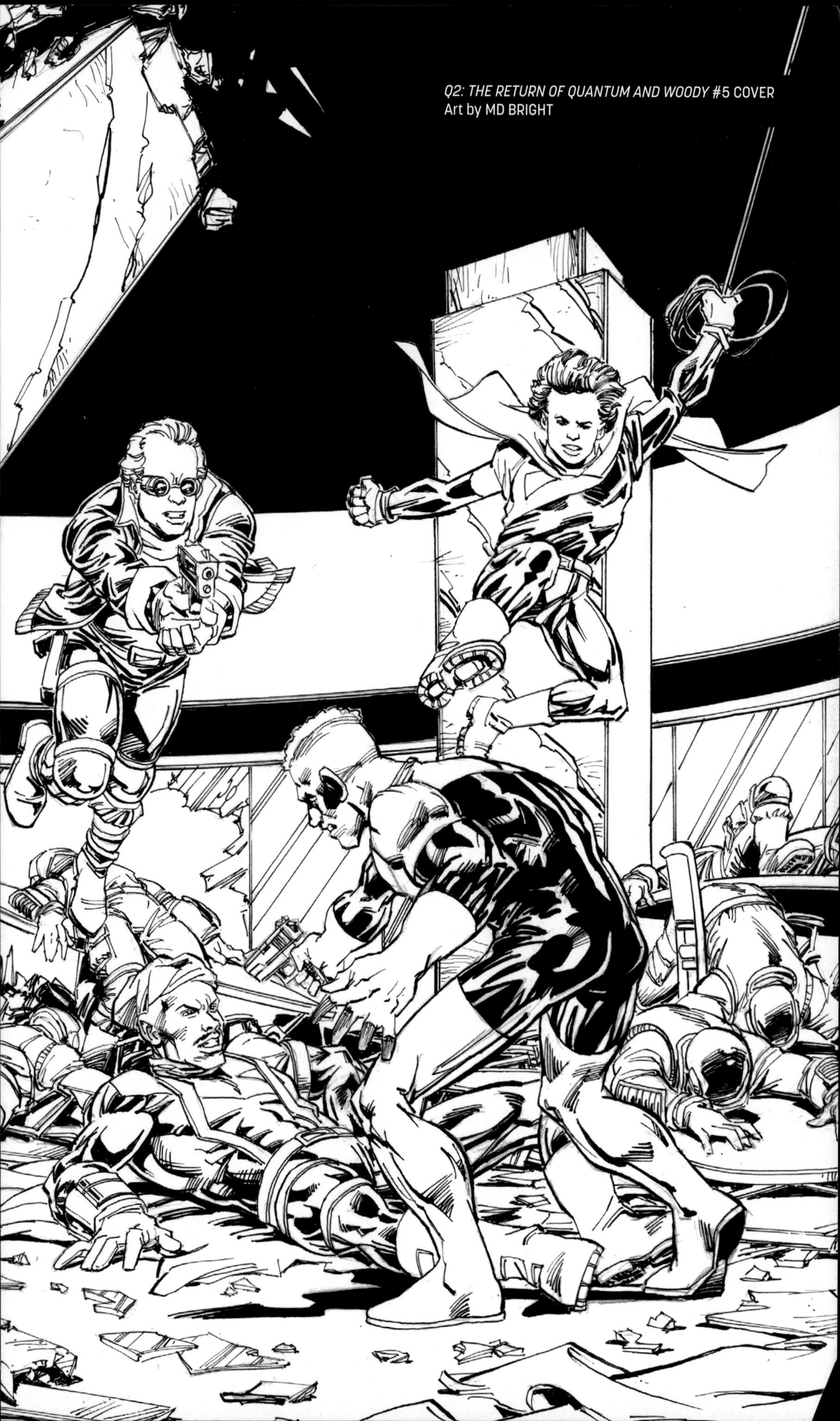

Q2: THE RETURN OF QUANTUM AND WOODY #5 COVER
Art by MD BRIGHT

EXPLORE THE VALIANT UNIVERSE

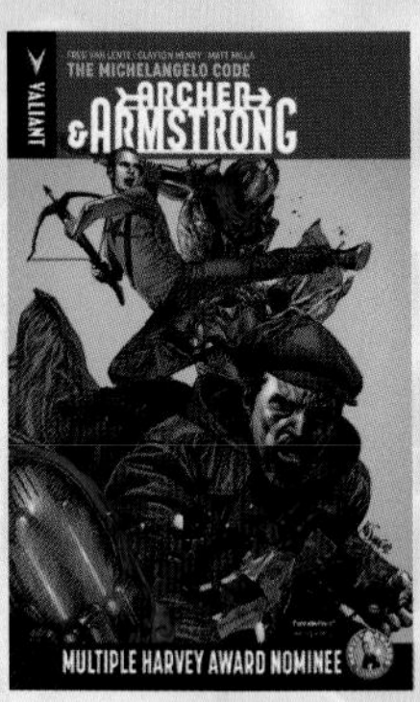
VALIANT
THE MICHELANGELO CODE
ARCHER & ARMSTRONG
MULTIPLE HARVEY AWARD NOMINEE

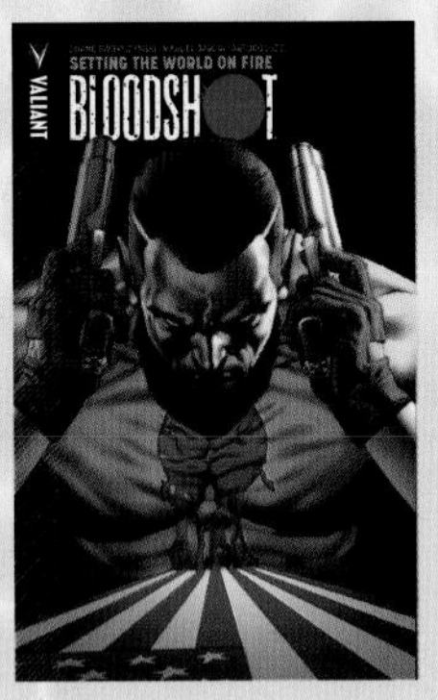
VALIANT
SETTING THE WORLD ON FIRE
BLOODSHOT

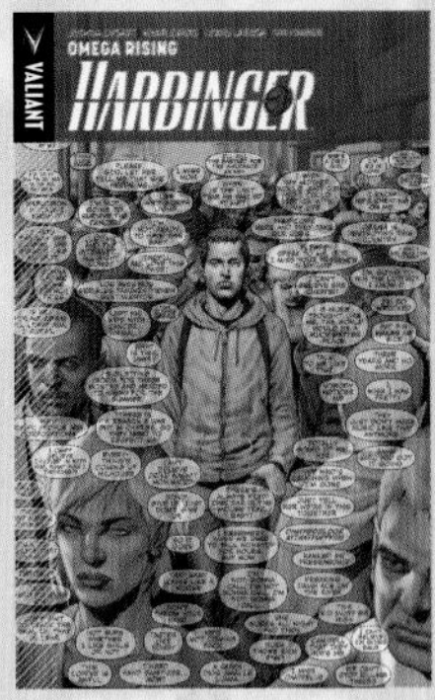
VALIANT
OMEGA RISING
HARBINGER

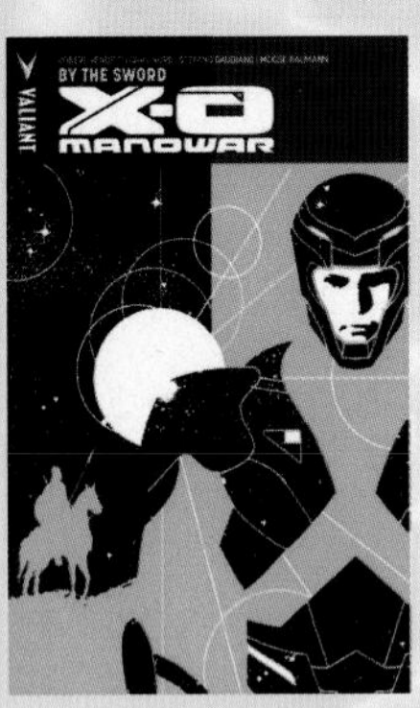
VALIANT
BY THE SWORD
X-O MANOWAR

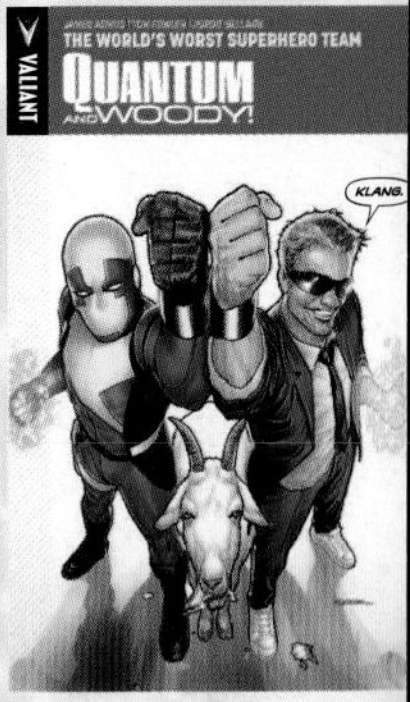
VALIANT
THE WORLD'S WORST SUPERHERO TEAM
QUANTUM AND WOODY!
KLANG

ARCHER & ARMSTRONG

Volume 1: The Michelangelo Code
ISBN: 9780979640988

Volume 2: Wrath of the Eternal Warrior
ISBN: 9781939346049

Volume 3: Far Faraway
ISBN: 9781939346148

Volume 4: Sect Civil War
ISBN: 9781939346254

Volume 5: Mission: Improbable
ISBN: 9781939346353

Volume 6: American Wasteland
ISBN: 9781939346421

Volume 7: The One Percent and Other Tales
ISBN: 9781939346537

ARMOR HUNTERS

Armor Hunters
ISBN: 9781939346452

Armor Hunters: Bloodshot
ISBN: 9781939346469

Armor Hunters: Harbinger
ISBN: 9781939346506

Unity Vol. 3: Armor Hunters
ISBN: 9781939346445

X-O Manowar Vol. 7: Armor Hunters
ISBN: 9781939346476

BLOODSHOT

Volume 1: Setting the World on Fire
ISBN: 9780979640964

Volume 2: The Rise and the Fall
ISBN: 9781939346032

Volume 3: Harbinger Wars
ISBN: 9781939346124

Volume 4: H.A.R.D. Corps
ISBN: 9781939346193

Volume 5: Get Some!
ISBN: 9781939346315

Volume 6: The Glitch and Other Tales
ISBN: 9781939346711

BLOODSHOT REBORN

Volume 1: Colorado
ISBN: 9781939346674

Volume 2: The Hunt
ISBN: 9781939346827

Volume 3: The Analog Man
ISBN: 9781682151334

BOOK OF DEATH

Book of Death
ISBN: 9781939346971

Book of Death: The Fall of the Valiant Universe
ISBN: 9781939346988

DEAD DROP

ISBN: 9781939346858

THE DEATH-DEFYING DOCTOR MIRAGE

Volume 1
ISBN: 9781939346490

Volume 2: Second Lives
ISBN: 9781682151297

THE DELINQUENTS

ISBN: 9781939346513

DIVINITY

ISBN: 9781939346766

ETERNAL WARRIOR

Volume 1: Sword of the Wild
ISBN: 9781939346209

Volume 2: Eternal Emperor
ISBN: 9781939346292

Volume 3: Days of Steel
ISBN: 9781939346742

WRATH OF THE ETERNAL WARRIOR

Volume 1: Risen
ISBN: 9781682151235

HARBINGER

Volume 1: Omega Rising
ISBN: 9780979640957

Volume 2: Renegades
ISBN: 9781939346025

Volume 3: Harbinger Wars
ISBN: 9781939346117

Volume 4: Perfect Day
ISBN: 9781939346155

Volume 5: Death of a Renegade
ISBN: 9781939346339

Volume 6: Omegas
ISBN: 9781939346384

HARBINGER WARS

Harbinger Wars
ISBN: 9781939346094

Bloodshot Vol. 3: Harbinger Wars
ISBN: 9781939346124

Harbinger Vol. 3: Harbinger Wars
ISBN: 9781939346117

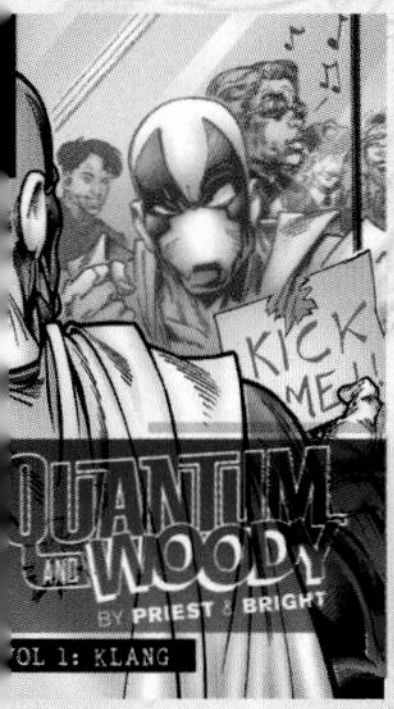
KICK ME
UANTUM
AND WOODY
BY PRIEST & BRIGHT
OL 1: KLANG

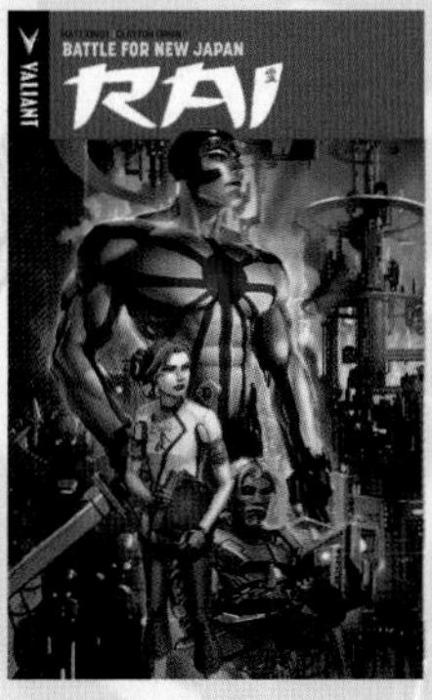
VALIANT
BATTLE FOR NEW JAPAN
RAI

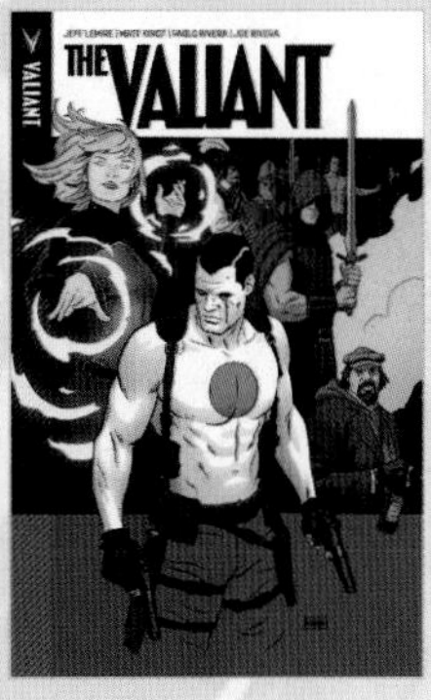
VALIANT
THE VALIANT

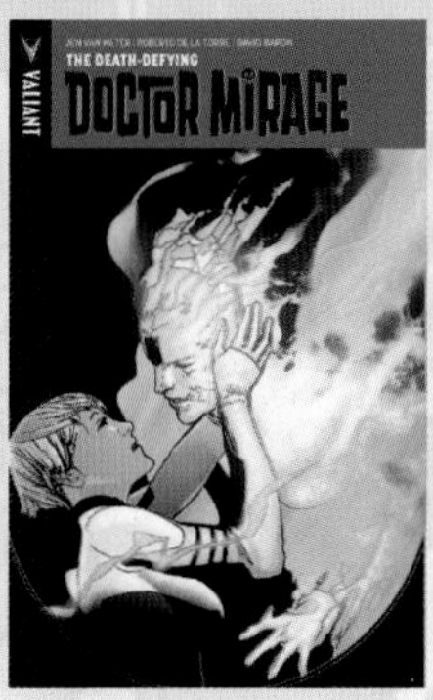
VALIANT
THE DEATH-DEFYING
DOCTOR MIRAGE

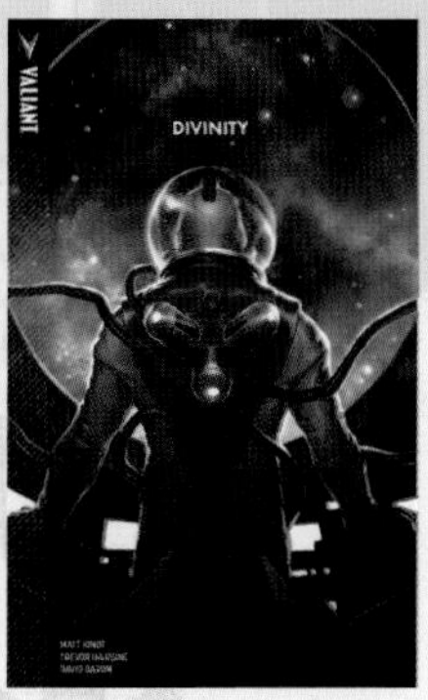
VALIANT
DIVINITY

PERIUM

ume 1: Collecting Monsters
N: 9781939346759

ume 2: Broken Angels
N: 9781939346896

ume 3: The Vine Imperative
N: 9781682151112

INJAK

ume 1: Weaponeer
N: 9781939346667

ume 2: The Shadow Wars
N: 9781939346940

ume 3: Operation: Deadside
N: 9781682151259

UANTUM ND WOODY

ume 1: The World's Worst Superhero Team
N: 9781939346186

ume 2: In Security
N: 9781939346230

ume 3: Crooked Pasts, Present Tense
N: 9781939346391

ume 4: Quantum and Woody Must Die!
N: 9781939346629

UANTUM AND WOODY Y PRIEST & BRIGHT

ume 1: Klang
N: 9781939346780

ume 2: Switch
N: 9781939346803

ume 3: And So...
N: 9781939346865

ume 4: Q2 - The Return
N: 9781682151099

RAI

Volume 1: Welcome to New Japan
ISBN: 9781939346414

Volume 2: Battle for New Japan
ISBN: 9781939346612

Volume 3: The Orphan
ISBN: 9781939346841

SHADOWMAN

Volume 1: Birth Rites
ISBN: 9781939346001

Volume 2: Darque Reckoning
ISBN: 9781939346056

Volume 3: Deadside Blues
ISBN: 9781939346162

Volume 4: Fear, Blood, And Shadows
ISBN: 9781939346278

Volume 5: End Times
ISBN: 9781939346377

IVAR, TIMEWALKER

Volume 1: Making History
ISBN: 9781939346636

Volume 2: Breaking History
ISBN: 9781939346834

Volume 3: Ending History
ISBN: 9781939346995

UNITY

Volume 1: To Kill a King
ISBN: 9781939346261

Volume 2: Trapped by Webnet
ISBN: 9781939346346

Volume 3: Armor Hunters
ISBN: 9781939346445

Volume 4: The United
ISBN: 9781939346544

Volume 5: Homefront
ISBN: 9781939346797

Volume 6: The War-Monger
ISBN: 9781939346902

Volume 7: Revenge of the Armor Hunters
ISBN: 9781682151136

THE VALIANT

ISBN: 9781939346605

VALIANT ZEROES AND ORIGINS

ISBN: 9781939346582

X-O MANOWAR

Volume 1: By the Sword
ISBN: 9780979640940

Volume 2: Enter Ninjak
ISBN: 9780979640995

Volume 3: Planet Death
ISBN: 9781939346087

Volume 4: Homecoming
ISBN: 9781939346179

Volume 5: At War With Unity
ISBN: 9781939346247

Volume 6: Prelude to Armor Hunters
ISBN: 9781939346407

Volume 7: Armor Hunters
ISBN: 9781939346476

Volume 8: Enter: Armorines
ISBN: 9781939346551

Volume 9: Dead Hand
ISBN: 9781939346650

Volume 10: Exodus
ISBN: 9781939346933

Volume 11: The Kill List
ISBN: 9781682151273

EXPLORE THE VALIANT UNIVERSE

VALIANT
JOSHUA DYSART | BARRY KITSON | CLAYTON HENRY | KHARI EVANS | RAFA SANDOVAL
HARBINGER DELUXE EDITION 2

VALIANT
ROBERT VENDITTI MATT KINDT JOSHUA DYSART JOE HARRIS ROBERT GILL DOUG BRAITHWAITE DIEGO BERNARD TREVOR HAIRSINE STEPHEN SEGOVIA
ARMOR HUNTERS DELUXE EDITION

VALIANT
VALIANT MASTERS
JIM SHOOTER | DAVID LAPHAM
CHILDREN OF THE EIGHTH DAY
HARBINGER
L8-AGIN

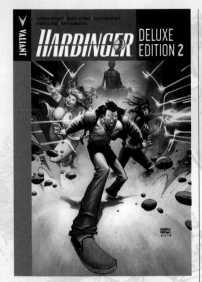

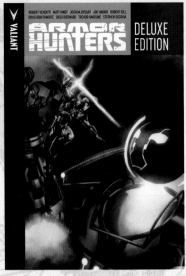

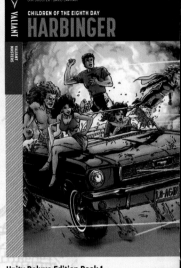

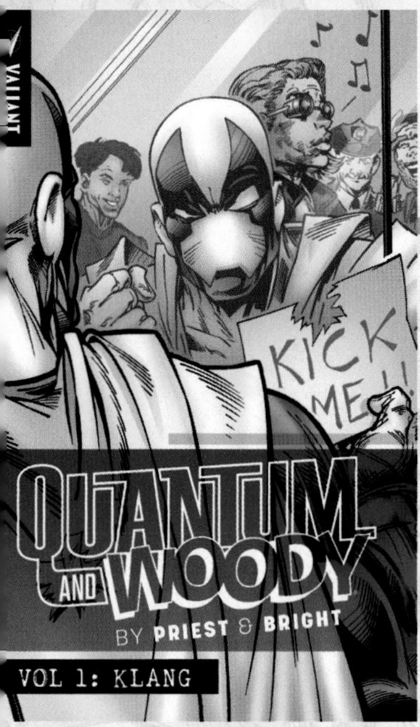
VALIANT
QUANTUM AND WOODY
BY PRIEST & BRIGHT
VOL 1: KLANG

Quantum and Woody by Priest & Bright
Vol. 1: Klang

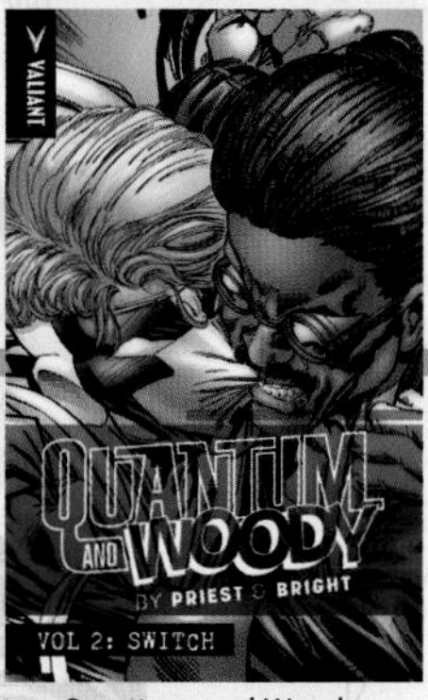
VALIANT
QUANTUM AND WOODY
BY PRIEST & BRIGHT
VOL 2: SWITCH

Quantum and Woody
by Priest & Bright
Vol. 2: Switch

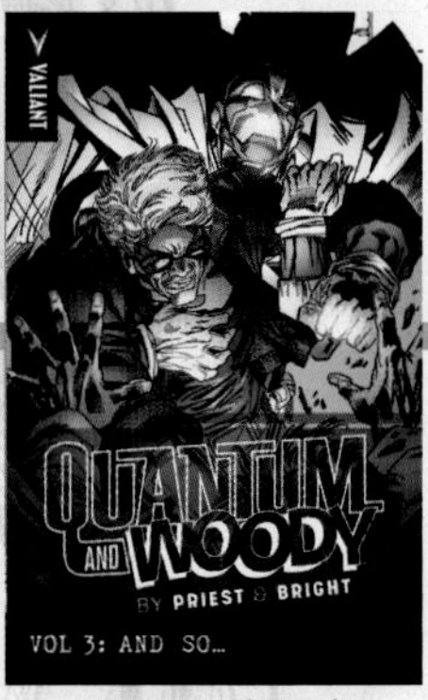
VALIANT
QUANTUM AND WOODY
BY PRIEST & BRIGHT
VOL 3: AND SO...

Quantum and Woody
by Priest & Bright
Vol. 3: And So...

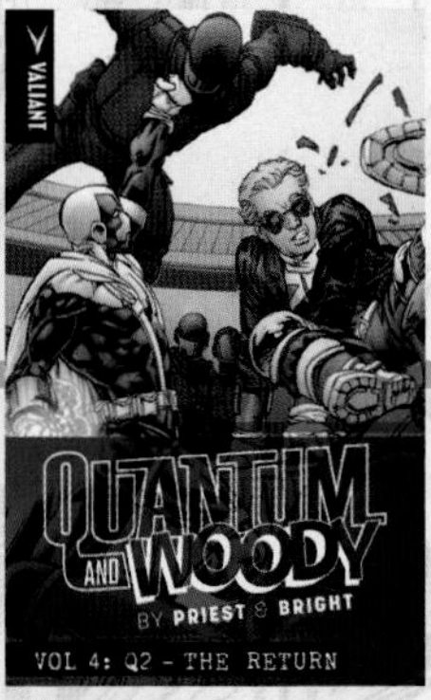
VALIANT
QUANTUM AND WOODY
BY PRIEST & BRIGHT
VOL 4: Q2 - THE RETURN

Quantum and Woody
by Priest & Bright
Vol. 4: Q2–The Return

ne of the funniest superhero mics ever..." - Kotaku

fun ride.... Unmissable."
Wired

The complete collected adventures of the original world's worst superhero team - now in trade paperback!

From legendary creators

CHRISTOPHER PRIEST ([*Black Panther, Deadpool*]) and **MD BRIGHT** ([*Green Lantern, Iron Man*])

VALIANT®

QUANTUM AND WOODY!®

VOLUME ONE: THE WORLD'S WORST SUPERHERO TEAM

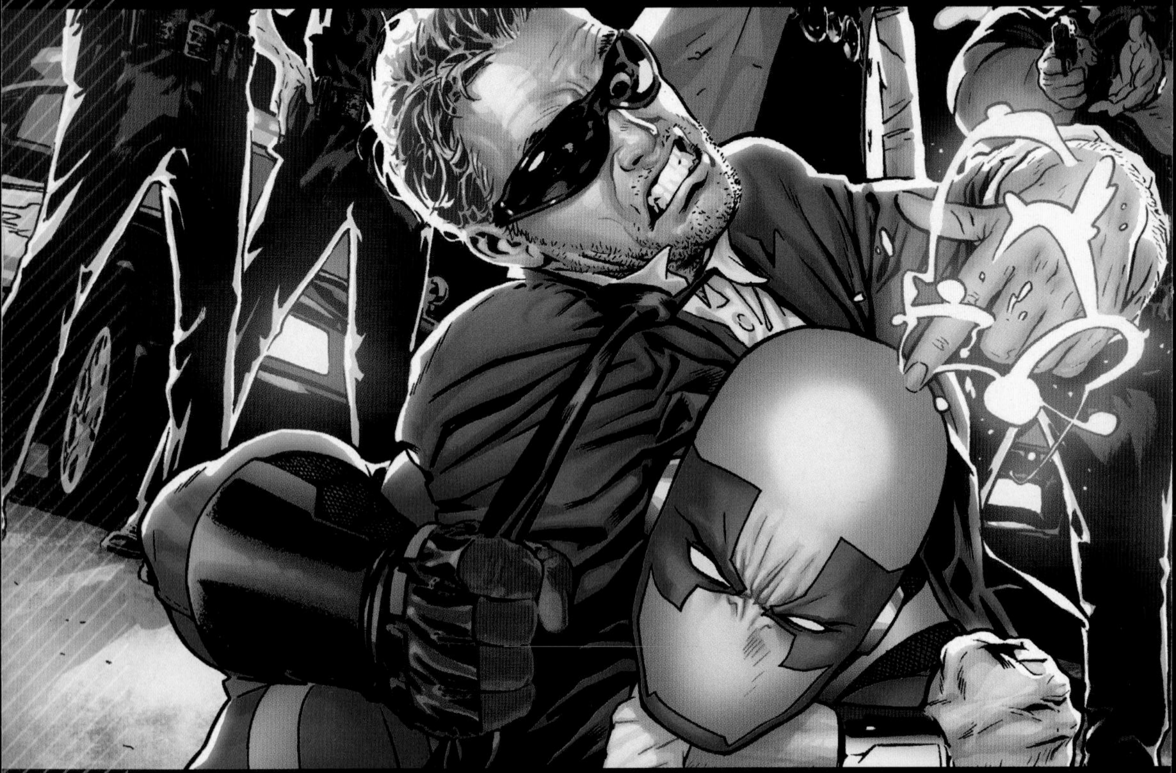

THOSE GUYS ARE THE WORST.

Once upon a time, Eric and Woody Henderson were inseparable. Adopted brothers. Best friends. Brilliant minds. Years later, they are estranged siblings, petty rivals, and washed-up failures. But when their father's murder leads them into the throes of a life-altering scientific accident, Eric and Woody will find themselves with a whole new purpose - and a perfectly legitimate reason to wear costumes and fight crime. Go big or go home, folks! Quantum and Woody are coming! (And, yes, there is a goat, too.)

Collecting QUANTUM AND WOODY #1-4 by creators James Asmus (*Thief of Thieves*) and Tom Fowler (*Hulk: Season One*), start reading here to jump into the action-packed, zeitgeist-shredding exploitation stunt comic that Comic Book Resources calls "yet another critically acclaimed hit for Valiant Comics."

TRADE PAPERBACK
978-1-939346-18-6

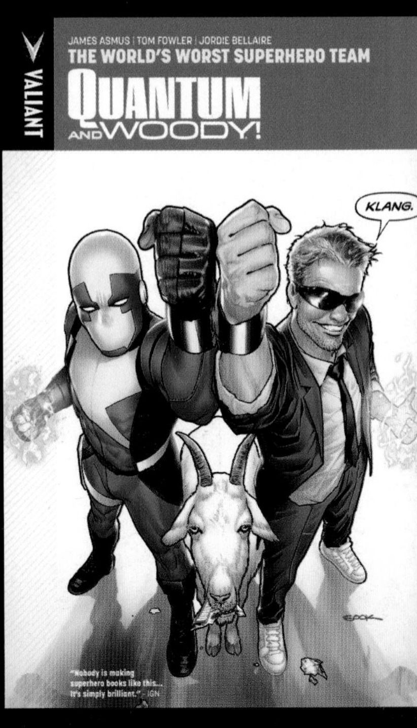

VALIANT
JAMES ASMUS | TOM FOWLER | JORDIE BELLAIRE
THE WORLD'S WORST SUPERHERO TEAM
QUANTUM AND WOODY!
KLANG.
"Nobody is making superhero books like this... It's simply brilliant." - IGN